REFORM iN CHINA

Challenges & Choices

REFORM IN CHINA

Challenges & Choices

A Summary and Analysis of
the CESRRI Survey

Prepared by the Staff of the
Chinese Economic System Reform
Research Institute

Edited with an Introduction by
BRUCE L. REYNOLDS

An East Gate Book
M. E. Sharpe, Inc.
Armonk, New York/London

East Gate Books are edited by Douglas Merwin
120 Buena Vista Drive, White Plains, New York 10603

Copyright © 1987 by M. E. Sharpe, Inc.
80 Business Park Drive, Armonk, New York 10504

Available in the United Kingdom and Europe from M. E. Sharpe,
Publishers, 3 Henrietta Street, London WC2E 8LU.

Library of Congress Cataloging-in-Publication Data

Kai Ko. English.
    Reform in China.

    Translation of: Kai ko.
    1. China—Economic policy—1976–   . I. Reynolds. Bruce
Lloyd, 1944–   . II. Chinese Economic System Reform Research
Institute. III. Title.
HC427.92.K32 1987   338.951   87–23537
ISBN 0-87332-458-7
ISBN 0-87332-459-5 (pbk.)
Printed in the United States of America

CONTENTS

LIST OF FIGURES

LIST OF TABLES

Introduction to the English Edition

Bruce L. Reynolds

Challenges and Choices presents the fruits of what is arguably the most extraordinary empirical investigation undertaken in twentieth-century China. In the spring of 1985, China was trying to evaluate the second major push on the "reform" front. In 1979–80, the agricultural sector had felt the force of the reformers' zeal, with electrifying results: stimulated by the strong incentive efforts of a return to quasi-private property, peasants increased effort (and output) to unprecedented levels. In October 1984, the party had issued a clarion call to push reform into China's cities—into the industrial sector. Here, reformers found the going considerably rougher than in agriculture, both because the issue of who shall "own" industrial capital is less tractable than creating quasi-ownership of agricultural land, and because industrial production involves coordination of a large number of specialized producers.

Thus in 1985, the question was: how is reform faring, and what should be done next? Storm warnings were up: the dramatic decentralization of decision-making power had generated massive imbalances. In foreign trade, China's imports had increased vastly more than exports; in early 1985, the resulting hemorrhage of foreign exchange led to a sharp recentralization of trade powers. Domestically, factory managers and local governments had used their new powers to launch new investment projects, build better housing, or simply raise wages; this wave of purchasing power generated an alarming burst of inflation.

It was in this context that the China Economic System Reform Research Institute (CESRRI) launched its research project. This fledgling organization, with a strikingly young staff (average age thirty-five), is lodged directly below the State Council (China's cabinet) and has won the strong patronage of Premier Zhao Ziyang. The enthusiasm of its members for sustained reform is clear. The older members of the group, aged fifteen to twenty when the Cultural Revolution broke out in 1966, were profoundly influenced by that event. Many see reform as the road to political pluralism and institutional constraints on the raw exercise of political power. But tempering their proreform bias is an equally strong commitment to Deng Xiaoping's famous dictum: ''Seek truth through facts.'' That ideal is reflected in the pride with which Wang Xiaoqiang, who spearheaded the research effort, reports that it ''collected fourteen million data.''

Six separate investigations were conducted:

—The main project, a field survey of 429 enterprises in 27 cities, generated 90 separate reports.

—CESRRI coordinated three separate attitudinal surveys: on reactions to price reform, attitudes toward job security versus job mobility, and young people's attitudes toward reform.

—A second factory survey administered a 70-item questionnaire in 900 enterprises in 7 provinces.

—CESRRI worked with three universities and the Chinese Academy of Social Sciences to conduct a series of studies of government administration in 12 cities.

Altogether, 447 people participated in the investigation— principally college students working under the guidance and with the inspiration of two dozen ERRI staff members.

This book, the product of that effort, is a ringing defense of urban reform. And what a departure from past practice: where traditional ''policy articles'' might occasionally allude to a single fact or anecdotal example to support their arguments, these young people have marshalled millions of facts and put them to work. In the process, they offer us an array of fascinating insights into how Chinese society functions, from the motivations of factory managers to the more familiar question of whether wives should work outside the home.

This book is organized into four parts. In part I, a summary report knits together the results of the whole research project. It addresses three questions: What has reform achieved to date? What are the major problems of the current reform period? And what should the next big step be? In parts II-IV, chapters by individual contributors, each one drawing on one or two of the different research projects, address these same three questions in more detail. Brief introductions to each part place these chapters in a broader context.

The book was published in Chinese in 1986, under the title *Gaige: Women mianlingde tiaozhan yu xuanze* (Reform: The Challenges and Choices We Face). Many people have contributed to the English edition. Cao Yuanzheng supervised the translation process. Chen Yizi and Wang Xiaoqiang provided CESRRI's enthusiastic support during this period. Carolyn Micklas typed a series of drafts. The American publisher was also very supportive.

As this volume goes to press, reform is in limbo. Hu Yaobang has resigned in the wake of the December 1986 student demonstrations. Major advances toward free political expression, achieved through 1986, have been dismantled. The effort to free enterprises from party intervention has faltered. The September 1987

National Party Congress is emerging as a crucial turning point for reform. As we speculate on the future of reform, this book is tremendously useful. It shows us how far urban reform has already advanced. It documents proreform attitudes and aspirations among youth and among enterprise managers. And the manner and spirit in which the book was written, in and of themselves, testify to a fierce dedication among some of China's "best and brightest" to policies based on careful analysis of the country's realities and the real needs of its people.

Preface to the
Chinese Edition

Wu Jinglian

V. I. Lenin once quoted J. Kautsky as saying that the study of economics must not be casual; one must know history and statistics and pose a myriad of questions. When we review economic studies generated since the founding of New China with this standard in mind, we find that although China, which has one billion people and is currently in the midst of unprecedented rapid development, is in urgent need of well-grounded economic theories, there are only a few works that rigorously base their theoretical analysis on facts. Therefore, the publication of these research reports, which are the result of a large-scale investigation conducted by close to three hundred young economists in twenty-seven cities over seven months, is very encouraging.

Old China was a semicolonial, semifeudal agricultural society. The self-sufficient economy and the underdeveloped exchange relations had impeded the development of economics; and the young and weak capitalist class had left behind almost no understanding about social and economic situations. Economics developed after Liberation. But under the impact of the erroneous "Left" ideology, academic studies waned. At that time, "Left" ideology occupied a dominant position; articles in newspapers were filled with "Marxism," which was used to establish various kinds of correspondences and even to show the correctness of the hypocritical theories of Lin Biao and the "Gang of Four." Other works, going along with the tide, merely quoted the classical writers rather than explaining things, or compiled numbers only to avoid expressing opinions on controversial issues.

After the downfall of the "Gang of Four," everything looked fresh and encouraging. Many really good works emerged. In the meantime, groups of young economists, trained or self-taught, joined in the research work, swelling the ranks of Chinese economists. This book is the research fruit of these young economists. Compared with similar works published before, this book has two characteristics:

1. New ideas were brought forth on the basis of facts and figures obtained during a large-scale investigation. This investigation was carefully prepared beforehand. The designing of forms and questionnaires as well as the taking of samples were all unprecedented. Modern social science methodology was adopted. The investigation covered not only economic factors, such as circulation, production, and enterprise performance, but also noneconomic factors that should not be overlooked, such as public reaction to price reform, young people's job preferences, people's attitudes toward life, and public comments on the guaranteed employment system. As the investigation reports included in the book contain more than ten million separate data, they necessarily hold water. Unlike some papers, which are full of superficial, empty points based on single facts, these reports relate to the actual situation. Although some of their points are merely hypotheses that require proof, their arguments are not groundless; they are supported by specific facts and documentation. This has paved the way for further study.

2. The report does not merely enumerate facts or present a superficial discussion. On the contrary, it quotes copiously from many sources, draws historical and international comparisons, links up theory with all the information acquired during the investigation, and on this basis draws policy conclusions. For example, the investigation report notes the importance of the underdeveloped capital markets in explaining excessive investment, declining scale of investment, and decreasing productivity of investment. There is a systematic analysis of a negative phenomena that emerged in the course of decentralization of investment decision-making power. This had already been perceived by many people, but this report has greatly deepened our understanding. In addition, quite new ideas are put forward on China's achievement in urban economic reform and its related problems; an analysis of the "two-track" system for distribution the means of production; elaboration of the status quo of the expansion of consumption mechanism; and constructive proposals on how to overcome the expansion of consumption and investment demand. Although some economists, including myself, may disagree with some of the explanations and inferences and point to shortcomings, they stimulate us to ponder questions often neglected in the past.

China is in the process of rapid transition from a "dual economy" with traditional agriculture as its center of gravity to a modernized economy. During this transitional period, more and more farmers, whose labor yields low economic returns (amounting to disguised unemployment), will be trained with modern technology and put to work in highly efficient nonagricultural units. To smooth the transition, it is imperative to have these rising economic returns ensured so as to raise the consumption level of urban and rural residents and therefore accumulate more funds. To guarantee the preconditions for the above-mentioned "take-off," besides having a better understanding of the speed of turning agricultural people to nonagricultural work, which means the *construction* speed, and the rate of improvement of the standard of living in both urban and rural areas, we need to strive for the realization of a change in the dual models of economic system and development strategy. During the intricate and complex process of transition and development, we must study and solve many theoretical and practical policy problems. However, it is not easy to solve problems that integrate theory with practice on our own. Individually, each of us is limited by our own ability. We are not likely to accomplish so arduous a task alone. Instead, we must rely on the collective efforts of all economists and economic research workers. United as one, those people who are devoted to the economic rejuvenation of the Chinese nation will surmount every difficulty, and complete the task entrusted to us by history.

The road of science is by no means smooth. Those who wish to scale the heights of science must be devoted. The 279 authors of this investigation report have displayed an empirical spirit, creativeness, cohesion, and devotion. If we can carry forward their spirit and make strenuous efforts, we will surely develop our discipline and succeed in socialist modernization.

Social Scientific Research Serves Reform

Chen Yizi

At present both China's economic development and its economic reform have entered a new stage. Since the beginning of 1979 the production responsibility system has been carried out throughout rural China. The country is no longer concerned over feeding its people. China's economy now aims to provide for a comparatively well-off society, as the country's consumption structure undergoes great change. To reach this goal, China's production structure must be readjusted. The Third Plenary Session of the Twelfth Party Central Committee, held in October 1984, marked a turning point; the focus of China's economic reform shifted from the rural to the urban sector, and the scope of reform was extended from a few fields to all the remaining ones.

The current reform involves developing a commodity economy under an overall plan and building a socialist economic system with Chinese characteristics. It is more a revolution than a reform. As the reform is carried out in an all-round way, it will not only influence everyone's income but will also change their social status and may even change their values. The reform of pricing, planning, and administration will cause a drastic change in production structure as well as a radical shift in government functions. As enterprises are given greater decision-making power and assume sole responsibility for their profits and losses, the social structure—including the relationship between the party and government, between government and enterprises, and between managers and workers—will be reshaped. To stimulate production, while reforms of prices, wages, taxes, and finance are carried out, reforms of the cadre system, the labor and personnel system as well as the social security system should also be conducted. Inevitably, other areas such as scientific research, education, medical care, and housing will

Chen Yizi, born in 1940, is a member of the State Economic System Reform Commission, director of the China Economic System Reform Institute, and a deputy director of the Economic Society of Beijing Youth. This article is an excerpt from his speech at "the summary meeting of the 1985 social and economic investigation."

be also affected by reform.

As the reform expands in depth and breadth, the economy becomes more and more difficult to control and the reform itself is more difficult to sustain. During the last quarter of 1984 and the first quarter of 1985 China's economic reform met some unexpected problems, such as the expansion of consumption and investment demand, an uncontrolled expansion of credit, a drastic decline in exchange reserves, and an uneasy public mood toward some measures. The situation reveals that China's economy is quite different from both the Soviet model and the Western market economy; and China's economic reform is more complicated than that of either Eastern Europe or other third world countries.

No doubt the current economic reform will decide China's ups and downs. If China's social science research workers want to serve their country and to meet the needs of the times, they must choose a most effective way to perform their research work. Methodology has become the priority question in academic work. Undoubtedly, they will choose to integrate theory with practice, since finding out the most effective and practical way to build a socialist country with Chinese characteristics is what China's reform is all about.

The Third Plenary Session of the Twelfth Party Central Committee proposed the framework of a "commodity economy under unified planning." However, its specific laws of motion are still vague. Much detailed research work on different economic systems must be done.

What is the biggest obstacle to research work on reform? The biggest problem is not "Left" thinking. It is whether or not theoretical research and strategical study or application research can meet the needs of the reform. It lies in the poor level of the country's research work. For example, at the beginning of the century, China was forced to open to all the big powers and was reduced to a semifeudal and semicolonial country. At that time not only was land a commodity, even people could be sold freely on the market. Clearly, at that time, people's thinking was even more "liberated" from "Left" thinking than it is today. And yet China remained a very poor country.

The logic of a commodity economy and the exchange of equal values is very simple. But we cannot get a ready answer to our practical questions through mere inference. The answer does not lie in books or in other countries' models either. Only through practice can we find the best way to build a socialist country with Chinese characteristics. For example, in its revolutionary practice, the Communist Party of China found it very important to set up rural revolutionary base areas. It used the villages to surround cities and then took the cities. In this way the New China was founded. The recent rural production responsibility system was also born in practice.

A systematic investigation into the actual situation is an essential part of the method of "integrating theory with practice." For example, it was research that penetrated deeply into the real situation that played a key role in the CPC Central

Committee's decision to carry out the rural reform. The urban economic system reform is much more complicated than that of rural areas. It is intellectually inconsistent to reject investigation into urban economic reform on the pretext of the low transparency of the urban economic mechanism. Whether investigation will play a key role in academic work, enabling it to serve the modernization program, depends on whether we employ a comprehensive scientific method.

China's research workers have to put great effort into three aspects in their work. First of all, we must combine investigation based on "typical examples" with the sampling method. The highly specialized urban economy is quite different from the rural natural economy. Individual cases, no matter how rational, cannot be universally applied. The traditional method of analyzing a typical example is not enough for a scientific survey. Scientific sampling must be employed at the same time. Second, we must combine the investigation at one point in time with investigation over a period of time. Finally, we must promote comprehensive, interdisciplinary research. Conducting research in one discipline with no links to other disciplines is one of the hallmarks of China's research work. The results of that kind of research are not desirable. Comprehensive research combining different disciplines will not only better serve reform but also play a key role in raising China's scientific research level.

With the above ideas in mind, the China Economic System Reform Institute and the Economic Society of Beijing Youth conducted a series of social and economic investigations under the leadership of the State Economic System Reform Commission and with the enthusiastic help of the relevant government departments. These investigations reveal China's social and economic development trends and expose some questions and problems in the current reform. The investigation not only offered a chance to train China's social research workers, it also made them realize the difficulties and complexities of reform. Through the investigation they have gained a deeper understanding of the party's guidelines and policies in recent years. They also realized that reform requires not only their enthusiasm and their strong sense of duty to the party and the country, but also a cool head and a scientific attitude in their work. The survey taught them to put forward questions practically, to design investigation schemes systematically, to select samples rationally, to connect the research in one discipline with that in others, and to do a comprehensive analysis on the basis of quantitative and qualitative analysis. In the survey they have once again realized that scientific research is no easy task. The spirit of devoting oneself to the cause of science, the firm pursuit of truth, and a rigorous work style is a precondition for performing sound scientific research.

All in all, the investigation has achieved significant results. We believe that more social science research workers and young friends will join us in the future in the great and glorious work of serving the reform and our country.

An Overview of the CESRRI Survey

Wang Xiaoqiang and Zhang Gang

Under the leadership of the State Committee on Restructuring the Economic System and with the enthusiastic help of various ministries and the relevant departments of local governments, the investigation on urban economic reform was conducted by the China Economic System Reform Research Institute (CESRRI) and the Economic Society of Beijing Youth (ESBY) between February and November of 1985. The whole process included eight procedures: planning, chart design, trial investigation, professional training, overall investigation, a group report, data processing and material analysis, and report writing. With participation from 21 units, including ministries, research institutes, and colleges and universities, the investigation employed a work force of 447 people including statisticians and college undergraduates and postgraduates. Fourteen million data were collected and 156 reports totaling 1.3 million words were written in the investigation.

The main components of the investigation were as follows.

1. The Urban Economic System Reform and Urban Economic Development

This section investigated the actual situation of urban economic system reform and the urban economic mechanism. The content includes the managerial environment of enterprises; the economic performance of enterprises; planning, material, finance and tax, banking, price, and commercial system reform; the speed and impetus of industrial development; the distribution of consumption

Wang Xiaoqiang, born in 1952, is deputy director of the China Economic System Reform Research Institute and deputy head of the Research Department of the Economic Society of Beijing Youth. Zhang Gang, born in 1949, is director of the Liaison Office of the China Economic System Reform Research Institute and secretary general of the Economic Society of Beijing Youth.

funds and demand and supply of consumer goods; the distribution of credit and the development of apparatus needing credit; the investment mechanism; labor and employment, the wage system, the dual system for means of production, and so forth.

Forty kinds of charts were designed. During the investigation 6,453 valid responses were recovered and 12 million data were collected, upon which 92 reports totaling 700,000 words were written.

The investigation was carried out in Chongqing, Tianjin, Shanghai, Dalian, Wenzhou, Qingdao, Fuzhou, Xiamen, Guangzhou, Jinan, Harbin, Shijiazhuang, Nanchang, Weifang, Hefei, Hangzhou, Lanzhou, Guiyang, and Kunming. All these cities are comprehensive pilot projects for urban economic system reform, except four that bear special significance for the survey. The following departments of each city were involved in the investigation: the economic system reform commission (or office), planning commission, economic commission, labor bureau, statistics bureau, tax bureau, finance bureau, materials bureau, commerce bureau, industrial and commercial administration, local branches of the People's Bank of China, the Bank of Industry, and the Bank of Commerce and Construction as well as five industrial bureaus in charge of various production industries and the fifteen factories under them. Altogether 429 enterprises from the above-mentioned 27 cities were involved in the survey, including 279 state-run enterprises, 131 medium-sized enterprises, and 188 small ones.

The participant units of the investigation include the Institute of China Economic System Reform, the Economic Society of Beijing Youth, the Rural Policy Study Office under the Secretariat of the CPC Central Committee, the Beijing Economic System Reform Committee, Beijing Sociological Research Institute, the Financial Research Institute under the People's Bank of China, the Financial Scientific Research Institute under the State Planning Commission, the graduate school of the Chinese Academy of Social Sciences, Beijing University, the Chinese People's University, Qinghua University, Beijing Teacher's University, the Central Finance College, Beijing Economic College, Nankai University, Fudan University, and the Economic Research Institute under the Shanghai Academy of Social Sciences. About 280 professional researchers, postgraduates, and students on in-service training programs participated in the investigation.

2. The Wishes and Aspirations of Factory Heads and Managers

Questionnaires were issued to 359 factory heads or managers concerning their management objectives, their incentives for these goals, obstacles to the realization of the goals, their preferences concerning sources of and funds as well as their personal ambitions. All 359 questionnaires were recovered and 40,000 data were collected.

3. The Public Response to Price Reform

The investigation was conducted by the fourth section of the CESRRI and the sociology department of Beijing University. It was designed to reveal urban residents' understanding and remarks on price reform, their choice of lifestyle, and their ability to adapt themselves to a commercial society. The investigation was conducted separately in February 1985 and July 1985. The first one was carried out among 2,409 households in 11 cities and 16 counties from Beijing, Hebei, Zhejiang, Hunan, and Anhui, obtaining 380,000 data; the second one was carried among 2,060 households in 10 cities from Beijing, Heilongjiang, Shaanxi, Sichuan, Shangdong, Zhejiang, Hubei, and Guangxi, acquiring 350,000 data.

4. Reform of the Social Security System

This study began in March 1985 and was carried out in two steps: (1) an analysis of the necessity of social security and employment system reform; (2) a survey questionnaire conducted among state enterprise workers and staff members. The analysis focused on the following questions: the problem of a structurally swollen enterprise work force, the relationship between the inflation of consumption funds and the guaranteed employment system, the employment of rural residents in cities and the introduction of contract workers, the opening of the labor market and the reform of the guaranteed employment system. The questionnaire contains such topics as the trend and the motive of job transfer among state-employed workers and staff members; their remarks on and abilities to deal with unemployment and the bankruptcy of their enterprises; the attitude of people of different ages, occupations, and localities toward the reform of the employment system, public welfare, and social security; and the feasibility of and social psychological preparation for the reforms in those fields. The survey, conducted by the fourth section of the CESRRI, the sociology department of Nankai University, and the sociology department of Beijing University, was carried out among 1,314 workers and staff members in Shanghai, Xiamen, Chongqing, Shashi, and Harbin, obtaining 400,000 data.

5. Young People's Attitude Toward Job Transfer and Their Outlook on Social and Economic Affairs

The investigation was conducted by the fourth section of the CESRRI and *Chinese Youth* magazine through questionnaires published in *Chinese Youth*. The project was designed to find young people's attitudes toward various occupations, job transfer, private income—earning versus broader social objectives—risk-taking, and work. The survey workers sampled 3,340 responses out of the 76,000 recovered, collecting 400,000 data.

6. The Quality of an Enterprise Manager

This study was done by the fourth section of CESRRI and the sociology department of Beijing University through a questionnaire survey. The survey included factory heads' or managers' ambitions in both career and life, their experience and training, arrangement of time, confidence about the future, opinions on the importance of family, courage in taking risks, and personal experiences.

The investigation was carried out in 900 enterprises in Beijing, Jilin, Shaanxi, Sichuan, Shangdong, Guangxi, Zhejiang, and Guiyang, obtaining 70,000 data from 1,000 valid responses.

7. The Functions of Government and Streamlining Government Organs

This study investigated the government function of administration, decision making, and supervision as well as the establishment of new government organs. It also explored the present situation and the prospects for streamlining China's government organs at various levels. The investigation was conducted in twelve cities—Wuhan, Chongqing, Guangzhou, Jiangmen, Shenyang, Harbin, Wenzhou, Nanjing, Lanzhou, Hangzhou, Fuzhou, and Shenzhen—and eleven counties—Gangcha, Huzhu, Changshu, Guixian, Linxian, Youngji, Haicheng, Guanghan, Yuanping, Guangxian, and Pingba.

The investigation produced 64 reports totalling 440,000 words. It was conducted by CESRRI, the Central Political and Law University, Chinese People's University, Beijing University, and the Chinese Academy of Social Sciences.

The main results of the investigation are presented in the report and the ten subreports prepared by the Comprehensive Investigation Group of the China Economic System Reform Research Institute. It should be pointed out that the Comprehensive Investigation Group was composed of a mere twenty-one researchers, most of whom came from the institute. It was these people who conducted such a large-scale and extensive economic and social investigation in such a short period of time. What is contained in these reports is only a minor part of the whole 14 million data and 140 investigation reports. It can only hint at the hard work done by some 400 young people.

The second point that should be made clear is that in processing the materials obtained during the investigation, the Comprehensive Investigation Group was not attempting to paint a rose-hued picture of economic reform. On the contrary, we tried to gain a better understanding of the situation, to test some theories that are important to the reform, to uncover problems that have cropped up in the course of reform. With regard to possible blueprints for reform, we are of the belief that in the last few years nobody has advanced a plan or raised a slogan that is utterly new. Nor does this investigation report propose something new, merely to be different. China's economic development and structural reform find themselves challenged by swelling consumption, investment hunger, imbalance of international payments, and the need to reorganize government institutions. We are confronted with all the dilemmas posed by reform in any socialist country or by economic development in any third world country. China's social science research is also challenged by sophisticated research projects around the world. At this time, when China is undergoing structural reform and the structure of production is undergoing vigorous changes, the "transparency" of our national economic performance has drastically declined. As far as our academic work is concerned, what is more important than logical inference based on established concepts is, through empirical research, to enrich our body of knowledge with basic facts. On this basis, we will gradually build up new concepts or models that conform to the actual Chinese situation. We will develop our own economics, sociology, political science, and other social sciences, which will not be copied from elsewhere and which will, therefore, be best able to serve China's economic development in succeeding generations. We now know that this calls for intelligence and hard work. Perhaps this is the most important conclusion of the investigation.

The third point that should be made clear is that the conclusions these reports attempt to propound are vulnerable at both a theoretical and an empirical level. First, from the contents of these reports we can see that this investigation presents nothing new technically and fails to make a macro analysis. Moreover, such questions as the balance of international payments, reorganization of government institutions and reform of the cadre system, relations between the central government and the various localities, and the nature of enterprise ownership were not studied. There are even big shortcomings with regard to what is covered in the report. For example, questions vital to enterprise performance, such as reform of the financial and taxation systems, the impact of the eight-grade progressive tax rates on the scale of enterprises, the impact of the regulation tax on the enterprise accumulation fund, the relations between management of nonbudgetary capital and the development of nongovernmental credits and financial reform, the readjustment of consumption policies (e.g., commercialization of housing), and the readjustment of the policy on creating new enterprises were all untouched.

What's more, many key conclusions of these investigation reports were deliberately cast in a vague fashion, as a matter of writing technique. Take for example the "motive force" of enterprise management. Our analysis of the relationships among per capita bonuses and per capita retained profit, total profit, and the growth rates of output value, profit, sales, and investment as well as our survey data on factory directors' decision making all point to the conclusion that enterprises now are more concerned than ever about profit. But despite this, we still lack sufficient evidence to equate Chinese enterprises' "profit motive force" with the classical "profit motive" of the market economy, with its desire for reinvestment. Is it possible that the real motive force behind Chinese enterprise management, as in some other socialist countries, is the desire to maximize per capita income? We found that factory directors are not very eager to expand their enterprises, and they view "reducing the income of workers and staff" as the most painful option in overcoming financial shortages (see subreport 3). But it would still be excessively arbitrary to conclude that Chinese enterprises' pursuit of profits is really an attempt to maximize per capita income. And yet our conclusions as to what motivates postreform enterprise management will be the micro basis for our entire analysis of China's industrial system and readjustment of policies. Thus, further study of this issue is obviously worthwhile.

Take as another example the policies pursued by enterprises subject to the dual system of distributing producer goods. This investigation report has stressed the role of marginal adjustments in increasing production and practicing economy. However, there is a difference between the long-term and the short-term adjustment of enterprises to their changing environment. The external factors that should be taken into consideration are also different in the short and long run. Judging from the simple logic of marginal analysis, the market prices that apply at the margin under the dual system serve as adequate signals for resource allocation, no matter what the market-plan split is. However, the report has not made clear theoretically under what conditions and to what extent these Chinese enterprises will follow the marginal principle rather than making decisions based on total or average cost. If this question is not answered clearly, it is impossible to predict accurately the regulatory role of price signals under the dual system. Although the report has confirmed the existence of a "threshold value," it says nothing about the theoretical basis of the value. All this must necessarily affect judgments concerning price reform.

Another instance is the decision on labor income. By attacking the logic that wages should be linked to economic returns, this investigation report actually regards labor as a commodity, makes a mechanical description of the structural increase of wages, and proposes that the market mechanism be introduced to determine wages. But whether wages in the public sector should include part of profit is still theoretically unclear. The distribution of profit is closely associated with society's capacity to accumulate capital. Furthermore, if wages include part of profit, a new barrier to labor mobility will be erected. But if wages are divorced from profit, this will affect the source of accumulation—the delivery of profit entirely to the government means we retain the traditional government investment system. Originally, demand for labor and competition in the labor market were included in the investigation. However, due to difficulties encountered during the investigation, these were not investigated or covered in the report. Under the existing Chinese cadre system, competition in labor supply, in the absence of any change with regard to demand behavior and without opening a true labor market, would still serve to contain the ceaseless increase of consumption demand. But this would involve unimaginable social and political costs.

Take investment as the final example. The original investigation plan included a survey of factors that cause excessive investment. But so many difficulties were encountered during the investigation that this question was actually not touched. The government is now not the only investor. The multiplying of investors has changed investment objectives and eventually the pattern, scale, and efficiency of investment as well. At present, enterprise investment is made largely in pursuit of profit and investment is yielding good economic returns. However, since enterprises own only a small amount of capital and have limited control over resources, they are in a position to make only small-scale investments. Moreover, enterprise investment mostly seeks short-term profit; they are reluctant to make long-term investments that yield "poor" economic returns. In making investment, the municipal government aims mainly at improving the appearance of the city; only a very small amount of the money goes to industry. When the provincial government invests, it often tries to keep a balance among local industries and also takes into consideration social targets such as job creation. Furthermore, the scale of municipal investment can be larger through "angling" or through linked projects. But often the economic returns from municipal investment are not good compared to the projects that enterprises finance by themselves. Arbitrary government apportionment and allocation of investment sometimes fills enterprises with discontent. If we pursue the logic of a commodity economy, enterprises will eventually be fully empowered to invest on their own. But how should this power be delegated to the enterprises? How should we determine the shares of the various investment agents in total investment, with an eye to the needs of both reform and development? This vital question remains unanswered.

It is said in the concluding part of the investigation report that China's economic reform has entered a new stage, moving from destruction to construction and from the introduction of the market mechanism to the establishment of a planned and organized market management system. During the new stage, the labor and capital markets will be expanded. In the future, markets for land and natural resources will likely be opened as well. But all this will occur only under the premise that we achieve a highly efficient and organized management. More importantly, even if we are blessed with an "atomistic market" for the first time in our history, the interrelationship between the market mechanism and development target—national rejuvenation by the year 2000—will have to go through a process of development that the international and domestic environment will not allow and could not stand. Therefore, the new stage of reform will feature efforts to cultivate new government functions and to intervene actively in economic life, to make up for the continued deficiencies of market development.

This new agenda for economic development and structural reforms presents those social science research workers who seek to serve reform with the task of upgrading their research quality. We must broaden the scope of social sciences. This historic movement has moved beyond economics alone. Sociology, political science, and administration and management must be applied to our practical problems. We must improve the quality of academic research. The stage of simply introducing the market mechanism has come to an end, and now we must learn and apply academic research from countries with a mature market economy. The times demand that the various social sciences, in a coordinated way, work out new standards, new concepts, and new target social systems. As young social science researchers, we are willing to do our part for this great and arduous task. This is why we are now publishing the raw fruit of our research, for comments from our readers.

I
REFORM

Past Achievements,
Present Challenges
and Future Policy Choices

Summary Report

Abstract

Reforms have imbued enterprises with greater incentive and accorded them more autonomy. The introduction of market mechanisms has enlivened the market and raised the sovereign status of consumers. But the expansion of consumption spending and of investment demand pose a serious challenge to reform.

The expansion of consumption spending is the result of the upward adjustment of wages intensified by the immobility of labor. The runaway consumption-oriented investment and the softening of the bank constraint both feature prominently in the issue of excessive investment growth, while the miniaturization of the investment scale and the tilt toward light industry in the composition of production-oriented investment will become a serious drag on economic revitalization in the days to come.

The problem lies in the micro mechanisms. The proper choice is, in step with a strengthening of administrative and indirect controls over wages and credits, to launch bold yet prudent microeconomic reforms. To keep wages from rising continuously, it is necessary to reform the systems of social welfare and security, throw open the labor market, take advantage of the abundant supply of labor, and encourage a certain degree of employment competition. To quench the thirst for investment and reverse the trend toward light industry in the industrial composition, such alternatives as a reform in the bankruptcy laws, strengthening horizontal ties among enterprises, opening nonbank financial markets, and encouraging the formation of investment consortia by enterprises

The organization, research for, and drafting of this report involved Cheng Yizi, Wang Xiaoqiang, Zhang Gang, Zhang Shaojie, Diao Xinsheng, Li Jun, Gai Nanfeng, Jiang Sidong, Xia Xiaojing, Jiang Yao, Ji Xiaoming, Xu Xiaobo, Xu Gang, Cao Yuanzheng, Zhao Yujiang, Shen Hong, Liu He, and others.

may be steps in the right direction.

China's economic mechanisms in the "switchover" period are more complicated than either the traditional model of the Soviet Union or the mature market economies of Europe and North America. Therefore, in our attempt at exercising effective macroeconomic control, it would be far from adequate to adopt the methods of the traditional model or to introduce the macroeconomic indicators of the developed countries before our microeconomic mechanisms have been correctly understood. Gaining an understanding of the current economic mechanism through positive, in-depth studies and investigations is the prerequisite.

The current report is a summary of the major findings of a number of surveys conducted in 1985 by the China Economic System Reform Research Institute. Covered in the report are the results of economic studies of 429 enterprises in 27 cities, two polls on the public reactions to the May 1985 price reform (2,409 and 2,060 questionnaires respectively), a survey on job preferences of young people and their basic attitude toward social and economic life (76,000 questionnaires), and an opinion poll concerning the reform of the social security system. The report attempts to make a general analysis of the present state of economic reform, its problems, and strategic priorities for the reform in the next stage on the basis of the above surveys as well as an overall assessment of the nationwide situation.

1. Achievements of Reform Thus Far

Since 1979, based on the idea of simplifying administration and decentralization, the reform of the economic structure designed to create a commodity market and deregulate and enliven the enterprises has made substantial progress. The reform of the systems of interenterprise distribution, planned resource transfer and allocation, and price control has gained noticeable results. Market mechanisms have begun to play an important role in the operation of the economic system.

The reform of the distribution system has highly motivated the enterprises to generate profit. In 1984, the enterprises studied retained 21.9 percent of the gross profit realized, and 36.7 percent of the retained profits was disbursed as bonuses. The correlation coefficient between the increased rate of retained profits and the increased rate of gross profits realized was 0.57, while the correlation coefficient between the increased rate of per capita bonus and that of retained profits was 0.29. The interests of the enterprises and their workers are closely related to the profits of the enterprises. Enterprises that for a long time sought mainly to fulfill production quotas have begun to react to a strong profit incentive. According to statistics derived from 359 questionnaires addressed to factory directors, "improvement of efficiency and benefit" topped the list of fourteen management objectives, followed by "improvement of quality" and "development of new products" in that order. "Fulfillment of production quotas" came eleventh, with "doubling of product value" bringing up the rear. Such an order of priority is borne out by the actual performance indicators of the enterprises: the annual growth rates of product value and of profits of the sample enterprises show a significant correlation, as do the rates of investment in fixed assets and profit (for the former, $r=0.3249$, and for the latter, $r=0.1373$, while investment and other indicators do not show such correlations).

The reform in the system of planned resource allocation has afforded the enterprises a certain degree of autonomy in their operations. In 1984, the planned production ratio of the sample enterprises (the proportion of the output under mandatory plans in relation to the gross output) was 23.97 percent, the planned supply ratio of major raw materials (the proportion of planned supply in relation to the gross materials consumption) accounted for 73.16 percent, and the planned marketing ratio of products (the amount earmarked for planned allocation in relation to gross sales) took up 57.42 percent, leaving as much as 32.81 percent to be marketed by the enterprises on their own. In the period from January to June 1985, the planned ratios of raw material supply diminished sharply. In the gross consumption of major raw materials, the proportion acquired by the enterprises autonomously through adjustment and cooperative arrangements between enterprises and in the market abruptly increased from 26.84 percent in 1984 to 43.8 percent, an increase of 17 percent within half a year.

As regards the overall situation in the enterprises, in 1984, 51 percent of enterprises studied had already gained varying degrees of autonomy, 77 percent of them found it necessary to adapt their production plans to market demand, and 90 percent relied to a certain extent on marketing at least part of their products by themselves.

The ''two-tier'' pricing system has obviously played a positive role. An important function of enterprise-coordinated prices and self-marketed prices is to reflect more truthfully the supply and demand situation of the market and, through the accompanying marginal effect, to regulate enterprise activities. Take steel, for example: to producer and consumer alike, the possibility of selling additional steel output or the need to buy additional steel products at the high free-market price would imply that with each extra ton of steel produced or saved, a given enterprise would experience increased sales, or reduced cost, calculated according to market prices. The data gathered from twelve medium-sized steel mills (table 1.1) suggest that as soon as the self-marketed portion of output exceeds a certain ''threshold,'' a great marginal effect is achieved.

The ''two-tier'' pricing system also has a noticeable effect on economizing on materials. In 1984, 300 steel-consuming enterprises reduced steel consumption for each 10,000 yuan of output value by 18 percent. The market has begun to exert a strong influence on enterprise production, supply, and marketing. Vested with more decision-making power, enterprises have to cater to market demand in order to realize profits. The correlation coefficient between the growth rates of output value and sales revenue of the sample enterprises is a high 0.74. The fastest growing lines of trade and enterprises are also the most successful sellers.

Table 1.1

Relationship between Self-Marketing Rate and Output Growth Rate of Twelve Steel Mills

Number of Enterprises	Self-Marketing Rate (%)	Average	Output Growth Rate (%)	Average
Lowest 6	0– 7.8	2.96	−10.98– 5.80	− 9.32
Highest 6	20.0–34.0	18.78	2.30–69.73	14.38
All 12	—	11.00	—	5.26

The city of Shashi, a model in this reform campaign, is known throughout the country. Its gross industrial output value increased by 7.1 percent in 1984, only half as much as the previous year and far below the national average increase of 14 percent. Other indicators of economic performance such as the utilization of circulating funds also failed to maintain the level of the previous year. The simple reason is that the textile industry, the output value of which accounts for 60 percent of the city's gross industrial output value, faced an unfavorable market. By contrast, the city of Xiamen registered a 57.7 percent increase in its industrial growth in the first half of 1985. The reason lies in the 890 percent increase in the industrial output value of the much sought-after electronic products, which account for 58.3 percent of the total increment in industrial output value.

The Hungarian economist Janos Kornai takes the ratio between the input inventory and the output inventory of an enterprise (referred to as "Kornai index" for short) as the most important comprehensive index capturing the essential difference between the resource-constrained sellers' market economy and the demand-constrained buyers' market economy (table 1.2).

The Kornai index of our sample enterprises was 4.5 in 1983, 4.4 in 1984, and 3.8 in the first half of 1985. The relative reduction of the input inventory and increase of output inventory of the enterprises imply a greater room for choice to the enterprises as buyers, and a greater constraint of market demand on enterprises as sellers. Different methods of computing all affirm the significant change in the effect the market mechanism has on enterprise operations. Along with the deepening of the reform, the sovereign status of enterprises as independent buyers is rising steadily, whereas the monopoly status of enterprises as sellers is gradually receding.

The introduction of market mechanisms has accustomed the people to life under a commodity economy and has won widespread support (see table 1.3). The interval between these two surveys was less than six months, but the score for strict state control over prices plummeted. Shortly after the opening of prices for nonstaple foodstuffs, quite a number of people turned from a negative attitude to show support for price management by market forces, thanks to their as yet

Table 1.2

"Kornai Index" for Six Countries[a]

Buyers' Market Economies	Years	Kornai Index	Sellers' Market Economies	Years	Kornai Index
Australia	1972–1977	1.5	USSR	1967–1977	9.2 –12.3
Sweden	1968–1972	0.7 –0.74	Poland	1975	10.3
U.S.A.	1960–1977	0.94–1.16	Hungary	1971–1980	7.26–8.53

a. Janos Kornai, "The Dual-Dependency of State Industry," *Economic Research* 10 (1985).

Table 1.3

Public Reaction to Price Control Alternatives

Alternatives	February Survey	July Survey
All prices should be fixed and strictly controlled by the state.	61.8%	34.7%
All prices should be open to market quotation.	5.9	6.7
Some prices should be open and some others subject to state control.	30.8	58.2

short experience with market practices.

In the survey conducted in February 1985 on the social and psychological effects of the price reform, we found that in the list of eleven factors affecting people's views on the reform, "evaluation by changes in the standard of living" (subjective indicator) scored the highest, whereas "evaluation by per capita family income" (objective indicator) scored the lowest. What is more, there did not seem to be any significant correlation between the two. People did not think that their standard of living was markedly correlated with their actual levels of income. This interesting phenomenon shows that in a sellers' market, where money cannot always get one what one wants, consumption ceases to be a direct function of income, and the level of income cannot be equated with the actual standard of living.

For this reason, it is far from adequate to base macrocontrol over inflation on commodity price indices which include many planned prices that do not reflect market supply and demand. What affected people's opinions most during the "switchover" period was their realized purchasing power and the actual improvement of their living standard. The second opinion survey last July reaffirmed the above conclusion. The prices of nonstaple foodstuffs have a direct

Table 1.4

People's Understanding of the Reform

Statement	Total & Partial Agreement	Total & Partial Disagreement or Uncertainty
As long as the reform measures are conducive to social & economic development, they are worthwhile even if entailing greater risks to one's own welfare	78.3%	21.7%
The reform may be somewhat disorderly at present, but it is better than "eating from the same big pot."	77.8	22.2
As long as one has skill and ability, one won't suffer from the reform.	80.7	19.3
If the reform succeeds in the end, we don't mind suffering a lower standard of living for the time being.	75.3	24.7

bearing on people's livelihood. At a time when wage adjustments had not yet fully caught up, when the very sensitive and risky reform of the price system had just been launched, people who claimed a "substantial" and a "slight" improvement of the standard of living still accounted for 73.4 percent (11.1 percent less than in the February survey). Is that attributable to the income subsidies? Our conclusions point to the contrary. Especially worth mentioning is the encouraging attitude of understanding and support of the broad masses toward the reform, as reflected in another survey entitled "the Social and Psychological Reaction of People to the Reform of the Social Security System" (see table 1.4).

It is safe to conclude that the reform over the last few years has been a great success. As far as the functioning of the economy is concerned, the goal of production has begun to shift from the fulfillment of state quotas to the satisfaction of market demands, and supply is actively responding to demand. The development of production has increasingly been motivated by profits and sales returns instead of output volume, output value, and growth rate. More autonomy to enterprises has led to changes in their operational objectives and enhancement of their managerial capability. The constraining effect of market demand on enterprises has to some degree edged the enterprise behavior away from the track set by the old mode of control. The introduction of market mechanisms has helped acclimatize people to life under a market economy and is steadily fostering ever greater support reform.

The achievements of the reform have provided favorable conditions for pushing reform efforts from product markets into factor markets and have laid a solid foundation for more effective and active government intervention in economic life while adopting the market mechanism as a guideline. The task we are facing now is not to reintroduce the Procrustean bed and shove our national economy back on to the old track, nor is it to brush aside the great breakthroughs already made in the reform and to start wholly anew. Rather, we should come to grips with problems in real life and resolutely carry forward the reform on the basis of what has already been achieved.

2. New Challenges

Having established the constraint that market demand now imposes on the orientation of the economic system, this report focuses next on trends and problems in consumption, investment, and microeconomic mechanisms. The expansion of consumption spending, and the "thirst for investment" which seems to be embedded in the system, have become serious challenges to economic development and structural readjustment, just at a time when reform over the past years has begun to bear fruit. This is a syndrome common to economic reform in all socialist countries.

2.1. Expansion of Consumption Demand

Structural Wage Inflation. "More work, more pay" is a fair demand by workers. Wages should rightfully be determined by market supply and demand. Such a system would draw forth well-motivated labor. But the lack of job mobility in China required that we motivate workers by linking wages to enterprise profit.

Unfortunately, the performance of an enterprise is affected not only by the enthusiasm of its workers but also by a mix of various other factors. The planned allocation of factors of production, enforced over a long time in the past, has resulted in extremely uneven operational conditions among the enterprises in China. Take fixed assets for example. The ratio between the highest and lowest per worker value of fixed assets in the sample enterprises is roughly 200. Under these circumstances, average labor productivity, a main indicator of the productive enthusiasm of the labor force, does not reflect the quality or quantity of work, and in fact it shows a negative correlation with profit. The fifty-six sample enterprises whose profit increase rate is below −14 percent show an average labor productivity increase rate of over 10 percent, whereas for the forty-three enterprises with profit increase rate in excess of 120 percent, the average labor productivity increase rate is below zero. Presumably, these enterprises increased profit by increasing fixed assets. In this context, it would obviously be inadvisable to link labor to profits.

But in practice, it is hard for a profitable enterprise to resist pressure for wage hikes, in the absence of a labor market. When wages in one sector shoot up, workers in every other enterprise or industry press for "matching" wage hikes in their "home base," in an inflationary process that has been labeled "upward emulation." After the taxi companies in Beijing achieved wage raises, the bus drivers applied to be transferred to taxi companies. When their applications were turned down, they were usually compensated by a wage increase close to the level achieved by the taxi drivers. Whether we admit it or not, wages are already being determined by supply and demand. If there were enough drivers competing for jobs with taxi companies, wages there could not remain high. If the bus companies could enroll drivers from the community, then they would not need to raise wages without regard to economic efficiency.

This structural wage inflation due to the lack of a labor market has not yet received adequate attention. Wage reform is more inflationary than price reform. Although the removal of price controls leads to a rise in the general price level, the simultaneous reform of the system of planned allocation and the expansion of enterprise autonomy over supply, production, and marketing allows factors of production to flow and form new combinations. The resulting increase in supply of products helps to check the general price rise. But reform in the system of planned labor assignment and allocation has not even started. As a result the partial lifting of wage control is not accompanied by a labor reallocation that might mitigate wage inflation.

Since any one sector's wage increase is merely a result of the rigid economic mechanism, a call for "upward emulation" (matching wage hikes) naturally is received with sympathy by factory managers, local governments, banks, tax authorities, and auditing and other management departments. According to data covering 429 enterprises, in 1984 alone, enterprises were able through "negotiations" with these higher-ups to raise the percentage of retained profit in gross profit from 19.36 percent to 21.59 percent and to increase the percentage of bonus disbursement in retained profit from 25.43 percent to 36.70 percent. Despite great differences in profitability, labor productivity, and operating conditions, the sample enterprises sharply reduced the Gini coefficient of per person retained profit from 0.208 in 1983 to 0.182 in 1984. Undoubtedly, "upward emulation" has contributed to this situation. And these are only the facts on record in the accounts. Off-the-accounts "loopholes" are too numerous to stop up. According to our investigations, the enterprises employ more than forty different methods to dodge wage control and secure more bonuses and benefit. These include, inter alia: transferring funds through labor service companies or auxiliary companies, unmerited disbursement of income, illicitly diverting funds from the set purposes, disbursing administrative appropriations to benefit individuals and adding the amount thus spent to the cost, using the bank accounts of collective enterprises to escape detection, unauthorized marketing of products by enterprises and omitting part of the returns from account books, awarding shares to individuals and paying them dividends, and increasing the disbursement of tax-free bonuses. According to a rough calculation, "off-the-books" losses alone amount to some 20 billion yuan in the whole country.

Hidden Expansion of Consumption Funds. China's planned job assignment system combines employment with welfare and social security. Any redistribution of national income must take place at the point of employment. Consequently, social welfare and security expenses have become components of gross labor cost. Hence, the "upward emulation" and the resultant expansion of consumption funds in the form of wages are sure to kick off a substantial increase in various welfare funds. In the period from 1978 to 1984, the disbursements of wages and wage-related cost by the banks throughout the country increased by 11 percent annually; state subsidies for commodity prices increased by 36 percent annually (from 1978 to 1983); and the disbursement for labor welfare increased by 21 percent annually. In 1984, the state appropriated to various cities 60 billion yuan for workers' welfare and subsidies, which equalled 66 percent of wages. From 1978 to 1983, the per capita national income created by city workers increased by 9.28 percent, and their average cash and noncash income doubled in the same period. If the hidden expansion of consumption funds is also counted in, wage cost reaches 13 percent of total cost, equaling the level of Japan.

Consumption Demand Is Far in Advance of Level of Production. The expansion of consumption funds in the form of wages and the hidden expansion of consumption funds have led to an overall advance of consumption demand far ahead of the level of production. In the consumption of foodstuffs, the caloric intake per person per day in China was 2,877 calories in 1983, which amounted to the 1979 level of Japan and was 1.3 times that of the average level of all developing countries (1977). The intake of animal calories is also close to the world average, reaching Japan's level when its per capita national income was $413 (China's per capita national income in 1983 was only $231). In consumption patterns, the proportion of durable goods consumption climbed from 24 percent in 1979 to 44 percent in 1984. In 1985, the average level of possession by urban residents of such durable consumer goods as TV sets, electric fans, tape recorders, and sewing machines matched the level in Japan when its per capita national income was $1,600. Consumption in terms of housing, transportation, and medical care has also gone up with the tide. This concentrated and vigorous consumer demand exerts a heavy pressure on the market and a strong pull on industrial production and investment.

In 1984, the accumulated purchasing power of our urban and rural residents approached 200 billion yuan, amounting to 60 percent of the gross cash income of the residents in the same year and 36 percent of gross national income. In 1985, consumption demand increased by about 80 billion yuan. The irreversible momentum of the expansion of consumption spending, which has taken up 80 percent of national income outlays, poses a grave threat to structural reform, economic development, and social stability. It must receive adequate attention and be dealt with seriously.

2.2. Expansion of Consumption-Oriented Investments and the Shift of the Industrial Structure toward Light Industry

In 1984, extrabudgetary investment in fixed assets accounted for 80 percent of the gross social investment in fixed assets. The continued expansion of the retained segment of enterprise profits, the continued decentralization with respect to the authority to invest, the reduction of state budgetary investment, and the conscientious implementation of the policy of "substituting loans for budgetary appropriation" are reform objectives decided on for the Seventh Five-Year Plan period. These extrabudgetary investments, which have been increasingly determined by the interplay of supply and demand in the market, will become a major factor in the sectoral distribution of investment. The resource allocation pattern established thereby will, to a great extent, determine the fate of the overall economic revitalization drive after 1990.

Expansion of Consumption-Oriented Investment. A main characteristic of the current investment expansion is the rapid growth of consumption-oriented investment, and insufficient growth of producer goods. As of August 1985, nonproductive investment was 42.43 percent of the national capital construction during the Sixth Five-Year Plan period. It is now a common practice to divert funds for technological renovation and reform to housing construction. Even if funds for technological renovation and reserve funds were both lumped under productive accumulation, the investment rate in China has fallen from 29.14 percent (1976–79) to 24.41 percent (1981–84). By the end of 1985, it is estimated, the productive capital construction projects completed in the Sixth Five-Year Plan will have increased by only 6.4 percent over those of the Fifth Five-Year Plan, whereas the nonproductive capital construction projects completed will have increased by 128.76 percent. The increase in the nonproductive investment amounts to 87.75 percent of the gross increase in capital construction in the Sixth Five-Year Plan. According to statistics provided by nineteen cities under survey, in the period between 1983 and the first half of 1985, the proportion of nonproductive investment in gross investment was roughly 60 percent.

Investment in housing accounted for 70 percent of gross nonproductive investment in the whole country. From 1982 to 1984, investment in housing occupied 28 percent of gross social investment. More alarming still, the rapid growth in housing and similar nonproductive investment seems to be particularly insensitive to overall contraction of investment, perhaps due to the rigid employment system under which housing is a major fringe benefit. In the period of investment contraction from 1981 to 1982, the share of nonproductive investment in gross investment rose from 43.0 percent to 45.5 percent. In 1983 and 1984, as investment expanded, the share fell to 41.7 percent and 40.3 percent. The share rose again to 42.5 percent in the first half of 1985, during the renewed contraction in gross investment. Over the recent past, investment in housing has hardly been affected at all by state macroeconomic policies but has maintained a steady and rapid growth. And the share of such investment in the total tends to become greater when overall investment shrinks. Housing investment seems to be as "downward-inflexible" as wages. If such a trend is allowed to continue, the long-term development of the national economy will surely be hampered by insufficient productive investment.

The Danger of a Softening Bank Constraint: "Investment Thirst." Given expanding and inflexible consumption investment, to guarantee the necessary productive accumulation would presuppose an undesirable expansion of overall investment. The traditional thirst for investment in socialist systems poses another threat to economic development and to the relaxation of control over investment.

Conventional wisdom attributes the thirst for investment to the "everyone eating from one big pot" system that ignores economic accounting. However, it should be pointed out that the investment expansion today differs substantially from previous fiscal investment expansions, for it occurs at a time when the budget constraint on enterprises has become harder. At present, enterprises are still not really wholly responsible for their profits and losses, and the cadre system in enterprises has not been thoroughly reformed. Investment decision-makers are in the enviable position of engaging in profit-seeking adventures and being credited with success in operation without having any qualms about investment losses rebounding on themselves. The factory directors are not afraid of bankruptcy and workers do not fear unemployment—this is what fuels investment expansion. And yet, with the progress of the reform, the constraint on the enterprise has after all become more stringent. Except for a few priority projects, the era of wrangling for free fund appropriations and resource transfers is no more. Investment decision-makers have at least to bear the burden of paying bonuses to workers and staff as long as their enterprises still remain in operation. Such developments should at least have eased to a certain extent the thirst for investment. Then how can we explain the reemergence of an investment upsurge that shows no visible signs of abating?

We believe that the rampant investment expansion in 1984 and thereafter was to a large extent brought about by excessively liberal bank lending. National investment in fixed assets financed by domestic loans in 1984 increased by 47.3 percent over 1983. In the period between January and August 1985 an increase of 129.8 percent was registered (despite the high increase in 1984), while investment through enterprise self-financing rose by only 49.6 percent. The proportion of extrabudgetary capital construction and technological renovation financed by loans was respectively 18.7 percent and 29.3 percent in 1982, and these figures abruptly jumped to 20.5 percent and 35.0 percent in 1984; and again to 26.5 percent and 44.3 percent in the first half of 1985. As a result of the general tightening of credits and loans, the banks have readjusted their loan structures. According to itemized reports from the banks in eighteen cities, the proportion of loans for fixed assets in the sum total of loans was 6.3 percent in 1983, 6.8 percent by the end of June in 1984, 7.7 percent by the end of 1984, and 8.9 percent by the end of June 1985. Our sample enterprises financed 31.84 percent of their gross investment in fixed assets by bank loans. The loans for investment by rural enterprises have increased by a similar margin.

When we asked factory directors to rank operational constraints, "inadequate financing" won second place in a list of sixteen alternatives. Asked to rank their preferred sources of funds, "to borrow from a bank" scored first out of eight options. And each of fourteen enterprise subgroups without exception named it as their first choice. This shows that the reform has hardened the fiscal constraint, while bank loans have become an important source of capital funds. Of the loans provided by the construction banks in seven cities, the overdue arrears in repayment of loans by the end of 1984 increased by 6.6 percent over the previous year, and the figure shot up by 44.7 percent by the end of June 1985, as compared with the same period of 1984. The data in table 1.5 show the same pattern. All these statistics testify to the softening of the bank constraint, once the most rigid area of the Chinese economy. The softening of the bank constraint poses an even greater threat than fiscal investment expansion. Within government finance, an increase in the fiscal reserve must necessarily be accompanied by a decrease in consumption. However, the banks possess unlimited power to create money and can achieve high accumulation at the same time as consumption expands. Nowadays, it has become common practice for enterprises to pay bonuses and welfare expenses from their own funds and carry on construction projects on borrowed money. The profit retained by the enterprise is mainly earmarked for consumption, which generates additional investment demand through the accelerator mechanism. The resulting effects—a shortfall in productive investments and accelerated investment prospects—in turn exert a two-pronged pressure on bank financing, compelling the banks to grant loans and finally compelling the central bank to issue currency. In this pattern, there seems to emerge a new economic mechanism, which satisfies through bank loans both the enterprise's welfare needs and its production needs. For the local banks, a handsome investment turnover might be expected. But what seems rational and feasible at a micro level is not necessarily healthy for the macroeconomy. While the microeconomic entities are rejoicing over their respective gains, the softening of bank control may have kicked off a general inflation characterized by excessive money supply.

The lesson of Yugoslavia is that when enterprises assume responsibility for their own financial gains and losses, the consumption spending from enterprise-retained funds lurches forward, a piling up of bank loans for investment follows closely behind, and the issuance of money brings up the rear. Compared with 1970, in 1976 in Yugoslavia individual consumption increased by 273 percent, collective consumption increased by 330 percent, investment in fixed assets increased by 290 percent, and accumulation by 40 percent. The cost of this dual satisfaction of welfare and production needs was a high foreign debt and infla-

Table 1.5

Insolvency Losses of Construction Banks in Eighteen Cities

	June 1983	Dec. 1983	June 1984	Dec. 1984	June 1985
Ratio of insolvency to arrears	24.29%	36.93%	41.90%	47.66%	51.80%

tion, which could hardly be due to fiscal expansion.

"Stunted Trees": The Miniaturization of Unit Investment Scale. The expansion of overall investment is only one aspect of the problem. Along with the increase in the share of enterprise-retained profit, decentralization in investment authority, and expansion of the overall level of investment, the neglected question of miniaturization of the scale of investment projects looms increasingly large.

In 1984, of the extrabudgetary funds of twenty-three cities, the enterprises and their upper management bodies accounted for 76 percent of the income and 89 percent of the outlay. The objective of the reform is to strengthen and not weaken the trend of enterprises controlling their own resources. However, because 90 percent of China's enterprises are small in size, the growth of enterprise-controlled funds implies a scattering of these funds over hundreds of thousands of enterprises, and thus a reduction in the amount of money available to any one unit. Of the enterprises we investigated, 57 percent are large and medium-sized, which is a much higher proportion than the national average. The profits they retained averaged 1.53 million yuan, only 0.5 million of which was earmarked for the development of production. The retained profits of the small enterprises averaged 0.26 yuan, and funds for the development of production only 0.1 million yuan. These are tiny amounts.

In China today, the financial market has not yet developed. There is no way of concentrating financial funds. The division of labor among enterprises is not well-developed, and mechanisms for enterprise integration and merger are rudimentary. Thus, the scattered distribution of investment funds inevitably leads to their scattered utilization. Enterprises cannot lend or borrow funds, so they use what they happen to have. Our survey found that for ten cities, of 3,212 capital construction projects in 1984, only 5.5 percent exceed 10 million yuan, and 52.0 percent were lower than 0.5 million yuan, averaging 0.237 million yuan. The projects that fell between 10 million and 0.5 million yuan averaged only 1.18 million yuan. If we look farther away from the central cities, we find the situation even less encouraging. (Consider, for example, the situation in Sichuan Province illustrated by Fig. 7.1 on page 121.)

The data all came from state-owned entities. Investment by urban and rural collectives and individuals amounts to 35 percent of gross social investment in fixed assets. Here, the miniaturization problem is even more conspicuous. By the end of 1984, the fixed assets owned by rural enterprises averaged 35,000 yuan each in terms of their original value, less than 0.5 percent of the average for state-owned enterprises.

The miniaturization of the scale of investment has seriously hampered economic performance. During the period of high economic growth in Japan, nongovernmental investment created the then world's biggest iron and steel works, chemical complexes, shipyards, automobile works, and so on. Generally speaking, large-scale investment stimulated by a promising economic environment, on the one hand, and large-scale production and expansion of the scale of investment, on the other, are two sides of the same coin. The reality we are facing today, however, is the expansion of gross investment coupled with a decline in the scale of investment. Take for example, those projects that have caught the fancy of many investors. The minimal optimal production scale of a washing-machine factory should be 200,000 units per annum. In 1984, of 130 washing-machine factories in the whole country, only 9 reached such a capacity. Of 110 refrigerator factories nationwide, average output was 4,600 units per annum, which is far below the national scale. There are over 110 motor factories in China, distributed all across the country except in Tibet and Ningxia. Their average scale is 2,000 cars per annum. Only a few state-financed automobile works established in former years operate up to the requirements of scale economy.

The minuscule unit investment scale is a challenge to current strategic thinking on reform. The emergence of more than 1,000 "bucket-size blast furnaces" has sounded the warning. In one sense, the problem reflects the success of the price reform. As the "two-tier" price system for steel generated an accurate price signal, market demand stimulated supply. It is impossible to revitalize the national economy by relying on a nationwide blooming of "stunted trees" like these.

"Short-term Investment and Quick Turnover": The Light-Industrialization of the Industrial Structure. Within productive investment, extrabudgetary financing is biased toward short-term payoffs. Since 1978, our country's policy has given priority to the development of consumer goods, which has helped improve the economic situation and contributed to social stability. But in the long run, the proposition that the economy of a big country can depend on light-industrial growth is not borne out by any historical precedent. As matters now stand, the increased demand for durable consumer goods is exerting a strong pull on production and investment. Combined with the miniaturization of investment scale resulting from decentralized investment, this has led to inadequate investment in the heavy and chemical industries. This is yet another problem that endangers long-term development.

The tendency shown in figure 1.1 is increasing. The present pattern of China's industrial investment is far different from that of five advanced countries (United States, Japan, Britain, France, and West Germany) when their per capita national income was $1,000. The average structural differential is as high as 22.56

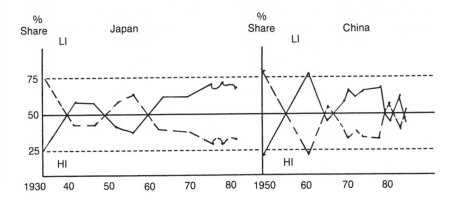

Figure 1.1

Percentage Shares of Light and Heavy Industry in Japan and China

percent. In 1965, the production of Japan's chemical and metallurgical industries accounted for 30 percent of the gross industrial output value, while those two sectors in China accounted for only 20 percent of gross industrial output value and 20 percent of gross investment in 1984. It is evident that the structural gap is becoming wider.

The scattering of investment will cause further light-industrialization of industry. The increase in general-purpose investment has far surpassed investment in energy, transportation, and other priority construction activities. From January to June 1985, the proportion of delivered investments in the energy sector in relation to gross investment fell from 23.8 percent for the same period in 1984 to 19.7 percent. In transportation and telecommunications the ratio fell from 15.1 percent to 13.9 percent for the same periods.

Meanwhile, the net increments of productive capacity in the railroad, highway, steel-making, electricity generation, and other sectors in the Sixth Five-Year Plan period have all declined. The development of the raw materials industry is falling even farther behind the needs of economic development. In the first half of 1985, based on the share of the metallurgical industry in gross industrial output value (the annual average of which was 0.084 from 1980 to 1984) and the investment output ratio of the metallurgical industry (0.66), investment in the metallurgical industry should have been 10.4 billion yuan. However, the actual investment in the metallurgical industry in the period mentioned was only 3.384 billion yuan, representing a shortfall of 207 percent. The insufficiency of investment in the metallurgical industry will undoubtedly hinder the effort to reverse the increasing dependency on imports for the development of our domestic industry.

As to the age of the productive equipment of China's metallurgical industry, the equipment of the 1970s only comprises 15 percent, that of the 1950s and '60s comprises 70 percent, and that of the 1940s still occupies 15 percent. The need for investments in energy and transportation sectors is even more pressing. With the further advance of the reform and the increase in the retained profit of enterprises (which implies a reduction of the portion for state fiscal use), investment will more and more be undertaken using scattered extrabudgetary funds. In the light of the trend toward short-term returns in extrabudgetary financing, it is safe to predict that the light industrialization of the industrial structure will in time become a most serious drag on the national economy.

3. Alternative Directions of Reform

3.1. Introduction

In the Seventh Five-Year Plan period, we are faced with three strategic tasks: Reform, development, and improvement of living standards. Reform—that is, simplification of administration and continued decentralization—presents three touchy problems.

(1) "Relaxation of control always breeds expansion." Reform conflicts with economic stability. Reform requires the delegation of power to enterprises, for without authority over such matters as wages and investment, the enterprises will have no genuine room to maneuver. At present, there is still no mechanism to check the structural wage inflation induced by "upward emulation." With any renewed reform, the expansion of consumption is bound to provoke a new upsurge of investment and an overheated growth rate. Meanwhile, the banks may soften their lending policies, resulting in an inflationary spiraling of consumption and investment.

(2) Reform conflicts with the need to emphasize heavy industry. Reform means using indirect economic levers to stimulate particular industries, regions, or enterprises. But the mechanism of "upward emulation" quickly turns any local incentive policy into a widespread consumption expansion, threatening a loss of macro control.

(3) Reform conflicts with effective long-term economic development. Reform seeks to lodge the investment decision in those enterprises that are responsible for their own losses and gains. But miniaturization of the scale of investment caused by this decentralization, the expansion of nonproductive investment, and the shift toward light industry all deviate in varying degrees from long-term development goals.

The rising expectations for income, the entrenched "upward emulation" mentality, and the experience with markets in recent years have combined to imbue the broad masses with a desire and an expectation to change jobs or choose professions, which was out of the question under the "big pot" system. The attitude of people toward employment has switched from seeking security and avoiding risks to seeking opportunities in spite of risks. This has laid the foundation for the formation of a labor market. Meanwhile, the thirst for investment and the miniaturization of the scale of investment will induce enterprises to pool resources and to open wider channels for the concentration of capital, making them more inclined to integration. This in turn prepares the ground for formation of a capital market, reform of the financial system, and active intervention by government. We consider each of these issues in turn in the rest of this section.

The macro imbalance that confronts us is severe indeed. Until we are able to curb the "two expansions" (expansion of consumption and expansion of investment), some remedial measures are unavoidable. For the sake of preserving reform, this recentralization must be carried out resolutely. With so many problems arising from our microeconomic mechanisms, rashly to change mandatory administrative control into indirect economic regulation at the macro level would run the risk of "one move amiss, the whole game a mess." Besides, the capacities of macro control, even in Western countries with full-fledged market mechanisms, are limited. So, the correct direction is to strengthen administrative control over aggregate wages, credit, and loans while resolutely deepening the reform of the micro mechanisms.

A prerequisite to containing the expansion of consumption funds is the unemployment of some workers. Similarly, the prerequisite to quenching the "thirst for investment" is the bankruptcy of some enterprises. During the Seventh Five-Year Plan period, then, we should face these challenges squarely. On the basis of a product market and a reformed price system, we must push forward to the next stage: establishing a labor market and a capital market, along with adjustments in consumption policies and industrial organization policies.

3.2. Introducing a Labor Market

China's reality is the coexistence of large-scale "on-the-job unemployment" in the cities and a large surplus labor force in the countryside. Cheap labor should count as a great advantage in China's industrial revitalization. But under the present rigid employment system, the expansion of consumption funds is turning this advantage into a disadvantage. A continually rising labor cost is a very harmful thing. To check fundamentally the expansion of consumption funds and the continuous rise of the aggregate wage level, we must utilize our "unlimited supply of labor" (an advantage unavailable to the Eastern European countries in their reform drive), by prudently and gradually breaking down barriers to job mobility, encouraging a flow of workers between different ownership systems and between the cities and rural areas, and, in general allowing the surplus labor force to enter into employment competition.

Forming a labor market and labor mobility will not only create a direct check on wage increases through employment competition. It will also help lower people's expectations and self-evaluation, thus indirectly checking wage increases through weakening the "upward emulation" mentality. Under any kind of employment system, this "upward emulation" mentality will always be present. But under the rigid job assignment system, when labor is bound to one place, many people envy and covet other people's jobs and wages, which are beyond their reach mainly because they do not have the choice, not because they do not have the ability. The single most powerful antidote to the "upward emulation" disease is the employer's ability to say: "You are free to leave this job and compete for another with higher pay."

The "upward emulation" mentality covets both economic gain and social status. Under the rigid employment system, as there is very little opportunity to change jobs to achieve higher social status (vertical mobility), the masses' aspiration for doing so (e.g., developing one's special talent and pursuing one's special interests) becomes keenly felt. According to the "Survey on Job Evaluation and Preferences by Young People," young people's ranking of jobs is based mainly on social status, not on economic gain. The correlation between ranking and social status is high ($p=0.9272$); there is no correlation with economic gain. In the inquiry on job selection criteria, "give play to one's special talent," "provide educational opportunities," and "raise social status" occupied the three leading places, and "good pay" came a poor fifth on a list of six criteria. Of the people questioned, 62.6 percent opted for a "job, with prestige," even if it implied less pay; 85.5 percent mainly wanted their jobs to fit in with their interests; and 95.5 percent were most concerned about bringing their abilities into full play. Given these attitudes, it is clearly possible to use job satisfaction to diffuse wage pressure. Many peasants and self-employed entrepreneurs yearn for a chance to abandon higher income opportunities in order to acquire the status of a "permanent salary or wage earner." Why? Because social goals dominate economic goals. If we open up the labor market and allow them to acquire jobs that offer less remuneration but higher social prestige, we will at the same time weaken the demands for "upward emulation" of those already in such jobs.

The rigidity of China's employment system arises from the fact that employment provides not just a wage, but social welfare and social security as well. A job provides rationed grain, free medical service, and other social benefits, and also a retirement pension, unemployment security, and social security. This has led to the establishment of a set of allocation systems, including that of labor. Thus public finance finds itself at the mercy of employment.,and labor has therefore necessarily been centrally allocated.

Yet, ironically, our survey shows that young people do not wish to have such a "three-in-one" package deal. Some 74.5 percent of respondents support a retirement pension system, but 50.8 percent and 50.5 percent respectively are skeptical or negative toward permanent employment and free medical care. Thanks to the

Table 1.6

Attitudes Toward Labor Mobility

Questions	Yes	No
Do you wish to change your job?	48.2	24.1
Do you wish to transfer to another unit?	50.2	23.5
Do you wish to select your job freely even at the risk of unemployment?	51.2	48.0

achievements of the reform over the past few years, people's understanding of many major issues involving their own interests has gone beyond our expectations.

The present employment system is even less appreciated by the young people, who make of 60 percent of the working population. The percentage of youth who wish to choose their jobs freely even at the risk of unemployment is as high as 51 percent (table 1.6). Factory directors are no less emphatic when voicing their demand for job mobility. In their replies to the inquiry about sixteen operational constraints, the directors named "shortage of talents" as the number one constraint, and "inappropriate personnel policy" as constraint number three, preceding "poor raw material supply" and following "shortage of funds."

According to our investigations, the social risks involved in dismissing workers are not so appalling as previously imagined. Our questionnaire asked: If a factory needs 1,000 workers but has a work force of 1,200, should the surplus of 200 be dismissed? Some 71.8 percent of those questioned said yes; 28.1 percent said no. When the person questioned is hypothetically included in the dismissed 200, only 16.5 percent of the respondents would appeal to the leadership for a job assignment, 5.8 percent would choose to live on relief funds, 64.3 percent (!) would look on their own for other jobs, and 13.3 percent would try to become self-employed entrepreneurs. Unemployment insurance is the indispensable prerequisite for labor mobility. At present, already 48.2 percent of the people questioned support the establishment of an unemployment insurance system funded jointly by enterprises and individuals; 26.6 percent hold that as long as the pay is good, they can manage to pull through on their own in the unemployed days; and 24.7 percent think they would have to rely on state relief.

If we give employers the power to dismiss workers, do we risk a sharp decline in the overall employment level? More probably, we would first see a structural adjustment of employment that would be extremely conducive to industrial adjustment and improved efficiency. In one survey of enterprise directors, we asked them to order a list of sixteen operational constraints. Although these directors very strongly wanted the power to hire and fire, they gave twelfth, fourteenth, fifteenth, and sixteenth places respectively to "too many redundant persons," "employees not reconciled to their work," "shortage of qualified workers," and "too many retirees." When we hypothetically gave them authority to decide personnel affairs, the ratio between the total number of persons the 359 factory directors would wish to fire and those they would hire was 1:1.2. They mean to hire more than they would fire. This process of hiring in some areas and firing in others would work toward a structural adjustment of the labor force.

In reality, the labor market is already quickly taking shape, willy nilly. The job mobility now enjoyed by scientific and technical personnel and the widespread practice of "reserving a post without pay" have substantially changed people's views on employment. Moreover, quite a large number of enterprises, while leaving idle some employees on the state payroll, take on large numbers of contract laborers, temporary workers, and even peasants without assuming obligations for their social security. All this places the reform of the systems of employment, social welfare, and security squarely on the policy agenda.

In short, during the Seventh Five-Year Plan period, along with the strengthening of administrative control of aggregate wages, consideration could be given to the establishment of unemployment security according to age groups (the survey has proved the importance of a stratified approach, for people of different ages may have drastically different views on this), professional categories, post classifications, ownership systems, levels of employment, and organization in different sectors. At the same time, we should consider how to recognize and convert the covert welfare subsidies into overt subsidies, and how to unlink social welfare and security from the job relationship, so as to facilitate labor mobility and gradually form a competitive labor market. Consideration might be given to the possibility of allowing a certain number of peasants into the cities in a prudent and planned way to enliven employment competition in the labor market while maintaining strict control through residence certificates.

Admittedly, the establishment of a labor market per se will not eliminate consumption expansion. But the removal of barriers to labor mobility will certainly destroy the main raison d'etre of the troublesome "upward emulation." Unlinking employment, social welfare, and security will at least militate against the hidden expansion of consumption and consumption-oriented investment. Labor mobility will not only act as a check on the expansion of consumption funds but also facilitate enterprise management and operation, strengthen enterprise vitality, improve employment patterns, and promote the adjustment of industrial structure. In addition, this move will effectively remedy a big drawback, that is, the reform campaign has up to now only exposed people to new risks and costs (such as fluctuation of prices and wages) and has not brought them new opportunities (for example, chances to find new jobs that bring them more pay or higher social status). Therefore, the opening of a labor market will satisfy people more and predispose people toward continued reform.

3.3. Introduce Capital Markets to Reform the Financial System and Perfect the Investment Mechanism

The perfection of the investment mechanism involves the supply of financial resources, the channels for concentrating funds, and the investors themselves. The tightening of financial control over enterprises, easing of the thirst for investment, improvement of investment and production scale efficiencies, and acceleration of the structural adjustment of industry all call for improved mobility of funds and a profound reform of the financial system. If, along with the reform of the government-dominated investment system, we wish to develop a new type of far-sighted and powerful investor, we should cultivate an environment conducive to the development of enterprise groups. This cannot be achieved by "decentralization" alone. An advisable line of action may be comprehensively to restructure the investment mechanism through a combination of reform and control.

The Two-Tier Financial System: A Reform Objective. The two-tier banking system should take as its foundation the commercialization of local banks. As things stand now, the bank system is responsible for all the socioeconomic functions of currency circulation, including state fiscal revenue and taxation, wages and salaries of administrative organs and public establishments, social relief, and national defense expenditures. How these functions are to be separated would be the subject of another study. The commercialization of grass-roots banks should logically be predicated on the condition that all industrial and commercial enterprises have already become independent profit/loss entities. As China's banks at present provide financial surveillance and management control over most of China's enterprises, a rash commercialization of banks could lead to loss of control. Precipitous commercialization could also give rise to speculation, monopolistic exploitation (due to their monopoly in the supply of funds), and other bank abuses.

While the plan for banking system reform was still being weighed and pondered, especially in the tight-money atmosphere after the beginning of 1985, new forms of nonbank fund-raising emerged. Their common characteristic is that they all involve horizontal relationships for pooling funds among enterprises, investors, and grass-roots government units. They deal in all aspects of short-term and long-term financing activities, mainly covering the following areas: (1) Short-term financing, especially in the form of commercial credits between enterprises. Judging from the situation in the sample enterprises, it is obvious that the commercial credits between enterprises have become an important prop of the economic activities of our country. The scale of commercial credits in 1984 was equivalent to 35 percent of the loans from the revolving funds of the banks. And in 1985 they have expanded to 42 percent, accounting for about 20 percent of the funds acquired by industrial enterprises from revolving fund sources. This expansion of credit has made up for the shortage of financial resources, playing the role of a paracurrency outside of the plan that is responsible for the sustained super-high 1985 growth rate in spite of the tight money situation. (2) Medium and long-term fund-raising. The recent years have witnessed an upsurge of fund-pooling by local governments, projects that seek investors far and wide, and fund-raising by enterprises from internal and outside sources. In some economically more advanced areas, the funds raised for capital construction equal 50 percent of bank loans. In their questionnaire replies concerning the choice of financial resources, factory directors gave the second place to "intraenterprise funding" (next only to bank loans) out of eight choices. "Community fund-pooling" came in sixth. (3) Cooperative financial organizations. For instance, the business and service companies in the rural area of Jiangsu province have advanced from providing pre- and postproduction services to providing financing as well, and have become the financial mainstay to rural enterprises. Some textile industries in Shanghai and fourteen companies in the industrial zone of Shekou have established financing coordination centers, which execute the function of intraenterprise-group banking. (4) Local investment and development companies. The above-mentioned financial organizations and forms of financing are marked by their operational flexibility, responsibility for their own losses and gains, and a greater choice for the partners. Their development not only reduces the dependence of enterprises on funding by the state, stimulates the division of labor in financial operations, and diversifies financial assets and forms of financing, but also helps to open up more room to maneuver in the reform of the entire financial system.

Strengthen Command Control Over the Aggregate Credits and Loans. Fostering nonbank channels of credit and loans is feasible and relatively risk-free. To make this idea a reality, it is imperative to strengthen bank control in order to cede to the market an area within the unified financial system. In other words, we should build a "two-tier system" similar to that dealing with the producer's goods. In practice, the financial "two-tier" system will be more difficult to establish, because central control over bank lending is not as strong as central control over the producer's goods supply system. Some argue that as credits and loans transacted "outside of the bank" become new channels for credit expansion, some enterprises and individuals may take advantage of this to lend out money borrowed from the banks and profit from interest rate arbitrage. But if direct bank loans can expand endlessly (by pandering to the dependent mentality of enterprises and government bodies), then we will be unable to develop a nonbank financial market. So administrative control over the state banks must be tightened. The implementation of the tight-money policy in 1985 suggests that if control by administrative command is forcefully applied, it is possible to effectuate a sure check on financial flows at one end, and at the other to avoid abuses arising from the comingling of bank and nonbank lending. Note that when nonbank financing is well developed, an "across-the-board cut" in bank system credit will not cause such excessive damage to economic development. A two-tier system will also give us a market interest rate that truly reflects the demand and supply of funds. This will greatly improve the prospects for trying out various indirect macrocontrol measures and will create preconditions for the subsequent reform of the banking system as a whole.

Reform in Connection with Enterprise Bankruptcy. According to a study of the only four bankruptcy cases of state-owned enterprises, we have come to realize that the proper handling of enterprise bankruptcy must overcome the problems faced by the employees of the bankrupt enterprise. As to deciding who goes bankrupt, in terms of ownership systems, debt settlement, and the disposal of fixed assets, this is comparatively easy to cope with. Reform in the social security system to provide unemployment insurance is therefore the prerequisite for reform concerning enterprise bankruptcy.

Our investigation indicates that allowing for enterprise bankruptcy enjoys a certain degree of public acceptance (see table 1.7). The understanding of enterprise bankruptcy by employees, and their choices, are unexpectedly clear-cut and definite. Once the reform of the social security system is underway, it seems we will not have to wait for long to proceed with the reform of enterprise bankruptcy.

Horizontal Constraints on Enterprises. Enterprises are subject to three financial constraints: a fiscal constraint, a bank constraint, and the horizontal constraints arising between enterprises or between the enterprise and the community. Given the increasingly stringent fiscal control through the conversion of profits into taxes and the likely softening of bank constraints, the horizontal constraint on enterprises has become the hardest of the three. Whether an enterprise can raise money from other enterprises or from individuals will depend not on its negotiating position within the traditional planning system, but on its credit worthiness and productive power. What is more, money so borrowed must be repaid, and there is no way to dodge repayment. As we develop these horizontal relations between enterprises, we will strengthen enterprise financial constraints and, more generally, improve enterprise behavior. In this sense, the establishment of a ''two-tier'' financial system at a time of tight money policy will also contribute to the hardening of constraints on enterprises.

Foster Enterprise Groups. A basic problem inherent in the present investment system is the lack of motivation on the part of enterprises for long-term development. Apart from the need to advance the reform of the enterprise system and to improve enterprise behavior, the thinly spread resources for investment constitute a major obstacle to the enhancement of scale efficiency and the promotion of heavy industry. To address this problem, the reform of the industrial structure, and government intervention in this process in particular, should be an important task in the Seventh Five-Year Plan period.

It has been proved in the developed countries that forming enterprise groups greatly boosts economic development, given a proper enforcement of antitrust

Table 1.7

Public Opinion toward Enterprise Bankruptcy

Questions	Answers	
Suppose an enterprise bankruptcy law is enacted. What should be done for a bankrupt enterprise's workers?	The state should provide for everything and assign the workers to work elsewhere.	50.3
	The state should provide for basic subsistence. The workers should try to find jobs themselves (including setting up self-employed enterprises)	49.7
If your enterprise went bankrupt, what would you do?	Look for a job myself	51.8
	Found a self-employing business	35.0
	Ask leadership for job assignment	10.0
	Live on state relief	3.0

measures. In Japan, for instance, the degree of industrial concentration is very high. Of the total number of enterprises, 0.1 percent account for 41.9 percent of total assets and 35.7 percent of total sales. These groups are the main force in the realization of government structural policies and development plans, in technological renovation, and in foreign trade. China's reform in the ensuing stages should stress the cultivation of these sorts of powerful investment groups with a long time-horizon—forerunners in technological development—by strengthening horizontal links among enterprises. Such groupings would be able to fund large-scale investment and would facilitate enterprise specialization, and at the same time "guidance planning" by the government would be easier.

The groundwork for enterprise integration already exists. The ever-increasing pressure of market demand and supply makes the enterprises more eager to cooperate. A survey on the "inclination for cooperation" of factory directors shows that 88 percent of the enterprises are willing to establish a kind of cooperative relationship with other enterprises, and 54 percent wish to merge or enter into joint-ventures with others.

In practice, there exist many growing points that could foster enterprise groups. For example, mutual financial assistance between enterprises can bind together small and medium-sized enterprises and form "small woods of stunted trees." Large enterprises may subdivide their accounting units and encourage those units to expand via horizontal economic grouping. Enterprises' efforts to control cost and product quality and to ensure raw material supply and product sales predispose them to form horizontal financial links.

Until the factor market is well developed, however, it will be very difficult to form large numbers of enterprise groups in a short time by merely relying on spontaneous organizing by enterprises themselves. Therefore, in policy decisions, priority should be given to projects that "fish for adherents" and those based on a conglomeration of many sources. Government and large enterprises should work to accelerate this process.

For instance, in the management of extrabudgetary funds, in the organization of investment projects based on wide participation of many fund holders, and in pilot projects based on partnership and stockholding it may be advisable to expand the horizontal ties between enterprises though commercial credits and to encourage interlocking stockholding among the enterprise. Or the state could encourage establishing internal financing coordination centers and fund groups as part of the fiscal decentralization during the Seventh Five-Year Plan period. In addition, as we reshape our policies concerning taxation (especially the progressive tax on enterprises), credits, and loans, we should constantly try to promote enterprise merger and grouping.

4. Conclusion

The alternative directions for reform suggested in this summary report can serve only as general guidelines. More research is needed before we can arrive at a concrete reform strategy. Conscious of the lack of market mechanisms in China, reform, first initiated in the countryside, has followed the fundamental principle of simplifying administration and decentralization and has scored great achievements in the past few years. The market mechanism may have begun to play a remarkably positive role in the operation of our economic system and has created favorable conditions for reform to penetrate deeply into the social and economic fabric.

Reform today is faced with grave challenges. We must pluck up our courage and, with "opening up" as our watchword, prudently handle the two challenges of structural wage inflation and "thirst for investment," by opening the labor and financial markets. Second, without depreciating the existing achievements of reform, we should go beyond a simplistic interpretation of the guiding phrase "opening up" and work out scientific policy solutions concerning how to overcome the difficulties caused by a still-underdeveloped market and by government intervention in enterprise behavior. Third, to guarantee the smooth fulfillment of the two tasks mentioned above, it is necessary, for a certain period, to continue and even intensify administrative control over aggregate wages, credit, and loans.

Practical experience tells us that the state of the microeconomic base determines the effectiveness of macro control. As we seek substantial and risk-free advances for reform, we must promote indirect control at the macro level through reform at the micro level. Opening up the factor markets, creating the microconditions for a change in the mode of macro control, and carefully developing the new organizational functions of government while maintaining certain necessary administrative control measures—by combining these three aspects, we can map out a dynamic reform strategy that has structure, continuity, and gradually evolving priorities. This strategy, different from but linked to the previous one of simplifying administration and decentralizing, will mark a new stage of reform and provide a logical point of departure for our future study.

APPENDIX: NOTES ON THE CESRRI SURVEY.

The investigations summarized here were conducted by the China Economic Reform Research Institute (CESRRI). The whole process, from designing, investigations, processing, and analyzing data to the drafting of reports, lasted seven months.

1. Investigation of the Reform of the Urban Economic System and Trends in Urban Economy

1.1. Scope

The investigation covered twenty-seven cities (Chongqing, Wuhan, Shenyang, Nanjing, Changzhou, Shashi, Beijing, Tianjin, Shanghai, Dalian, Wenzhou, Qindao, Fuzhou, Xiamen, Guangzhou, Jinan, Harbin, Shijiazhuang, Nanchang, Chengdu, Wuifang, Heifei, Hangzhou, Lanzhou, Guiyang, Kunming, and Xian), all of which, except Beijing, Tianjin, Shanghai, and Wenzhou, are designated experimental cities in the reform campaign.

The investigation in each city involved the planning commission, economic commission, statistics bureau, bureaus of finance, material resources, and commerce, branches of the People's Bank of China and the Industrial and Commercial Bank as well as other departments. It also involved five industrial management bureaus and fifteen industrial enterprises. Altogether 429 enterprises were investigated, including 279 owned by the state, 131 owned by urban collectives, and 19 by rural collectives, of which 241 were large and medium-sized enterprises and 188 small enterprises.

1.2. Content

1. The actual progress of the urban economic reform and the mechanism of current economic operations, mainly covering the operational environment and the behavior of enterprises; the state of the structural reform as it affects planning, finance and taxation, funding, prices, the supply and marketing of material resources, and commerce.

2. The trend of economic development and major economic problems, including the industrial growth rate, investment in fixed assets, the trend and demand of consumption funds, and the involvement and development of credits and loans.

3. Special studies on the mechanism of decentralized investment operations, labor employment and wage systems, and the "two-tier" pricing system for the means of production.

For the above issues, forty investigation forms were designed, including twenty-seven comprehensive forms, five forms addressed to different lines of trade and industry, and eight forms to enterprises. Altogether, 1.5 million data entries were registered.

1.3. Units and Persons Involved

China Economic System Reform Research Institute; Economic Society of Beijing Youth; Rural Policy Research Office of the CPC Secretariat; Committee on Economic Structural Reform of Beijing Municipality; Institute of Social Sciences of Beijing; Institute of Finance of the People's Bank of China; Institute of Fiscal Science of the Ministry of Finance; Postgraduate School of the Academy of Social Sciences of China; Economic Institute of the Planning Commission; Beijing University; People's University of China; Qinghua University; Central College of Finance and Economics; College of Economics of Beijing; College of Finance and Trade of Beijing; Central Party Training School; Nankai University; Fudan University; and Institute of Sectorial Economic Studies of the Shanghai Academy of Social Sciences. Two hundred seventy-nine professional researchers and post-graduates from the above units participated in the investigations.

2. Surveys of Factory Directors' Opinions

Concurrently with the above investigations, we conducted surveys of directors' opinions in 359 enterprises through questionnaires. The enterprises were selected from the above-mentioned 429 enterprises.

The questionnaires mainly asked about the managerial objectives and kinetic patterns of enterprises, constraining factors, selection of labor sources, sources of funds, inclination for integration and reasons behind it as well as personal goals of the directors. Forty thousand data entries were obtained.

3. Questionnaire Survey on Public Reaction to the Price Reform

This actually refers to two consecutive surveys in February and July 1985, jointly conducted by China Economic System Reform Research Institute and the Social Science Department of Beijing University, involving twenty-five of their staff members. The February survey covered eleven cities, sixteen counties and sub-urban areas in Beijing, Honan, Zhejiang, Hunan, and Anhui, obtaining 380,000 data entries from a sample of 2,409 households. The survey in July covered ten cities in Heilongjiang, Shanxi, Sichuan, Shandong, Zhejiang, Hubei, Guangxi, and the city of Beijing, obtaining 350,000 data entries from a sample of 2,060 households. The surveys were mainly to measure the understanding by the urban populace of the reform, their reaction to the price reform, their choice of life styles and adaptation to the life of a commodity economy.

4. Investigation on Reform of the Social Security System

The reform of the social security system is an important component of the urban economic reform. The study of this question was divided into two parts: (1) analyzing the objectives, modality, and necessity of the reform in the current employment security system, including such questions as "structural overmanning" of enterprises, the interrelation between consumption fund expansion and the employment security system, the implications of peasants joining the urban labor force and of the contractual labor system, and attitudes concerning opening up the labor market and commencement of the reform in the social welfare and security system; (2) conducting surveys through questionnaires on employees' inclination and motives for job mobility, their views on and adaptability to unemployment or enterprise bankruptcy, and their views on current systems of employment, social welfare, and security, and a survey on the different attitudes of laborers of different ages and in different regions. These surveys formed a basis on which to assess the sociopsychological conditions and the feasibility of the reform in the social security system.

The surveys were conducted in six cities—Beijing, Shanghai, Shamen, Chongqing, Shashi, and Harbin—and they obtained 410,000 data entries from a sample of 1,314 questionnaires. Involved in the surveys were twenty-eight staff members of China Economic System Reform Research Institute, the Social Science Department of Beijing University, and the Social Science Department of Nankai University.

5. Survey through Questionnaires on Youth Job Preference and Basic Attitude to Social and Economic Life

This survey was jointly conducted by China Economic System Reform Research Institute and *China Youth* magazine, concerning job evaluation and preferences of young people and their attitudes toward economic income, noneconomic job satisfaction, risks, and career development. Four hundred thousand data entries were registered from a sample of 3,340 replies extracted using a stratified sample from the 76,000 replies to the survey questionnaires.

6. Survey on the Quality of Enterprise Cadres

The reform set new and higher requirements for the factory directors and managers. The survey was aimed at assessing the personal qualities of present enterprise leaders through an examination and analysis of the selection of enterprise leaders, their goals in life and work, their knowledge structure, employment of time, confidence in the future, family values, attitude to risks, personal experience, theoretical knowledge, and so on.

The survey, conducted through questionnaires, covered 900 enterprises situated in Beijing, Jilin, Shanxi, Sichuan, Shandong, Guangxi, Zhejiang, Guizhou, and other areas. More than 1,000 factory directors and managers replied to the questionnaires, and 700,000 data entries were registered. This survey involved twenty-four staff members from and was jointly conducted by the Program on Social Studies of CESRRI and the Social Science Department of Beijing University.

7. Investigation on the Reform in Governmental Functions and Organs

The investigation, conducted jointly by China Economic System Reform Research Institute, the Central Party Training School, and the Central University of Political Science and Law, mainly examined the management, decision-making, supervision, and verification functions and the institutional set-up as well as the operations of government bodies at various levels during the economic reform, and was meant to be a tactical exploration of the current state and prospects of the institutional reforms.

II
ACHIEVEMENTS OF REFORM

Reform in China experienced early and rapid success in agriculture. There, the strong incentive effect of the move to the production responsibility system caused a sharp increase in output. In addition, reform permitted renewed specialization of crop growing, in response to centrally determined price signals.

In industry, the problem of reform is far more difficult. The degree of specialization is vastly greater, with tens of thousands of distinct products, and complex intersectoral interaction. Reform means that industrial producers are to gain new autonomy of action, responding to price signals. But with so many products and sectors, the job of "getting prices right" is virtually insurmountable. State price bureaus must in effect solve a very large set of simultaneous demand and supply equations. The usual experience in industrial reform efforts elsewhere has been a reversion to administrative control.

China has pioneered a new institution to cut this Gordian knot: the two-tier price system in industry. The first chapter in part II, by Diao Xinshen, describes the progress of this system. For a number of products, such as steel, coal, and trucks, the state continues to ration out a portion of annual output directly through the traditional planning mechanisms, at (low) state-set prices; but at the same time, producers are allowed to sell above-quota output on the free market at a high price. The reformers hope to hold the rationed share constant, or even reduce it over time, and also to adjust the state price upward toward the market price. No other centrally planned economy has experimented with a bridging mechanism of this sort. Ms. Diao's report shows that this system is widespread, so that virtually all enterprises are now to some extent market-oriented.

The next chapter, by Zhang Shaojie and Zhang Amei, presents data bearing on the extent to which enterprises have more discretionary power vis-a-vis central planners, and the extent to which enterprises now operate in a market environment. They use the "Kornai index" (developed by a Hungarian economist) to show that Chinese enterprises behave as though they were in a buyers' market, not the traditional sellers' market of a "forced-draft" planned economy. They suggest that some consumer goods enterprises are being pinched by an asymmetry: buyers' market for output, sellers' market for inputs. The principal cause of this is differing supply elasticities—low in the capital-intensive producer goods sector from which they receive their inputs, high in their own sector, where expansion can occur without much investment in new capital.

Inflation is the bugbear of reform. Sharp inflation in 1980 led the leadership to put reform on hold. The renewed push in 1984 generated double-digit inflation again. The authors of the third chapter in part II report that most people surveyed understand the need for price reform (a loosening of price controls, which permits inflation to occur) and support it. Most striking: support for price reform is higher in the August 1985 survey (after the burst of price increases) than in the earlier February survey. Correlation analysis suggests that support for price reform depends on whether the respondent feels that his standard of living is rising, stagnant, or falling.

The final chapter in part II, by Yang Guansan, Wang Hansheng, Liu Bin, and Wu Quhui, is an exceptionally valuable profile of the people who manage China's factories, stores, and other economic units. It presents detailed information about 1,286 cadre respondents and 1,061 worker respondents from 900 enterprises in 18 cities. Section 1 gives information about cadre characteristics and qualifications. It also presents evidence that enterprise cadre are strongly proreform—a very important finding. Section 2 shows how the cadres' outlook on appropriate management objectives and methods has changed during reform. Cadres are more concerned about market pressures, with little concern about finding funding or meeting state output plans. But they show a continued preference for strongly centralized management structures, for money rewards and penalties, and for appointing managers from above (from nominees generated by a workers' council). Section 3 explores a paradoxical finding: that although these cadres display substantial ambition and report that work is by far the most satisfying part of their lives, fully 78 percent would choose to leave management work if they could—mainly to enter the government bureaucracy. The principal reason is that these cadres feel conflicted—caught between the demands of the workers and the demands of the state—a dilemma that has sharpened as reform has increased their power and, thus, increased workers' expectations of what they can provide.

2

The Role of the Two-Tier Price System

Diao Xinshen

Price reform is one of the most crucial and difficult links in China's economic reform. As a way of softening the considerable impact brought about by readjusting the economic structure and the relations between various interests, the two-tier price system became the most important part of the reform in its previous stage. Naturally, the current study of the reform of the urban economic structure took the two-tier system as the central issue within the broad category of price reform.

1. The Two-Tier Price System—A Successful Approach to the Reform

The two-tier system in the pricing of industrial products emerged as state mandatory planning gradually receded in production, supply, marketing, and other major operations of enterprises. *The Ten Points on the Expansion of the Decision-Making Power of State-Owned Industrial Enterprises*, which was instituted in 1984, was a key factor in greatly accelerating implementation of the two-tier price system. A survey of 429 industrial enterprises indicates that 51 percent of them acquired decision-making power in varying degrees in production, supply, and marketing in 1984. The rest became autonomous in at least one of these fields. In most enterprises, part of the production is no longer planned by the state. The enterprises themselves take care of the marketing of part of their products and purchase part of the raw materials directly on the market. In 1984, the average rate of independently marketed products of the 429 enterprises (the share of products marketed by the enterprises on their own in aggregate sales) was 32.08 percent; the average rate of market-purchased principal raw and other materials (the share of materials acquired through inter-enterprise exchange and cooperative deals, or purchased on the market, in total supply) was 16.4 percent.

Table 2.1

Breakdown of Enterprises' Use of Raw and Other Materials by Percentage of Market Purchases

Percentage of	Percentage of Enterprises	
Materials Used	1984	Between Jan. and June 1985
0	9.6	6.5
0–20	49.6	41.9
20–40	16.8	21.5
40–60	9.1	10.3
60–80	3.2	4.7
80–100	11.7	15.0

Between January and June of 1985, this rate rose sharply to 43.8 percent; that is, the share of market-supplied raw and other materials rose by 27.3 percentage points (table 2.1).

As the prices for that part of output over and above the stage plan are allowed to fluctuate, the enterprises' independent operations in production, supply, and marketing are inevitably regulated by market prices that reflect changes in supply and demand (table 2.2). We can conclude, therefore, that with the reform of the planning system and the expansion of the enterprises' decision-making power, the two-tier price system has been extended to practically all industries and most of the enterprises, that virtually all enterprises are now in various degrees geared to the market, and that in this process their capacity to bear up against and respond to changes in market prices is constantly increasing.

2. The Two-Tier Price System—Characterized by a Supplementary Regulatory Role

With the restructuring of the distribution system in the enterprises and the expansion of their decision-making power, and with all-round implementation of the two-tier system, market prices are beginning to have an impact on the supply and demand of industrial products and the allocation of resources. It goes without saying that the effects produced by market prices under the two-tier system have features different from those under the unitary market price system. A grasp of these features is necessary to a discussion on how to carry the price reform forward.

2.1. The Marginal Regulatory Role Played by the Two-Tier Price System in Short-term Supply and Demand

Basically, the two-tier price system means the existence at the same time of two prices for commodities, one being the list price set by the state and the other being

Table 2.2

Breakdown of Enterprises' Rate of Independently Marketed Products

Percentage of Independently Marketed Products	Percentage of Enterprises	
	1984	between Jan. and June 1985
0	14.9	16.2
0–20	20.1	15.7
20–40	16.4	12.0
40–60	8.2	7.2
60–80	33.7	38.2
80–100	11.7	15.0

the fluctuating market price decided by market forces or agreed on by the parties engaged in a transaction. The part of output or inputs that changes hands under the state plan is allocated, purchased, sold, or distributed at state-set process. Any amounts that are in excess of the figures set in the state plan are marketed or purchased at market prices. In such a context, when an enterprise increases or decreases its output or input, the impact of this marginal change is calculated at market prices. In other words, for every additional unit of output above the plan, which is sold at the market price, the enterprise obtains extra revenue, whereas every unit of raw materials saved means one unit less to be purchased on the market, at the market price, hence means less cost-reduction for the enterprise. The enterprise, therefore, in making decisions regarding production, should evaluate its increase in production or economizing on materials in terms of market prices instead of state-set prices. This means that market prices have assumed a decisive role in the incremental output and input decisions of the enterprise, and that through this marginal role they have become signals and levers that help to readjust short-term supply and demand.

It has never been possible to measure precisely this marginal role, because it is very difficult to identify and exclude the impact of factors other than prices on the increase in production. Still, the data collected from the survey of the 429 enterprises show that, although many nonprice factors are involved, the supplementary role of market prices is already a reality in the actual economic situation.

Over the past few years, one of the commodities for which the state-set and market prices show a rather sharp divergence is steel. This wide divergence is a sign of the serious imbalance between supply and demand. Theoretically, market prices should play a prominent role in regulating short-term supply and demand. In reality, one would be surprised to see a high market price promptly prove its marginal role by stimulating short-term supply. After all, steel has been in short supply for a long time in China, and we observed a very high utilization rate of existing productive capacity. Furthermore, it takes a long time for investment to

Table 2.3

Relation Between Independent Marketing Rate and Output Growth Rate

Number of Enterprises	Independent Marketing Rate	Average Independent Marketing Rate	Output Increase Rate	Average Output Increase Rate
6	0–7.8	2.96	– 10.98–5.80	– 9.32
6	10–34.0	18.78	2.30–9.73	14.38
12	—	11.00	—	5.00

create new capacity. And yet, despite all this, the iron and steel works (twelve in all) we investigated clearly reveal the strong marginal role played by market prices.

In reality, even within the state plan, part of these goods are transferred at market prices. This, however, produces quantitative, rather than qualitative, changes in the marginal role of the market price and hence is ignored in our theoretical discussion of the marketing rate and the annual output growth rate. Linear regression shows a correlation coefficient between these two of 0.763. (As for the relationship between independent marketing and the level of output, or between the degree of planned production and output growth rate, the correlation coefficients were − 0.294 and 0.418 respectively). The result indicates on the one hand that the independent marketing rate has a greater effect on increasing output than the degree of planned production has. On the other hand, it indicates that, through the decision-making power of the enterprises in product marketing, market prices act mainly on the above plan output (the production of steel products in excess of quotas) and have little influence on gross output.

The independent marketing rate does not show its effect on the output increase rate until it reaches a certain threshold. Among the iron and steel works investigated, none of those with an independent marketing rate of lower than 10 percent registered an increase of over 6 percent (a negative increase being recorded for two of the enterprises), whereas those with an independent marketing rate of above 10 percent have mostly boosted their production at a double-digit rate (with only two of the enterprises registering a single-digit rate), as indicated in table 2.3.

The relation between the independent marketing rate and the output growth rate demonstrates how the effect of market prices on supply hinges on the extent to which the two-tier price system is implemented in actual economic activities. If the portion subject to the regulation by market prices is too small (i.e., the proportion of the products independently marketed by the enterprises is too small) to reach a certain ''threshold,'' then market prices will be restrained from

Table 2.4

Steel Consumption in Sichuan Province Machine-Building (1984)

(1) $a_M \div a_T$	2.30
(2) incremental $a_M \div$ incremental a_M	1.74
(3) incremental $a_M \div a_M$	0.71

playing their marginal role in regulating supply.

On the demand side, market prices have a certain positive regulatory effect on short-term demand, although changes in consumption of steel products are restricted by nonprice factors, particularly given the enterprises' "soft" budget constraint. Here, we shall attempt an approximate explanation in terms of the changes in the consumptions of steel products per 10,000 yuan in enterprise output value.

The 1984 consumption of steel products per 10,000 yuan in output value dropped by 18 percent in 300 users of steel products in the machine-building industry in Sichuan province (table 2.4). In the table, a indicates the steel input-output coefficient (in value terms), in machine-building (a_M), and in all industry (a_T): the yuan of steel used per yuan of output. "Incremental a" is the ratio of increased steel use to increased output: how much additional steel was required to generate one yuan of additional output. The first entry in table 2.4 shows that machine-building used 2.3 times as much steel per yuan of 1984 output as did industry as a whole. But in incremental terms, the figure is lower (1.74), suggesting that these machine-building enterprises, compared with the rest of industry, were particularly effective in economizing on steel use in 1984 as compared with 1983. The third entry, which is mathematically equivalent to the elasticity of machine-building output with respect to steel, shows this economizing from another angle: a 1 percent rise in machinery output required only a 0.71 percent rise in steel inputs.

Consider an enterprise that produces two products, A and B. Suppose that the enterprise produces A and B by combining certain key inputs (which flow partly through state allocation and partly through free- market channels) with other inputs. Suppose further that $MC_a = MC_b$ (with inputs evaluated at market prices), but the market price of A exceeds that of B. One might expect a profit-maximizing enterprise to eliminate production of B, in response to these market signals. But this overlooks the fact that key inputs are usually allocated at below-market prices. The state can impel the enterprise to produce B instead, by manipulating input prices. Typically, allocation of subsidized inputs for B will be linked to the enterprise's output target for B; in this case, the enterprise might produce B for the state, but would market only A. (Of course, all this assumes that key inputs are not fungible between A and B, for either technical or legal reasons.)

This shortcoming of the two-tier system deserves special attention. The planned allocation of major raw and other materials tends to preserve not only the original structure of subsidies but also the original structure of output. In this sense, preserving the portion of inputs allocated according to plan means strengthening the force of inertia in the original industrial structure. If resources cannot be redistributed in response to market supply and demand, the readjustment of the industrial structure will be damped to a degree corresponding to the share of planned allocation, thereby aggravating the frictions in the process of readjustment.

2.2. The Role of the Two-Tier System in
Regulating Long-term Supply and Demand and the
Allocation of Resources Is Limited

Marginal cost and marginal revenue play a decisive role in determining short-run supply and demand, whereas in regulating long-run supply and demand, total cost and total revenue play a greater role. An enterprise, in deciding whether to alter its production structure or form a new factory through investment, compares the profit gained after the structural change with that gained before it. But market prices relate only to the enterprise's marginal output; total revenue and total profit are affected by state prices as well. Under the two-tier system, therefore, both market prices and state-set prices help determine the long-range economic behavior of the enterprise. Only if there is a considerable difference between state-set and market prices will a high market price dominate the decision.

Take coal for an example. Between 1982 and 1984, China's coal output increased by 105.1 million tons, of which 55.9 million tons (53.19 percent) came from the town-run enterprises, 22.6 million tons (21.5 percent) from state-owned coal mines under local administration, and 26.6 million tons (25.31 percent) from state-run mines with output subject to unified state distribution (table 2.5). The big increase in output achieved by locally administered, state-owned enterprises and by town-run enterprises is mainly due to increased investment. In 1983, as much as 770 million yuan was raised locally to finance the construction of local coal mines. Most of the funds were used to build or extend mine shafts. The newly added production capacity of that year was 10.54 million tons. The number of collectively owned, town-run coal mines increased by 40,000 in just one year. Of these mines, the big ones alone showed an increase of 10 million tons in their newly added production capacity. This shows that, when the difference between state-set and market prices is relatively big, the more the producers benefit by the market prices, the greater incentive they have to invest. The town-run enterprises, being completely regulated by the market, are the most sensitive to the changes in market prices and respond most promptly in investing in production of the goods in short supply. In contrast, the locally administered state enterprises,

Table 2.5

Changes in Coal Output

	1984 Output Increase Over 1982	Percentage of Country's Gross Output	
		1982	1984
Country's gross output	15.86	100	100
Of which output from:			
1. Coal mines with output subject to unified distribution	7.75	52.51	48.33
2. Locally administered state mines	13.26	25.57	25.00
3. Town-run enterprises	38.30	21.92	26.17

restricted by state-set prices to some extent, do not respond so well to market price changes, whereas large state enterprises, which are under the greatest restriction of state-set prices, find it most difficult to react positively.

3. Proportional Two-Tier Price System—A Grave Defect in the Two-Tier System

One of the major factors preventing the two-tier price system from playing its full role in regulating long-term supply and demand in state enterprises is the proportional two-tier system practiced in most of these enterprises. A typical form of this is to fix yearly the proportion of planned production, supply, and sales in the total for a given enterprise, taking those of the year before as the base. This means that both in the newly added investment and in the newly established production structure, a portion always remains under the planned distribution and regulation by state-set prices. Viewed dynamically, this means the proportion of the planned distribution will not diminish gradually with the growth and expansion of production unless the state chooses to make readjustments. Naturally, it is very difficult for the enterprise to develop long-term economic initiatives.

A survey of the degree of planned production in 429 enterprises indicates that the overall proportion of planned production between January and June of 1985, measured in the actual output of the year, rose by 0.11 over 1984. But if measured by comparing the 1985 planned output targets with the output of 1984, the proportion would show a rise of 0.20.

Perhaps an analogy from the experience of rural reform would be in place here. In summing up the responsibility system linking remuneration with output in the agricultural production, the farmers would have said most clearly, "Give the state and the collective their due and let us keep all the rest." The state's due refers to the guaranteed quota of produce to be sold to the state which, once fixed as the base in a contract, would remain unchanged for a number of years. Of the output in excess of the base quotas, a certain portion is retained by the collective. All the rest goes to the producers. This gives them an incentive to engage in long-range planning. To ensure an increase in revenue from year to year during the contract period, they will have to invest in medium- and long-term inputs. In some cases, they must even increase investment at the expense of immediate consumption, in expectation of a larger revenue in the future. If the responsibility system had adopted the principle of "proportional distribution" instead of "contracting quotas to producers," the increased output in any given year would probably be included in their obligations to be fulfilled to the state the next year. The farmers would adopt a short time-horizon, rather than invest at the expense of immediate consumption.

The external restraints on state-owned enterprises are much less rigid than those on farmers. And the reasons for their lack of long-range economic activity are much more complicated. The proportional two-tier price system, though not the main reason, has certainly contributed to the lack of improvement in the long-range behavior of the enterprises.

Another shortcoming in the system is that it makes it very difficult for the market to strengthen its restraints on the enterprises. As the government retains some power to change the quotas of materials allocated to enterprises, they in turn are in a position to "bargain" with the government for a larger supply of raw and other materials at state-set prices. Sometimes, in order to secure more of such materials, they would even offer to provide the state with more output at state-set prices. During the investigation the managers were more often heard to complain that the state supplied too few materials they needed, rather than that it purchased too many of their products at set prices. This supports our statement above.

For the local governments at different levels, the power to change the allocated quotas of materials greatly strengthens their control over enterprises. Especially when the increase in government revenue becomes directly linked to the performance of the enterprises, local governments will certainly actively employ this lever to further their own interests. Statistics show that local governments, at both the provincial and municipal levels, invariably feel an urge to expand the proportion of planned production.

As table 2.6 indicates, the coefficient of extension of the provincial mandatory plans to the central government plans is 0.73, (i.e., [21.51 − 12.44] ÷ 12.44 = .73; the scope of mandatory planning was extended by 73 percent when moving from the central to the provincial level). The coefficient of the provincial guidance plans to the central government plans is 2.73, and that of the provincial guidance plans to the central government plans is 2.07. The coefficient of extension of the municipal mandatory plans to the provincial plans is 0.12, and that of the municipal guidance plans to the provincial plans is −0.08 (the negative number implies that part of the guidance plans were converted into mandatory plans).

Table 2.6

Share of Planned Production in Enterprise Output in 1984

	Central Govern- ment Plans	Provincial Plans	Municipal Plans
Proportion under mandatory plans	12.44	21.51	23.97
Enterprise own sales	9.48	29.12	26.91

Note: Total output is taken as 100. The municipal plans contain the provincial plans, which in turn contain the central government plans.

The expansion of the local plans beyond the central plans increases both the government's control over the enterprises and the enterprises' dependence on the government. As a result, the materials "exchange market," which existed under the original system, has not vanished because of the opening of the free market; instead, it has tended to be strengthened and enlarged with respect to certain products. A survey of the utilization and purchase of raw and other materials in the 429 enterprises shows that, of the materials acquired in 1984 beyond the supply quotas, 56 percent were obtained by the enterprises through mutually benefiting exchange and other cooperative arrangements between enterprises. The proportion of materials purchased directly on the market was not large. In the case of steels, timber, and cement, which are in very short supply, the proportion of direct market purchase of these materials is even smaller.

When the "exchange market" is brisk and the free market inactive, for enterprises that have a high capacity for exchange of materials, market prices, even though considerably higher, will neither become a strong check on demand nor provide a powerful stimulus to supply. The result is that the shorter the supply, the more active the exchange, and the more active the exchange, the shorter the supply. On the other hand, those enterprises with little or no capacity for exchange (mostly the town-run enterprises) finding it impossible to acquire the needed inputs by paying with money because they are nowhere to be bought, resort to various illegal means of payment of a nonprice nature (the most common of which is bribing individuals or enterprises). A study of the "principal restraints on the development of enterprises" shows that, in the seventeen principal restraints mentioned, the acquisition of raw and other materials was placed at the head of the list by town-run enterprises that rely totally on the market, whereas state-run enterprises placed it fifth.

4. Lack of Factor Markets—The Greatest Obstruction to the Development of the Goods Market

The price reform aims at straightening out the twisted price system so that prices can function as a guide to the regulation of supply and demand and the distribution of resources. The present stage of price reform centers on reform of product prices. In that context, equilibrium product prices that reflect the situation in supply and demand are beginning to take shape in the market. They are already playing an important role in regulating enterprises' short-term supply and demand behavior. They are also acting to a certain extent on the distribution of the newly acquired factors of production. However, for the recombination of factors already in use and structural redistribution of existing and newly acquired factors, it is obviously not enough to have market prices only for products and not for productive factors. The formation of market prices for factors is premised on the open market. There being no capital market or labor market of any significant size in China at present, the distribution of these factors still depends on nonmarket forces. Because of the underdevelopment of factor markets, it is most difficult for enterprises to respond fully to the signals given by market prices for products.

The impediments are of two sorts. First, when supply falls short of market demand, surplus labor, capital funds, and other factors in one industry cannot flow smoothly into other industries where these factors are in short supply. Second, even when surplus factors are transferable, in the absence of a mechanism to pool together the scattered factors (e.g., capital funds), those industries where economies of large-scale production are crucial will receive a suboptimal share of reallocated factors. The best case in point is steel. Over recent years, demand for steel products has steadily outstripped supply, resulting in a continual rise in their market price. Theoretically, at such a high price, the producer could not fail to obtain very high returns from any new investments. But because of the underdeveloped capital market (in addition to system and technological factors) and in the absence of a mechanism or medium for pooling together capital funds and other productive factors, no single enterprise has the resources to act, because steel production is characterized by such prominent scale economies.

In other reports analyses have been made of the implications of an undeveloped factor market for the investing and allocative behavior of enterprises. The present report intends to emphasize that, if there is only a product market with no accompanying factor market, then despite powerful signals sent out by product prices, the original supply structure will display a tenacious inertia, keeping resources irrationally allocated.

As for the product market, lifting control over prices without at the same time perfecting the organizational setup of the market will leave the role of market prices restricted in one way or another. This is another crucial aspect in which the price reform has failed to achieve the desired results. China has practiced for decades a system of allocation of goods and materials and rationing of products, which makes it very difficult for the organizational setup of commodity circulation, such as the departments handling commerce and goods and materials, to adapt to meet the needs of market circulation. Furthermore, the vertical administrative setup (extending from central authorities through local ones down to individual enterprises), which has been maintained for years, makes the relationship between enterprises very different from a market-regulated relationship. As mandatory planning is minimized and relationships formed through central allocation become weaker, the market system and market relationships are established and developed. But all this will take time.

5. Some Ideas on Furthering Price Reform

5.1. Lift Controls Over Prices
Instead of Readjusting Them

The two-tier price system has contributed substantially to the improvement in the market supply and demand situation over the recent years. The crux lies in the lifting of control. It was through this that market prices made their appearance. To bring market prices into fuller play should be the orientation for further reform. Arbitrary readjustment of prices would lead either to the loss of market prices (through the formation of unified state-set prices)—to a price system that, much different as it may appear, is in essence the same as the one before the reform—or to the preservation of the two-tier system (a scheme to readjust prices in small steps), the only difference being a smaller disparity between state-set and market prices. The assertion of ''readjusting prices to market prices'' is in itself not scientific at all. Market prices are dynamic. What results from fixing market prices at what they happen to be at a certain time is another batch of arbitrarily set prices, which, as soon as they are set, will begin to deviate from actual market clearing prices. Moreover, without real market prices, there would be no standards whatsoever to go by in the readjustment of prices ''to market prices.''

Without, therefore, the lifting of control as the prerequisite for reform, not only will the readjustment of prices lead nowhere, but the reform itself will be costlier. It is better to lift control step by step than to readjust prices step by step. This should be one of the basic ideas for the reform.

5.2. The Task for the Near Future Is
to Perfect the Two-Tier System

In the course of its implementation, the two-tier system has revealed many shortcomings. As a source of price signals, its most serious shortcoming does not lie in the oft-cited ''speculation and profiteering,'' which is totally outside the scope of prices, but in the above-mentioned fact that market prices cannot under this system function fully as a guide to the distribution of resources. To eliminate these drawbacks depends eventually on the formation of a unitary (market) price system, the creation of factor markets, the perfection of the market mechanism and the organizational setup, and the strengthening of budgetary restraints on enterprises. Failing a rapid move to a unitary market price system, the price reform should focus on further improving the ''two-tier system'' during the first half of the Seventh Five-Year Plan. Indeed, there is plenty of scope for improvement in this area.

One approach to perfecting the system is to turn the proportional two-tier system into a base-figure two-tier system, and to strengthen the role of market prices in guiding the behavior of the enterprises, especially their long-range economic behavior. We believe that the base-figure two-tier system not only conforms to the overall reform scenario of reducing mandatory planning gradually during the Seventh Five-Year Plan, but also will help overcome some of the shortcomings in the existing proportional two-tier system, especially those in connection with the long-range regulation of supply and demand and the distribution of resources.

Essentially, the base-figure two-tier system means "contracting to enterprises comprehensive fixed quotas" (the base-figure responsibility system), which would remain unchanged for a number of years, in regard to the planned share of production, supply, and marketing. All incremental output and all incremental production capacity would be placed under market prices. This will help gain two ends at once: to make it less possible for local government to exert direct control over the enterprise as well as to lessen the urge of the enterprise to bargain with the government. Moreover, this will also make it less difficult for the enterprise to manage its production, supply, and marketing.

5.3. Accelerating Reform in the Nonprice Areas

It is correct to regard the price reform as the precondition for reforms in other areas. But price reform can by no means replace other reforms; rather it may be restricted by them. The present report, along with other supplementary reports, has discussed this problem from various angles, pointing out that the role of prices alone is not enough to solve such problems as the readjustment of the supply and demand structure, the optimization of resource distribution, and the rationalization of the behavior of enterprises. It naturally follows, therefore, that reforms in other areas must be stepped up during the Seventh Five-Year Plan, with a view to consolidating the achievements in price reform and giving greater scope to price signals. It is also necessary to form a capital market to lessen the resistance of industry to output shifts, and to form a labor market to lessen the rigidity of production costs to change.

The Present Management Environment in China's Industrial Enterprises
Zhang Shaojie and Zhang Amei

Since 1970 the economic system reform in China's cities has sought to streamline administration and give enterprises more power. To this end, we have transformed arrangements regarding planning, pricing, marketing of products, supply of raw and semi-finished materials, labor and wages, financial affairs, and taxation. We hope to improve the management environment, bring into play the market's regulatory function, and make the enterprise responsive to market signals, so as eventually to build up a self-adjusting economic mechanism.

How deep has the reform so far gone in this direction, and what are the present major tasks? In this respect, opinions differ. This subreport outlines the present management environment and its effect upon our country's industrial enterprises, and it also briefly discusses some problems that may lie ahead. The areas of labor, wages, and investment are covered elsewhere. This subreport stresses problems related to marketing.

1. Great Changes in the Enterprise's Management Environment

The policy decision on invigorating the enterprise and expanding its decision-making powers involves two basic aspects: (1) reducing the government's administrative interference in the enterprise's affairs, particularly mandatory plans for day-to-day business activities; and (2) expanding the market's influence on the enterprise by generating rational price signals and making demand a binding force on supply. Obviously, these two aspects are closely connected with each other. The reduction and eventual elimination of mandatory plans is the prerequisite for the regulatory role of the market mechanism.

According to the survey of 429 industrial enterprises, the role of planning in the supply of raw materials and the production and marketing of products has been reduced considerably in recent years, resulting in an expansion in enterprise autonomy. In 1984, output produced under mandatory plans accounted for 25.92 percent of the total, while output under guidance plans made up 26.91 percent, for a total of 52.83 percent. As for marketing, enterprises had 57.42 percent of their output distribution directly by the state, 9.77 percent purchased by commercial or administrative departments, and 32.81 percent sold by themselves. Finally, regarding supply of raw and semi-finished materials, the portion supplied under central planning was quite high, accounting for 73.16 of the total. The government controlled materials-supply much more tightly than it did the enterprises' production and marketing.

In 1985 in these enterprises, the share of planned production and marketing both picked up, whereas the share of planned supply dropped drastically. The proportion of major raw and semifinished materials obtained by way of coordination and cooperation with other industrial enterprises or purchased on their own from the market skyrocketed from 26.84 percent at the end of 1984 to 43.8 percent by June 1985, up 17 percentage points in six months. The disproportion between planned supply and planned production and marketing was somewhat alleviated.

In 1984, about 51 percent of the randomly sampled industrial enterprises enjoyed some degree of autonomy in materials supply, production, and marketing (see figure 2.1). Seventy-seven percent of the enterprises had to keep the market situation in mind when mapping out their production plan, whereas enterprises that got their supply of raw and semifinished materials, at least to a certain degree, from the market made up 90.4 percent. Enterprises that had the above-plan products to sell on the market on their own made up 97 percent of the total.

The reduction in the proportion of planned supply, production, and marketing means that the enterprise's decision-making powers have been expanded and that the enterprise has to adapt itself to the market conclusion. In 1984, the correlation coefficient between the growth rate of output value and the growth rate of output value and the growth rate of their income from self-sales was 0.74. At the same time, the finished products stockpiled in warehouses represented 11.2 percent of the total, which is obviously proportional to their products sold on the market on their own ($r=0.1809$). In addition, the proportion of their products sold on the market on their own is also comparable with the growth rate of their profits ($r=0.1511$). All this indicates that as the percentage of planned supply, production, and marketing dropped, the enterprise found it more difficult to sell its products, and that whether the enterprise is able to sell its products has begun to affect its profits.

Whether an enterprise responds well to market change depends on whether its productive capacity is flexible. Reform in this respect has been quite spectacular, though the change is not as conspicuous as that in the products market.

Concerning flexibility of funds, the enterprise's funds come from various

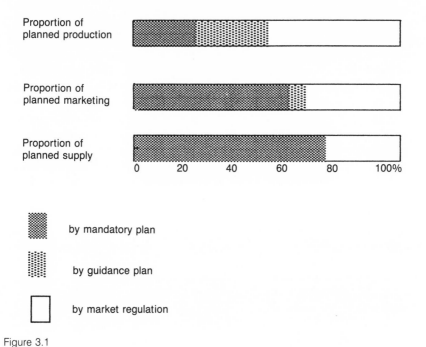

Figure 3.1

Planned Supply, Production, and Marketing as Seen in Randomly Sampled Enterprises in 1984

channels. The share of budgetary funds has dropped, and in addition, bank funds are no longer the sole other external source of funds. In the supply of short-term funds, enterprise commercial credit has developed rapidly. For these enterprises, the percentage of money that the enterprise put aside in advance to pay bank loans accounted for 19.53 percent in 1983, 35.91 percent in 1984, and in 1985 up to 41.38 percent of its total bank loans, or about 20 percent of its total circulating funds. In the supply of long-term funds, the horizontal investment between enterprises has also developed extensively. In the sample enterprises, funds that the enterprise itself collected for investment in fixed assets accounted for 45.59 percent of the total, of which the enterprise's own funds accounted for 64 percent. That is to say, 17.46 percent of the enterprise's funds for investment in fixed assets come from other sources than the state budgetary allocation, bank loans, and self-raised funds.

Regarding the labor force, the enterprise's management environment has experienced two outstanding changes. The first is the widespread employment of contract workers and casual laborers. The rapid development of auxiliary enterprises (labor service companies, for example) brought about a certain degree of maneuverability in the increase or reduction of the payroll and in the use of the labor force as well. The second is that the competition between enterprises for labor, especially for specialists and skilled laborers, has become intense, resulting in some free flow of labor. According to a survey of thirteen industrial enterprises in Nanjing and Hangzhou, in eight factories since 1984, workers and staff members, especially young workers, have sometimes left their posts without asking for permission, accounting for 20 percent of the total number who quit their positions in those enterprises.

Generally speaking, great changes have taken place in the production environment of our country's industrial enterprises. The regulatory role of the market mechanism in the product market has been strengthened greatly, and its regulatory role in the factor markets has made some initial progress. Such changes in the management environment have made the enterprise more responsive to the market and at the same time brought some pressure to bear upon the enterprise to improve its management to suit the market. There is little doubt that such changes in the management environment conform to the direction we projected for our economic reform.

2. "Assymmetrical Market"—A Major Feature of the Present Management Environment of Industrial Enterprises

Although the management environment of China's industrial enterprises is, to a certain extent, subject to some market regulation, the degree varies. This had led to a serious asymmetry. Some enterprises are confronted with one supply-demand relationship in the output market and quite a different one in the input market. A majority of enterprises sell their products in a buyers' market but face a sellers' market for the raw and semifinished materials they buy. While their agents go everywhere purchasing, they send out other agents everywhere selling. Such a market structure is what we can an "asymmetrical market."

The survey proves the existence of this asymmetrical market. The Hungarian economist Kornai suggested using the ratio between the stock of inputs and the stock of output (a ratio we will call the Kornai index) as the basic parameter determining whether a country has a "sellers' market economy" or a "buyers' market economy." In the buyers' market economy, where buyers have a wide range of choices and sellers compete with each other for sales, the enterprise will find it easy to buy but hard to sell, and so the enterprise usually has a big stock of output as against a small stock of inputs, and the Kornai index is low. In the sellers' market economy, the enterprise has a strong incentive to hoard raw and semifinished materials, and its products will be in the position of "the emperor's daughter [who] has no difficulty finding a husband." Therefore, where there is a lower stock of output than of inputs, the Kornai index should be high. Table 3.1 shows how several countries' Kornai index stands.

For the Kornai index of sample enterprises, see table 3.2.

According to table 3.2, the Kornai index of China's industrial enterprises

Table 3.1

Kornai Index of Some Countries

Buyers' Market Economy	Period	Kornai Index	Sellers' Market Economy		Kornai Index
Austria	1972–1977	1.5	USSR	1969–1977	9.2–12.3
Sweden	1968–1972	0.70–0.74	Poland	1975	10.3
USA	1960–1977	0.94–1.16	Hungary	1971–1980	7.26– 8.52

Table 3.2

Changes in Stockpile Ratios for Sample Enterprises

	1983	1984	First Half of 1985
Stock of input goods vs. stock of output products	4.6	4.5	3.8
Stock of input goods vs. annual sale value	0.1533	0.1473	0.1579

fluctuated between 3.8 and 4.6 in the period from 1983 to 1985. An investigation of twenty state-owned industrial enterprises by the Economic Research Institute of the Chinese Academy of Social Sciences and the World Bank indicated that during the period from 1980 to 1982, the ratio between the stock of input goods and the annual sale value was 0.154. The result of this survey shows that compared with three widely recognized sellers' market economies, China's industry, despite a rapid growth rate, does not show a strong hoarding tendency. This suggests that China's industrial enterprises have made extremely important progress toward using market mechanisms in recent years.

But table 3.2 also shows that for the present, China's Kornai ratio is still distant from the typical figure for a buyers' market economy. Presumably, because inputs in the "asymmetrical" markets forced by these enterprises are still in short supply, a hoarding tendency persists, raising the Kornai index.

Table 3.3 shows what proportion of the labor force was idle in each year. As the table reveals, when asked to explain the failure fully to utilize this labor, enterprises were much more likely to cite a lack of inputs than a lack of buyers for their product. Again, we see the "asymmetrical market" structure.

We see this same phenomenon reflected in the management goals of the directors of these enterprises and the constraints they cited. Of the first three management goals listed by the factory directors, two are connected with marketing, with "quality improvement" second and "development of new products"

Table 3.3

Utilization of Manhours in 182 Sample Enterprises

	1983	1984	First Half of 1985
Percentage of nonproductive manhours in total	6.7	5.47	5.29
Percentage caused by shortage of materials and power	31.59	41.47	39.44
Percentage caused by lack of a production task	21.22	23.44	18.97

third in their order of priority. On the list of constraints, they put "unstable supply of raw and semifinished materials" in fourth place, next to "lack of skills," "lack of funds," and "unsuitability of the labor and personnel system," which are listed in the first three places.

In the present reform, the asymmetrical market has three effects. First, as compared with a traditional overall buyers' market economy, the asymmetrical market stimulates the enterprise's technical change, compels supply to conform to demand, and strengthens the consumer's power. When it is difficult to have an overall buyers' market, the asymmetrical market constitutes a second-best environment for promoting reform. Second, the asymmetrical market has a two-pronged influence upon prices. First, it helps check a rise in the price of output, and second, it does *not* help control production costs. These combine to produce an unfavorable effect on profit. In the first half of 1985, the fact that some industrial enterprises tried hard to speed up production, so as to offset the disadvantage brought about by price hikes of raw materials, reflects this situation. Third, such a market structure in other ways (especially for input-producing enterprises) will dampen the producer's responsiveness to the markets and will reduce the pressure for technical advances that the market ordinarily brings to bear upon the enterprise. Therefore, it can be said that such a market structure will have a two-pronged influence, good and bad, upon the economy as a whole.

3. Causes of the Asymmetrical Market

Causes behind the shaping of the asymmetrical market are diverse and intricately complicated. The most important causes, however, are: (1) the unevenness in the rate of reduction of the planned share, in supply, production, and marketing; (2) the uneven application of reform in different sectors of industry; and (3) differing supply elasticities in different industrial sectors.

3.1. Uneven Rate of Reduction of Planning in Supply, Production, and Marketing

At present, the degree to which planning persists varies greatly from supply to production and marketing. For enterprises under different kinds of ownership, the shares of planned supply, production, and marketing can be several dozens of

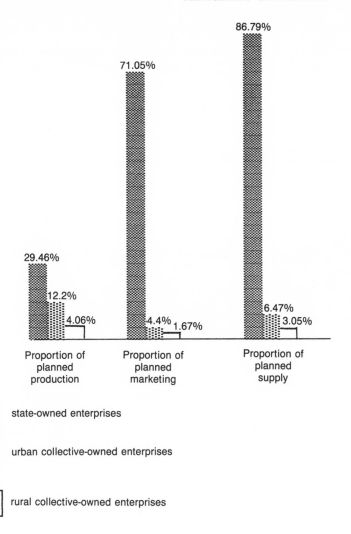

Figure 3.2

Proportion of Planned Supply, Production, and Marketing for Industrial Enterprieses Under Different Kinds of Ownership, 1984

times different from each other (see figure 3.2).

For enterprises of varying sizes, there is also an extremely striking difference in the proportion of planned supply, production, and marketing. In 1984, the proportion of planned production, supply, and marketing for big and medium-sized enterprises was, respectively, 28.38 percent, 84.47 percent, and 67.97 percent, whereas it stood respectively at 3.55 percent, 4.47 percent, and 3.02 percent for small enterprises.

The difference in planned production, supply, and marketing has an obvious

Table 3.4

Kornai Index of 141 Producer Goods Enterprises

	1983	1984	First Half of 1985
State-owned enterprises	5.69	4.85	3.97
Collectively owned enterprises	2.64	1.68	1.71

relation to an asymmetrical market. Table 3.4 shows how the Kornai index stands for 141 state-owned and 52 collective-owned enterprises that produce means of production. It shows a much higher index for state-owned enterprises. In the light of figure 3.2 we can surmise that because for state enterprises input supply is largely still centrally planned, they are relatively more likely to face a sellers' market there, and, consequently, they will hoard large input stocks. The collectively owned enterprises, by contrast, buy more than 90 percent of their inputs on the market; they know that they can always get what they need (at a price) and so need not hoard.

A sectoral analysis will help us to understand this issue better. We divided the products of the enterprises into consumer goods, investment goods (including production-related machines, complete sets of equipment, vehicles, ships, and building materials), intermediate products (including various components, parts, and attachments used as input goods for production; ordinary chemical materials; yarn; and grey cloth), and basic raw and semifinished materials. (Obviously, the first two categories are finished products, and the last two are basically intermediate products.) The survey statistics show that *the difference in proportion of planned supply, production, and marketing for different enterprises stems from the difference in proportion of planned production of different categories of products.* Figures 3.3 and 3.4 show that planned control is tightest for production and marketing of *raw materials and intermediate products.* Since these products are what constitute the bulk of ''supply'' to Chinese industry, it is natural that planning is more dominant, in industry as a whole, in supply than in production or marketing.

As seen in figure 3.3, the proportion of planned supply and raw and semifinished materials is more than 100 percent, which means that the combined production task by mandatory and guidance plan is more than the enterprise's actual output.

Both the central and provincial authorities have played an extremely important role in maintaining a planned supply of raw and semifinished materials. The function of the city authorities is, for the most part, to adjust the production of consumer goods and intermediate products. Table 3.5 indicates how the proportion of mandatory plan by the central, provincial, and municipal authorities stands for different categories of products.

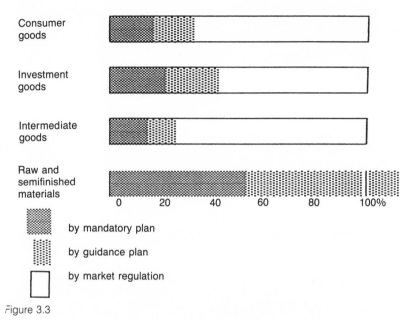

Figure 3.3

Share of Planned Production for Different Categories of Products, 1984

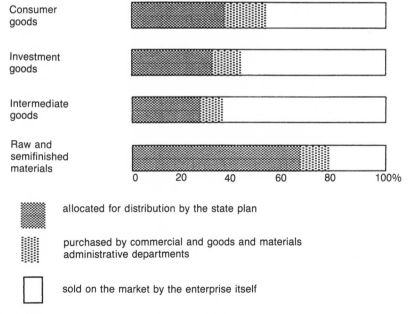

Figure 3.4

Share of Planned Marketing for Different Categories of Products, 1984

Table 3.5

Proportion of Mandatory Plan by Governments of Different Levels, 1984

	Central Government	Provincial Government	Municipal Government
Consumer goods	44	31	25
Input goods	42	48	10
Intermediate goods	59	4	37
Raw and semifinished materials	54	57	− 11

The enterprise's planned production tasks differ as the supply of raw and semifinished materials and demand for products by the governments of various levels differ. The supply of basic raw and semifinished materials is usually coordinated within a province or even within the country as a whole, whereas production and marketing of other intermediate products are now mainly coordinated within a city.

The Unevenness of Reform Across Sectors. This refers to a characteristic shared in common by most countries under reform. It is true even in the well-organized Hungarian economy. Simply put, reform applies more to the collective sector than to the state-owned sector. Collectively run enterprises operate largely on a market basis. Under the "two-tier price system" for inputs, they face high prices for inputs in short supply; they tend to draw back and economize, reducing the tendency for a sellers' market to develop. But because many state enterprises obtain a large share of their key inputs under state plans at low prices, and because they can pass along high prices (due to a "soft budget constraint"), the role of price in checking demand is obviously limited. It is obvious that such a situation is not good for reducing the short supply of raw and semifinished materials.

Differences in Supply Elasticity. At present, the manufacturing sector has more of its capacity lying idle than the raw and semifinished materials sector. This has led to a large gap in the input-output ratio for newly added investment between different industrial sectors. Take motorcycle production, for example. The scope of fixed assets during the Sixth Five-Year Plan period expanded by only 14.75 percent, with an annual rate of increase of only 2.79 percent, while its annual average growth rate increased by as much as 84.5 percent. However, the input-output ratio in the metallurgical, oil, and basic chemical materials sectors was quite low, making it difficult for their investment in technical transformation to spur their production. The construction period of new projects lasted usually as long as five to ten years. At the same time, it is hard for small investments to flow at the capital-intensive raw and semifinished materials sector. This operates to restrict any increase in supply of raw and semifinished materials for these sectors. Among these industrial sectors, the coal sector is the only exception. The rapid development of small coal mines in recent years has greatly increased the coal sector's capacity and alleviated the imbalance between supply and demand for coal, with the result that coal prices have tended to normalize.

From the above discussion, we can now conclude: (1) The basic cause behind China's asymmetrical market is the big difference in supply elasticity for different industrial sectors. This is connected not only to the country's original structure of production capacity, but also to the underdevelopment of its fund market. (2) To ensure a proper distribution of some badly needed raw and semi-finished materials, the country maintained a quite high degree of planned adjustment over their supply, production, and marketing, an adjustment which has not only maintained the consuming enterprises' dependence on the government and the tendency to hoarding, but has also held back the producing enterprises' responsiveness to the market. (3) The uneven application of reform means that the market's stimulation and restriction is not brought to bear on some enterprises to force it to control its production cost. This has made it difficult to develop a sellers' market in basic raw and semifinished materials.

4. Four Proposals for Further Study

To promote competition between enterprises and compel them to improve their products and update their equipment in response to the market, we must create a buyers' market which, in return, will bring pressure to bear upon the producer. The formation of a buyers' market, however, depends upon not only a proper relationship between overall supply and overall demand, but also the detailed operation mechanisms within the national economy. Such being the case, while overall macro control is strengthened, it is also necessary to reform further the operation mechanism of the economy. The task of promoting the formation of an overall buyers' market links up micro reform and macro control.

During the Seventh Five-Year Plan period, a gradual reduction in the proportion of planned adjustment with regard to supply, production, and marketing of basic raw and semifinished materials will help weaken the enterprise's dependence upon the government and the government's restriction over the enterprise. We need to reform the planning, supply, production, and pricing of raw and semifinished material. For the present, one possible approach is to implement further the two-tier price system, with the enterprise being responsible for its own materials, supply, production, and marketing. For the consuming enterprises, once the basic quota for supply of raw and semifinished materials is set, it will no longer change. For the producing enterprise, once the output quota to be allocated for distribution by the state is set, it will no longer change, or if there is any change, the quota can only become smaller. The above-quota portion will be left with the enterprise and subject to market regulation. The government can use various economic means, such as financial subsidy and preferential loans, to guide the enterprise in its production. The present practice of guidance plan by controlling the supply of raw and semifinished materials should be abandoned step by step.

To transform the unevenness between stimulation and restriction toward the enterprise represents an important link in the transition from the asymmetrical market to a buyers' market. The transformation is, however, an extremely difficult and long process. During the Seventh Five-Year Plan period, especially during the first half of the period, whose major task is to stabilize the economic situation, favorable policies for the strengthening of restriction should be given the first priority. The important policies in this aspect should include one aiming at strengthening the effect of interest rates upon production cost and after-tax profits, and also one aimed at gradually eliminating the present practice of paying the investment loan ahead of the tax. They should also include a policy that while the enterprise is to be exempted from adjusted tax for its income from sales on its own, it will not enjoy preferential tax treatment for those raw and semifinished materials it purchases on its own at a high price. The system that a bankrupt enterprise should clear off its debts should be further promoted. "Openness" and "pressing" are two aspects that should not be ignored in the reform of the enterprises' performance.

To strengthen the supply elasticity of the economy as a whole will help alleviate the disproportional structure of the national economy and strengthen the economy's responsiveness to demand. In this respect, to strengthen the flow of productive factors is an extremely pressing task. The formation of a relatively elastic funds market and a labor market will prove very important for strengthening the responsiveness to the market of the supply of basic raw and semifinished materials industry.

Before an overall buyers' market is created, to keep the asymmetrical market from retrogressing to an overall sellers' market should be the minimum target of the present policy. Therefore, it is necessary to study what conditions we should create so as to retain the present asymmetrical market. In this sense, the maintenance of the drawn-out structure of some industrial sectors, especially some final product sectors, may be useful for reforming the economy as a whole.

The Public Response
to Price Reform

Yang Guansan, Yang Xiaodong
and Xuan Mingdong

Abstract: The two surveys on social psychological response to the price reform, conducted in February and July 1985, indicate that most residents understand and support the price reform. The understanding and support has much to do with the rise of people's standard of living brought about by a series of reforms in the past few years. (See section 1 of this report.) When the price of nonstaple food, with which people are most concerned, was raised, people had some complaints about inflation (section 2). However, recognizing and appreciating the ascendancy of "consumers' sovereignty," people's enthusiasm for the reform was not fundamentally damaged, and most of them approved the price hikes for nonstaple food. What is more, in this short experience with a market economy, the Chinese people have already adapted to a commercial economy, creating a good foundation for future reforms (section 3). However, some problems remain (section 4).

People's understanding and support are very important to the smooth implementation of the reform. Whether people can gain the ability and attitudes required by a modern economy, and whether the change in their opinions can keep up with the process of reform, are key factors in the success or failure of the reform. To make every step of the reform scientific and feasible, it is very important to be abreast of public opinion on every measure of the reform and to identify people's psychological obstacles to the development of the reform.

To do so, two nationwide questionnaire surveys on response to the price reform were conducted separately in February and July 1985, before and after the price readjustment of nonstaple food carried out in May of the same year. The February survey was carried out in eleven cities and sixteen counties from Beijing, Henan, Zhejiang, Hunan, and Anhui. The organizer of the survey issued 2,600 questionnaires and recovered 2,409 valid responses, a 92.65 response rate. The July survey was conducted in ten cities from Beijing, Heilongjiang, Shanxi, Sichuan, Shangdong, Zhejiang, Hubei, and Guangxi. The organizer of the survey issued 2,400 questionnaires of which 2,060 responded, a response rate of 85.83 percent. The characteristics of the respondents are shown in table 4.1.

Table 4.1

Characteristics of the Survey Samples

	February	July
Location:		
Large city	49.6	48.7
Medium city	21.8	26.0
Small city	9.1	25.1
Rural	19.3	—
Occupation:		
Professional	16.2	12.0
Leading cadre	8.1	13.3
White collar	17.4	26.5*
Blue collar	25.7	24.8
Service	6.9	16.7
Farmer	15.8	—
Other	8.6	5.5
Urban Job: Type of Ownership:		
State	66.0	76.0
Collective	25.4	18.8
Private	5.0	2.8
Average Age	41	39
Sex:		
Male	62.8	55.6
Female	37.2	44.4

*Includes 7.8% primary or middle school teachers.

1. Standard of Living and Support for Price Reform

Most people agree that their standard of living has been rising in recent years, and they support price reform.

According to the February survey, over 80 percent of those surveyed thought their living standard had gone up in recent years, of whom about 20 percent considered the raise quite remarkable. Only 4 percent complained that their living standard was down.

Although the July survey was conducted right after the price readjustment for nonstaple food, which resulted in soaring prices of pork, eggs, beef, and vegetables, more than 70 percent of those surveyed admitted that their living standard had risen more or less over the last few years.

February Survey
Q: What would you say about the living standard of your family in recent years?

A: 1. Rising remarkably   18.6% ⎫
   2. Going up slightly   65.9% ⎬   84.5%
   3. No change   10.3% ⎭
   4. Falling slightly   3.8% ⎫   4.3%
   5. Going down drastically   0.5% ⎭

Q: What do you think of the living standard of your family since 1979?

A: 1. Rising remarkably   9.1% ⎫
   2. Going up slightly   64.3% ⎬   73.4%
   3. No change   12.5% ⎭
   4. falling slightly   13.7% ⎫   13.9%
   5. going down drastically   0.2% ⎭

After the prices of nonstaple foods were raised, more than 70 percent of the respondents still thought their food-consumption level had not declined, and a few of them even said it had risen slightly; less than 30 percent reported a decline.

Of those who give the former answer, 40 percent attribute their ability to maintain or increase their food consumption to higher income. Of all factors proposed, they ranked family income first.

July Survey

Q: What is the most important factor enabling you to maintain your food-consumption level after the price readjustment?

A: | Factors | Comprehensive Point | Order |
|---|---|---|
| Increased family income | 0.984 | 1 |
| Government subsidy | 0.672 | 2 |
| Giving up plans to buy durable goods | 0.600 | 3 |
| Reducing expenses on clothes and items of daily use | 0.561 | 4 |
| Reducing bank deposits | 0.426 | 5 |

Of those who thought their food-consumption level had fallen, 12.4 percent explained this by saying that they were not willing to reduce their expenses on clothes and items of daily use, 10.2 percent cited plans to buy durable goods, and 7.1 percent were unwilling to reduce their bank deposits. Only 6.1 percent attributed the lowering of their food-consumption level to a decrease of family income.

Q: What is the main reason why you can't maintain your original food-consumption level since the price reform?

A: *Reasons*	*Comprehensive Point*	*Order*
Unwilling to cut down on expenses of buying clothes and items of daily use	0.254	1
Saving money to buy durable goods	0.233	2
Decrease in family income	0.231	3
Unwilling to reduce bank deposits	0.148	4

The rise in the standard of living in recent years has enabled residents to withstand the impact of the price readjustment for nonstaple food. The increase in family income to a large degree offsets the effects of inflation. The majority of residents understand this clearly.

In July 1985 a multiple correlation analysis was made on the comprehensive point of people's attitude toward price reform and ten independent variables. The analysis shows that of all the factors influencing people's attitude toward the price reform, their evaluation of the standard of living was the most important. The higher the evaluation, the more firmly they support the reform.

July Survey

Evaluation of standard of living	*Comprehensive point of people's attitude toward the reform*
Increasing remarkably	67.66
Going up slightly	61.48
No change	57.28
Falling slightly	55.18
Falling greatly	55.00

Note: The higher the comprehensive point, the more firmly the respondents support the reform.

Of the 2,409 people surveyed in February, about three-quarters expressed their definite support for and understanding of the price reform.

February Survey

Q: What do you think is the purpose of the price reform?

A: 1. To activate the national economy 74.3%
   2. No idea   16.9% } 24.0%
   3. The state wants to increase its revenue 7.1% }

Q: Some people think the price reform will ultimately benefit the prosperity of the country. Do you think so?

A. 1. Yes   76.8%
   2. No idea 17.8% } 21.5%
   3. No   3.7% }

The July survey was conducted after the increase in the price of nonstaple food but before the wage increase expected in a wage reform a few months later. However, the majority of the 2,060 people surveyed still expressed their understanding of and support for the price reform.

July Survey

Q: What do you think is the reason the state needs a price reform?

A: 1. Many current prices conflict with
      the demands of the law of value   60.9%
   2. The state suffers financial
      difficulty   19.1% } 37.1%
   3. No idea   18.1% }

Q: Do you agree that the prosperity of our country requires price reform?

A: 1. Quite agree   10.1%
   2. Agree   57.1%
   3. Don't agree   22.7%
   4. Strongly disagree 2.3%

Although the price of nonstaple food rose, which stirred people's resentment and lowered some people's living standard, more than 60 percent of the respondents to the above two questions held a positive attitude toward the price reform.

People's positive opinion of the reform is further proved by another survey, conducted in July 1985, under the title "Public Reaction to Reforms of the Employment System, Public Welfare, and Social Security" (reported elsewhere in this volume). A total of 1,341 managers and workers from different enterprises were questioned, and the majority gave an encouraging answer.

Statements	*Agree*	*Disagree*
1. Although the reform is in a bit of disorder, it is better than the old days when everybody "eats from the same big pot."	77.8%	10.9%
2. If the reform can succeed, we can stand a temporarily low standard of living.	75.3%	16.7%
3. If the reform can benefit China's social and economic development, individuals should share some risks for the country.	78.2%	12.3%
4. You can't be damaged by reform if you are really capable.	80.7%	7.2%
5. If everybody is allowed to compete freely (for example, free job choice), everyone will live a better life.	62.9%	11.5%

The majority support the reform and hold an optimistic opinion about the future of the reform and that of themselves. This is a most significant finding because it provides a better chance for overall reform to succeed.

2. Complaints about Price Reform for Nonstaple Food

The price reform for nonstaple food affects people's standard of living and provokes their complaints.

Q: Since the price readjustment, how has the structure of your food consumption changed compared with that of one year ago?

A:	*Pork*	*Fish*	*Eggs*	*Vegetables*
Eating more	17.3	4.4	36.0	41.6
No change	38.3	21.2	39.3	40.0
Eating less	42.7	70.1	21.9	15.8

Most families have changed their food structure. They eat less fish and pork, but more eggs and vegetables.

To maintain the original food-consumption level, 27.9 percent of those surveyed reduced their expenses on clothes and daily used goods, 27 percent gave up plans to buy durable goods, and 20.6 percent even cut into their bank deposits. As a result about half of those surveyed felt their living standard had declined.

July Survey

Q: Taking into account the new state subsidies, what's the influence of the price reform on your total living standard (including food, clothes, and daily used goods)?

A: 1. Rising   12.4% ⎫
   2. No change   39.2% ⎬ 51.6%
   3. Falling   41.8% ⎫
   4. Going down greatly 4.7% ⎬ 46.5%

In the "falling" category, most felt their living standard had gone down slightly, not drastically. It is coincidental with the fact that most of these families' expenses on food did not increase drastically. Only 6.3 percent of those surveyed thought that the share of their expenditures on food in their total expenditure had increased more than 4 percentage points after the price reform; 58.7 percent thought the increase was between 1 and 5 percent, and 28.2 percent said they suffered no increase in food expenses.

Still, about half of those surveyed in July considered that their standard of living had fallen. This is bound to influence their attitude toward the reform.

Attitude toward reform

Evaluation of standard	Satisfied	Optimistic	Unsure about future	Worried about future
Rising	9.9	55.6	28.2	6.3
No change	6.4	47.9	39.0	6.4
Going down slightly	3.3	34.0	50.9	11.7
Going down drastically	3.1	15.5	52.6	28.9

Those whose living standard is falling feel uncertain about the future and are even skeptical about the reform.

Although some people's living standard is lower, and they naturally complain, most people rest their hopes on the development of production and further reforms. Given the following alternatives, they oppose "taking the road back."

July Survey

Q: If your living standard has fallen, what would be the best way to compensate for it?

	Accumulative frequency	Comprehensive point	Order
Increasing production, lower prices	68.3	1.69	1
Increasing wages	64.9	1.65	2
Increasing state subsidies	34.6	0.64	3
Rolling back the prices to original level	29.5	0.51	4
Earning more money through spare-time jobs	18.9	0.32	5

In the above survey, 68.3 percent of those surveyed hoped the development of production would lower prices naturally, 64.9 percent hoped the wage increase expected in a wage reform a few months later would offset the impact of the inflation, and 34.6 percent hoped the state would increase its subsidies to each family. Only 29.5 percent of those surveyed hoped the government would pull back the prices to the original level. Most people do not agree with them. They are unwilling to return to the old days when they had to stand in long queues to buy vegetables. The ample market supply, which appeared after the price readjustment, is a big attraction. They are looking forward to further reforms because they have been pleased by the one implemented already.

July survey

Q: What is the influence of the price reform on China's overall economic reform?

A: 1. It's very conducive to the overall reform.	11.3%	84.5%
2. It plays a positive role	73.2%	
3. It has no effect	10.9%	13.2%
4. It plays a negative role	2.3%	2.3%

People consider the price reform a success. Although there are some complaints among the residents about inflation, their enthusiasm for the economic reform is not fundamentally wounded. They do not take a negative attitude toward reform. In the process of reform, it is natural that some people have complaints about some phenomena brought about by the reform. What we should do is to educate people that the reform is not a smooth and easy process. Ups and downs should be expected. At the same time we should train people to cope with competition and challenge. We should urge people to respond to challenge, not to complain about it. Only in this way can the reform gain the support of the people.

Social stability cannot be achieved by issuing state subsidies. The only way to remove people's complaints is to raise people's living standard. To do so, apart from the development of the national economy, people must be given new opportunities—the opportunity to improve their financial conditions on their own.

In most cases, China's urban residents live on their salary. Since they are not allowed to transfer their jobs freely from one enterprise to another that issues a larger bonus, people cannot determine their income through their own effort. To cope with inflation, they have to turn to the state for subsidies or to their enterprises for a higher salary and a fatter bonus. As a result, there is an outcry for free job-transfer and for reform of the employment system.

The above analysis indicates that most people have a positive attitude toward the reform, although more than half say their living standard is somewhat influenced by inflation. This valuable attitude must be treasured and protected. To accelerate the process of reform is the demand of most people and the only way to remove people's complaints; to suspend the benefits provided by the reform will incur people's greater resentment and even run the risk of losing their support for the reform.

3. Ascendancy of "Consumers' Sovereignty"

The clear ascendancy of "consumers' sovereignty" caused people's appraisal of the price readjustment to be much more favorable to reform than expected.

The February survey indicates 84.2 percent of those surveyed were worried about the price of nonstaple food, vegetables, and fruit. Thus, price readjustment carried out in May 1985 touched a most delicate and sensitive field. There was much talk in society about people's resentment against the soaring prices. Hearing these rumors, the organizers of the survey scarcely expected a high evaluation of price reform in July. But the results of the July survey were contrary to expectations. The following list shows responses to the statements, where a high score indicates agreement.

July Survey

	Comprehensive score	Order
1. The market has become brisk.	5.740	1
2. You can buy what you want although it is expensive.	5.415	2

3. There is a big variety of nonstaple food.	5.332	3
4. The price reform was carried out at the right time.	4.218	4
5. The price reform was successful.	4.126	5
6. The price reform was rational.	3.920	6
7. The society is calm about the reform.	3.760	7
8. The government implemented the reform well.	3.675	8
9. Everybody applauds the reform.	3.415	9
10. The state has given enough subsidies to residents.	2.760	10
Average comprehensive point	4.236	

People were deeply impressed by the brisk market and the large variety of goods brought about by the price reform. In the past the residents sometimes had nowhere to purchase what they intended to buy even if they had enough money; now they have a much bigger variety from which to choose. This indicates a remarkable ascendancy of "consumers' sovereignty." That is, consumer dollars are now allowed to draw forth goods. People appreciate this very much (the comprehensive point of statements 1–3 is much higher than the middle value). On the other hand, people complain about low level of subsidies. Local governments issue different subsidies to residents according to the local inflation index and local financial conditions. The highest amount is 12 yuan a month per person and the lowest is 1.8 yuan. No matter how much the subsidy is, people always regard it as inadequate (the comprehensive point on this issue is much lower than the middle value). How do these two opinions influence people's evaluation of the price reform? Which one has a greater effect on people's evaluation? A rank correlation analysis was done on the question. The result of the analysis indicates that the key reason why the price reform was possible at a low cost in public opinion lies in the appearance of a brisk market and a wider choice for customers in the marketplace. It also shows that to introduce the market mechanism into pricing is in keeping with people's interest and will. The state subsidies, though necessary, do not effectively remove people's complaints about inflation.

People's attitudes are composed of three parts or structures: understanding, feeling, and behavior. For the first part, understanding, people show their support for price reform: 74.3 percent of those surveyed think the purpose of the price reform is to activate the economy, 76.8 percent think the reform will ultimately lead to the prosperity of the country, and 69.6 percent believe the reform is conducive to rising living standards. The July survey shows that 60.9 percent hold that the reform is necessary because "many prices don't meet the needs of the law of value," 67.1 percent think the price reform must be carried out if the national economy is to prosper, 54 percent do not agree with the notion that "fixed price is one of the superiorities of the socialist system," and 77.5 percent think different commodities should be priced according to their quality.

People have various feelings toward the reform. Some are happy because they are optimistic about the future of the reform, some are indifferent, and others are quite resentful. A prosperous market causes people to have positive feelings toward the reform, and inflation stirs their negative feelings. In the February survey 86.2 percent of those surveyed thought that "although things have become expensive, you have a wider choice when you go shopping" while 56.7 percent hold "I would rather have my salary not increase than let prices go up." In the July survey 81.6 percent of those surveyed felt that although things are expensive, a prosperous market provides convenience, while the "I would rather have my salary be fixed than let price go up" category increased to 62.8 percent. These two contradicting feelings seem to coexist all the time.

As for the behavior structure, some people keep expressing their complaints while others try to increase their income by transferring their jobs or by doing spare time jobs. Most people, 78.4 percent of those surveyed, denounce the tendency of "slacking off at work if the rise in wages can't keep up with that of prices." The analysis of these three structural components of attitude toward the price reform shows that most people have a high evaluation of the reform.

Our investigation contradicts common hearsay about the reform. That is because the former is the result of a comprehensive scientific survey, whereas the latter is an exaggerated expression of people's feelings—their complaints about inflation—that neglects other aspects of people's real attitude toward the reform. Everyone tends to exaggerate his dislikes. People of different countries and different times all hate inflation. But those who witness their national economy changing from a sellers' market into a buyers' market are happy with a price reform that brings about a prosperous market and a wider choice for customers.

4. Social Psychological Obstacles to
Further Reform

Although people have gained some experience in coping with a market economy, social psychological obstacles to further reform still exist.

One can expect that the price reform has to pay a "public opinion" price, because no one is happy with inflation. The analysis of the results of the two surveys, carried out before and after the price reform, however, shows an encouraging change in people's opinion about pricing and management of the market. The change is significant for the coming reforms and the long-term economic development.

The February survey shows most people, although supporting the price reform, don't agree with the idea that prices should be regulated by the market.

February Survey

Q: Of all the following schemes, which one do you prefer?

A: 1. All prices are controlled by the state.   61.8%
   2. All prices are regulated by the market.   5.9% ⎫
   3. Prices are partially controlled by the state   ⎬   36.7%
      and partially regulated by the market.   30.8% ⎭

Many people support price reform but do not want the market to play an important role in pricing. However, the purpose of the price reform is to give the market mechanism greater play. Therefore, these people's views are internally inconsistent.

After a short experience with the market economy, many people changed their opinion about the market's role in pricing. The change can be seen in the July survey:

Q: Of all the following schemes, which one do you prefer?

A: 1. All prices are controlled by the state   34.7%
   2. All prices are regulated by the
      market   6.7% ⎫
   3. Prices are partially controlled by   ⎬   64.9%
      the state and partially
      regulated by the market.   58.2% ⎭

The July survey shows that many people got rid of some traditional concepts. For example, they accepted the idea that prices can vary in a socialist country.

July Survey

Q: Some people say "fixed price is the reflection of the superiority of the socialist system." Do you agree?

A: 1. Quite agree   6.8% ⎫   32.7%
   2. Agree   25.9% ⎭
   3. No idea   11.9%
   4. Don't agree   48.6% ⎫
   5. Totally agree   5.4% ⎭   54.0%

Most people feel that commodities should be priced according to their quality.

July Survey

Q: The bicycles with well-known brands are in great demand. Compared with the price of ordinary bicycles, do you think theirs should be:

A: 1. Much higher   11.4% ⎫
   2. A little bit higher 66.1% ⎬   77.5%
   3. The same level   19.4% ⎭

   These opinions could not have been expected just a few years ago. People's thinking has really changed. The accumulation of such changes will prepare public opinion for further reforms.

   The investigation, however, also indicates that people's attitudes toward challenge, cultivated by a "natural economy" and the influence of eqalitarianism, is not easily removed. The tendency is clearly reflected in people's thinking about taking risks. Most people would rather live on a low income than accept a challenge in order to earn more.

Choice of Lifestyle	February 1985	July 1985
1. Living a stable life at the expense of earning less.	77.3%	79.8%
2. Living a life full of challenge but with a bigger opportunity to earn more.	11.2%	18.6%

The survey shows that most people prefer to live a stable life. People's psychological preparation for further reforms is influenced by their choice of lifestyle.

   A questionnaire survey including ten items was conducted in July 1985 to investigate people's psychological preparation for further reforms. The higher the comprehensive point, the firmer the preparation is.

July Survey

Choice of Lifestyle	Comprehensive point for Preparation for Further Reforms
1. Stable pattern	56.97
2. Challenge pattern	76.13

The figures above show that people who welcome a challenging pattern of life are much better prepared for further reforms than the others. The most effective way to encourage this tendency is to accustom people to a market economy.

Although people give a high evaluation of the price reform, it does not mean they have no anxiety and are not worried about further price reforms.

July Survey

Q: What is your opinion about further price readjustment?

A: 1. Prices need to be further
      readjusted.   31.4%
   2. Prices should not be changed
      for at least one or
      two years.   27.1% ⎫
   3. Prices should be kept stable   ⎬   67.5%
      for a long time.   40.4% ⎭

Obviously, most people hope prices will remain stable for some time. The following indicates that people are worried most about rapidly rising prices for daily necessities.

Q: For which goods would a price increase worry you the most?

| | February 1985 | | July 1985 | |
	Comprehensive Class	Order	Comprehensive Class	Order
1. Nonstaple food, vegetables, and fruit	4.31	1	2.567	1
2. Grain	4.10	2	2.076	2
3. Rent, water, and electricity	2.94	3	2.025	3
4. Fuel	2.73	4	1.391	4
5. Clothes	2.51	5	0.438	5
6. High-grade consumer goods	2.50	6	0.419	6
7. Stationery	2.09	7	0.146	7
8. Service fees	1.82	8	0.289	8
9. Cost of transportation	1.77	9	0.178	9

Surprisingly, the results of the two surveys are almost identical. Although the prices of nonstaple foods have been lifted a great deal, people are still worried most about them. Apart from the efforts to increase production and marketing, the mass media has a lot to of work to do to reduce people's uneasiness.

The investigation of "social psychological response to the price reform" was conducted by the sociological research section of the China Economic System Reform Research Institute and the sociology department of Beijing University. Twenty-five people participated in the February survey, and the same number of people were involved in the July survey.

The report of the February survey, carried in issues 3, 4, and 5 of the Economic Structural Reform Research Report, was written by Bai Nanfeng and Liu Yongohan.

5

Enterprise Cadres and Reform

Yang Guansan, Lin Bin,
Wang Hansheng, and
Wu Quhui

This chapter presents the results of a survey investigation of enterprise cadres and workers. The responses are separated into four parts. In section 1, we present information on the characteristics of the respondents. In section 2, we present information about enterprise cadres' attitudes toward reform. They are strongly and unambiguously in favor of it. Section 3 deals with cadres' opinions on the optimal way to structure work relationships; generally, they strongly support hierarchical methods. Section 4 presents information suggesting that enterprise cadres feel extremely stressed by the conflicting demands on them, and their own powerlessness.

1. Nature of the Survey; Cadre Characteristics

The investigation was conducted in July and August 1985 by means of a questionnaire survey in 900 enterprises in eighteen cities: Beijing, Qiqihar, Changchun, Anshan, Luoyang, Xian, Chengdu, Zigong, Guiyang, Nanning, Guilin, Wuhan, Hangzhou, Shaoxing, Ningbo, Wuxi, Yantai, and Suzhou.

The investigation was divided into two sections: cadres and workers. In the former section, 2,300 questionnaires were issued and 1,386 responses were received, with a response rate of 60.2 percent. In the latter, 1,300 questionnaires were issued and 1,061 were recovered, totaling 81.6 percent of those surveyed. All the responses reported here (with the exception of a few questions, as noted) are from the cadre survey. Of the 1,386 cadres surveyed, 80.1 percent came from state-run enterprises and the remaining 19.9 percent from collectively run enterprises. Of those surveyed, 93.1 percent are male and 6.7 percent female. The investigation collected 400,000 data.

Tables 5.1–5.12 show the characteristics of the respondents to the survey. They are distributed quite evenly across industry, with regard to both industrial sector and size of plant. Two-thirds of them are managers or deputy managers,

Table 5.1

Occupational Distribution of Respondents

Occupation	Percent
Light industry	29.3
Machine-building industry	29.0
Metallurgical industry	5.0
Chemical industry	7.1
Electronics industry	7.1
Construction industry	2.9
Textile industry	10.2
Commerce	5.0
Medical circles	3.2

Table 5.2

Size of Enterprises Surveyed

Number of Personnel	Percent
Fewer than 250	10.3
250–1,000	42.8
1,000–3,000	34.1
Over 3,000	12.6
Unknown	0.2

Table 5.3

Positions Held by Those Surveyed

Position Held	Percent
Factory head or enterprise manager	27.7
Deputy head or deputy manager	38.5
Secretary	21.5
Deputy secretary of party committee, general branch and branch in these enterprises	9.4
Consultant	2.3
Other	0.1

Table 5.4

Age Distribution

	Under 30	31–35 years	36–40 years	41–45 years	46–50 years	51–55 years	Over 56
Factory head or managers	1.0	5.8	16.3	26.0	29.7	18.1	3.1
Party secretaries	1.0	6.1	9.9	18.4	28.9	30.6	5.1
Whole sample	2.1	8.6	17.6	25.7	25.1	16.5	4.3

Table 5.5

Educational Background

Ownership	Junior School	Middle School	Senior Middle School & Secondary Vocational School	Higher
State-owned enterprises	2.4	16.8	27.7	53.0
Collectively owned enterprises	7.8	39.6	31.5	20.7
Whole sample	3.7	21.3	28.3	46.5

Table 5.6

Average Education by Age Group

Under 30	31–35 years	36–40 years	41–45 years	46–50 years	51–55 years	Over 56
3.4	3.0	3.4	3.4	3.0	2.7	2.2

Note: Primary = 1; junior middle school = 2; senior middle school = 3; higher education = 4.

Table 5.7

Previous Occupations

Occupation prior to promotion in enterprises Percent	Percent
Technological personnel	34.6
Professionals	9.6
Grass-roots managerial personnel	28.4
Administrators	13.3
Demobilized military officers	7.3
Workers	2.9
Others	3.9

Table 5.8

Occupations of Fathers of Those Surveyed

Workers	Farmers	Intellectuals	Cadres	White Collar	Other
24.1%	31.3%	7.4%	11.0%	16.1%	10.0%

Table 5.9

Educational Background of Fathers

Primary school	1.9%
Junior middle school	54.4
Senior middle school or secondary vocational school	24.3
Higher education	8.4

Table 5.10

Process of Appointment to Present Position

Elected	4.4%
Appointed by superior authorities	60.1
Superior authorities choose cadres among candidates nominated by workers' conference	30.7
Workers' representative meeting elects cadres from candidates offered by superior authorities	1.0
Inviting the qualified from other units	1.8
Other means	1.3

Table 5.11

Years in Present Position

Less than 6 Months	0.5–1.5 Years	1.6–4 Years	5–8 Years	9–15 Years	More than 16 Years
1.7%	28.5%	32.2%	17.9%	12.2%	7.7%

Table 5.12

Years Spent in Present Factory

Less than 5 Years	6–10 Years	11–20 Years	21–25 Years	More than 26 Years
8.3%	10.3%	39.1%	16.5%	25.7%

and one-third are party secretaries or deputy secretaries. With regard to age, a quarter are under forty. The more senior their position, the higher the average age—especially for party secretaries. Fully three-quarters of the respondents had completed senior middle school, and nearly one-half had some education beyond middle school. The impact of the Cultural Revolution can be seen in table 2.18: average education by age group. Generally speaking, the younger cadres have more years of education, but this trend reverses sharply for the age group 31–35 years old.

More than 90 percent of these cadres received their jobs through appointment by higher authorities (in 30 percent of the cases, with some participation by workers' councils). This background may help to explain their preference for hierarchical management methods in industry (see section 3).

2. Enterprise Attitudes Toward Reform

This section presents the results of nine questions posed to cadres about their attitudes concerning reform. The results are most interesting. China's enterprise cadres are clearly very much in favor of reform. Three questions (2,3, and 9) probe this issue in different ways. In each case, the response is unambiguous. These cadres are saying that thoroughgoing reform, steadily carried out, is China's only hope.

Cadres clearly feel that they have a role and responsibility in reform (question 8). They are concerned that reform may not be carried out to the end (question 4). This may perhaps be due to their remarkable lack of confidence in enterprise cadres themselves: 84.5 percent of the respondents agreed that "The quality of most present enterprise cadres is not suitable for economic reform" (question 1)! But the cadres are fundamentally optimistic about the future of reform, as questions 5, 6, and 7 make clear.

Statement	Strongly Agree	Agree	Dis- agree	Strongly Disagree
1. The quality of most present enterprise cadres is not suitable for economic reform.	13.0	71.5	14.2	0.8
2. Without reform, China would have no hope.	42.1	49.9	5.9	1.6
3. Economic reform should be conducted in an all-round way, not partially.	29.9	63.8	5.4	0.5
4. I fear that economic reform will not be carried through to the end.	5.6	61.8	29.5	2.4
5. With so many current problems, China's economy is hard to change.	1.5	12.7	68.3	16.1

6. With such big obstacles in the way,
   reform actually has no hope of
   success.   0.7   5.9   78.6   13.9
7. If the present situation persists,
   economic reform is bound to win
   complete victory.   10.1   69.0   18.7   1.2
8. Enterprise cadres need only run their
   own enterprises well. They do
   not need
   to think about economic reform as
   a whole.   1.0   19.7   68.5   9.7
9. Reform should be carried out steadily.   25.9   61.4   11.1   0.7

3. Attitudes Toward Hierarchical Management Methods

The thirteen questions reported in this section relate in one way or another to the way in which enterprise cadres prefer to structural relationships within their factories. The overwhelming impression left by these responses is that cadres believe in strict "chain-of-command" management (questions 1–7). Seventy-three percent, for example, favor an administrative pattern based on "formulating strict work standards" for rewards and punishments. Two-thirds oppose democratic management in the enterprise. They favor relationships based strictly on rank, and workers who have one job and stick to it. The leadership group within the enterprise should be appointed directly by the manager, who in turn should be appointed from above (although from candidates nominated by the workers' council).

This attitude may stem in part from a jaundiced view of workers' motivations. Questions 8–10 show that cadres believe workers to be motivated principally by a desire for higher pay and bonuses, with a weak sense of collectivism and little loyalty to the factory. A desire to develop the enterprise is said (by cadres) to rank only fifth on a list of workers' goals. Interestingly, workers confronted with the same list rank enterprise development second, and "high wages and bonuses" only fourth.

The last two questions in this section cast some doubt on the picture of enterprise directors who function mechanically as interstitial cogs in a large industrial hierarchy. When asked "Which of the following do you try hardest to avoid?" only 23 percent were concerned primarily about legal breaches or harm to their own reputation, while 64 percent responded "Something contrary to conscience." This suggests a cadre who is internally motivated and directed. The final question asked cadres to rank eight pressures: Which affects you most heavily? Here, pressure from the market came first; the industrial hierarchy, in the form of "quota of the state production plan," came fourth; and "inadequate funds" was last.

1. Which of the following three administration patterns do you prefer?

1. Formulating strict work standards whereby to reward and
   punish workers and staff members.   72.6%
2. Helping employees develop a sense of satisfaction and
   security, and to get along with each other.   21.2
3. Factory leaders only arrange work for the workers, they do
   not need to supervise them in person.   6.2

2. Some people are of the opinion that at present, enterprises do not yet have the necessary conditions for democratic administration. Do you agree with this view?

Agree	19.1%
Agree partially	46.7
Disagree	17.5
Strongly disagree	16.7

3. The only way to raise organizational efficiency is to insist that relationships between workers and cadres on the job be strictly predicated on job ranking. Personal feelings should not interfere with the decision-making process. Do you agree with this point of view?

Completely agree	42.2%
Partially agree	40.1
Disagree	13.6
Strongly disagree	4.0

4. Some enterprise leaders don't allow employees to change the type of production work they perform. Instead they have them do the same job for a long time. What is your opinion about this method?

It is conducive to the raising of productivity.   72.4%
It benefits production management.   8.1
Enterprise leaders are entitled to decide workers' job
  assignments.   5.4
It undermines workers' enthusiasm.   14.0

5. What is the best way to organize the leadership of an enterprise?

The group should be appointed solely by the factory head.	62.4%
The leading members of the group should be recruited by contract.	10.7
The members should be appointed by superior authorities.	10.0
The members should be elected by workers.	6.0

6. How do you think the factory head should be selected?

The factory head should be selected by direct election.	11.3%
The factory head should be appointed by superior authorities	7.5
The factory should be recruited from other units by contract.	7.3
The superior authorities choose the factory head from among candidates nominated by the workers' council.	67.3
The workers' representative meeting elects the factory head from among candidates offered by superior authorities	14.5

7. Do you agree that enterprise leaders' decisions cannot be changed even if they are criticized by their inferiors?

Respondents	*Agree*	*Disagree*
Factory heads or managers	57.4%	42.2%
Party secretaries	46.6	53.0
Combination of the two	53.3	45.9

8. Cadres were asked, "In your opinion what is the workers' main pursuit in their work?" while workers were asked "What is your ideal job?" The following represents a comparison of the rankings of their responses.

Response	*Cadre Ranking*	*Worker Ranking*
High wage and fat bonus	1	4
Good working environment	2	1
Leaders'concern for workers	3	3
Opportunity to be promoted	4	7
To develop the enterprise	5	2
A stable job	6	8
Good individual relations	7	9
Interesting work	8	6
Being praised	9	11
Creative work	10	5
Participation in enterprise administration	11	10

9. (Cadres) What is your evaluation of your workers' sense of collectivism?

They have a very strong sense of collectivism.	2.7%
Their such sense is not so strong.	39.2
Their sense of collectivism is weak.	53.5
Their sense of collectivism is very weak.	4.5

10. (Cadres) Toward which of the following do the workers in your factory seem to feel the most responsibility?

Family	49.7%
Relatives	1.5
Friends	19.8
Colleagues	16.2
Factory	12.4

11. When opinions differ about a public problem, whose ideas do you believe the most?

	Cadres	Workers
Party and state leaders	1.931	1.722
Specialists in the field	1.582	1.821
Myself	1.389	1.049
Masses	0.801	0.728
Friends and colleagues		0.196
News media	0.08	0.277
Family members		0.209

12. Which in the following do you try hardest to avoid?

1. Something contrary to conscience	64.0%
2. Something giving others a hard time	10.9
3. Something harmful to your family's name	0.9
4. Something legally punishable	11.9
5. Something harmful to your own name	11.5
6. Others	0.8

13. When you come to make decisions, which of the following factors do you think brings the heaviest pressure to bear upon you?

	Cumulative Frequency	*Series Order*
Pressure from the market	71.0%	1
Prospects of your enterprise	65.4	2
Demand of the workers	48.9	3
Quota of the state production plan	36.5	4
Influence of what neighboring enterprises do	33.2	5
Support or not of colleagues	24.1	6
Risk you have to take	12.9	7
Inadequate funds	3.8	8

4. Evidence of Frustration and Conflict

Section 4 presents the most disturbing results of the survey. We found evidence that enterprise managers, although highly motivated and idealistic, are so stressed by the conflicts of their job that many do not wish to continue. Questions 1–3 paint a picture of managers who are eager to accept responsibility and challenge, who thrive on work, who believe that in principle, the factory head plays an essential role in the enterprise. And yet in question 4, we find that fully three-quarters of these cadres, if given the choice, would not wish to be enterprise managers; instead, they seek to move up (into the industrial bureaucracy) or out (into technical jobs).

We believe that the reason for this paradoxical attitude is that managers are unable to fulfill the responsibilities placed on them, in part because those responsibilities conflict, in part because they are not given true power. Questions 5–8 show that although cadres recognize that the needs of the state plan and of their customers have priority over the needs of the enterprise, workers don't agree. Only 8 percent of workers believe that enterprise managers represent the interests of the state; 80 percent state that the manager represents the interests of the factory or its workers. Small wonder that relations between workers and management are conflicted rather than mutually supportive (questions 7, 8). The result of this conflict, understandably, is a thirst for greater decision-making power for enterprise managers (question 9).

1. Of the following jobs, which do you prefer?

A job offering power and great responsibility but full of change.	71.1%
A soft job with little power.	27.5

2. In your opinion, what is the greatest enjoyment in life?

Being with friends	7.6%
Being alone	7.5
Sports and arts	5.3
Being with family	4.6
Being at work	73.6

3. Does a factory head's performance matter much to the management of his factory?

He plays an essential role in management.	80%
He plays an important role.	19
His influence is not great.	0.5
His influence is almost zero.	0

4. Of the following occupations, which one would you prefer if you could choose freely?

Enterprise manager	22%
Rural enterprise manager	2
Foreign trade businessman	2
Administrator of government department	10
Social activist	2
Professional or technician	26
Scientific research worker/university teacher	10
Head of academic organization	1
White-collar worker	15
Consultant to enterprise or government department	6

5. What is your first priority of the following three choices?

The interest and development of the enterprise.	26.5%
The needs of customers.	20.8
The fulfillment of state quotas.	51.9

6. (To workers) Whose interests does the factory head represent?

The state	8.3%
The factory	62.7
The workers	17.2
Himself	9.4

7. In some enterprises, factory heads' orders are often resisted by workers actively or passively. Does this happen in your factory?

Often	4.5%
Sometimes	50.8
Seldom	38.1
Never	6.4

8. What is your appraisal of the present relationship between cadres and workers?

There is a sharp contradiction between them.	4.2%
There are some conflicts, but not serious.	83.7
There are a few conflicts.	5.4
They understand and support each other.	6.4

9. What role should a manager play in enterprise management? And what about the actual role he currently plays?

	Vital Role (%)	Important Role (%)	Unimportant Role (%)	No Influence (%)
Ideal role	80.0	19.0	0.5	0.0
Actual role	41.0	42.0	15.0	1.5

III
PROBLEMS OF REFORM
Macroeconomic Imbalance

China's reformers like to say that they propose to dismantle the system of detailed government intervention in enterprise decision-making and replace it with intervention via "indirect levers": taxes, subsidies, and macroeconomic policy tools. But as urban reform has progressed, China has come to recognize that this indirect control depends for its implementation on specific government institutions—especially banking and budgetary agencies—which have developed in market economies over a long period of time, but which in China are weak or nonexistent. When the government loosened the constraints on the economy—allowing greater leeway to local governments and enterprises to set prices, initiate investment projects, or engage in foreign trade—it was as if it had slipped the tether on a frisky colt without first constructing the corral.

The result has been significant macroeconomic imbalance, due to a sharp rise in imports of both producer and consumer goods, and a very large rise in investment flows (principally outside the government budget). These pressures led to price inflation in 1985 in the range of 12–18 percent. For a society that still remembers vividly the hyperinflation that accompanied the collapse of the Nationalist government in 1948–49, and the meticulous price stability of the subsequent thirty years, such a level of inflation is extremely unsettling.

In the first chapter of part III, Xia Xiaoxun and Li Jun take us from the initial impact of the reform—a big increase in retained profit and bonus payments to workers, described in section 1—to the consequences for consumer goods demand (excess purchasing power in 1983 and 1984), and then in section 3 to the resulting national macroeconomic imbalance. They argue that urban China is engaging in "premature consumption"—consuming some durable goods at Japanese levels even though China's income level is far below Japan's. Then, in section 4, they return to the details of "consumption funds expansion" and an excellent discussion of the intrinsic characteristics of a centrally planned economy which are conducive to "irrational" wage hikes. Section 5 proposes solutions.

The next chapter, on the investment mechanism, should be especially useful to those who are trying to understand the relationship between decentralization and macroeconomic imbalance (specifically between decentralization of control over investment funds and excessive investment spending). Nine tables document a shift from budgetary funds as the main source of investment finance to extrabudgetary and bank funding between 1983 and 1985. The authors cite easy bank credit as the villain. But they point out that local bank branches can hardly be blamed for funding a sudden glut of what, from their worm's-eye level, were eminently deserving producer-goods investment projects. As budgetary investment funds fell increasingly under local government or enterprise control, they were diverted away from producer-goods investment to consumer durables and nondurables, leaving many 'deserving' producer-goods projects unfunded. Meanwhile, the burst of consumer-goods-sector investment created a generalized investment boom within which the profitability of all investment projects, including those proposed to local banks, was enhanced. This is an extraordinarily valuable piece, in terms of both data and insight.

The third chapter, by Zhao Yujiang, focuses on extrabudgetary funding of investment projects. The author suggests that local fiscal departments in effect create money, when they "directly increase state-owned enterprise funds" without authority from above. Zhao analyzes the extent of this phenomenon, its impact, and possible countermeasures, based on data from a twelve-city survey of government administration.

China's macroeconomic dilemma will not yield to any rapid solutions. More than any other aspect of reform, constructing macro control institutions involves a long learning process. Corral-makers have to learn what a corral looks like, and how it fits together. To some extent, the corral cannot be built until it is clear in which direction the colt is inclined to go. And (most difficult of all), effective control institutions presuppose that the colt learns some lessons about self-control. It may be that a modest degree of price inflation is something China will have to learn to tolerate during the interval.

6

Consumption Expansion: A Grave Challenge to Reform and Development

Xia Xiaoxun and Li Jun

This subreport discusses the significance of the expansion of wage and bonus payments in recent years, based on insights from the enterprise survey. Section 1 reviews briefly the extent of the expansion. Sections 2 and 3 explain how this expansion has led to excess purchasing power, involuntary saving, and what we term "premature consumption" of consumer durables. Section 4 looks more closely at the systemic roots of the problem, and section 5 proposes solutions. We recommend strengthening financial constraints on enterprises, separating "efficiency" wage payments from "equity" payments, and opening up the labor market to dampen wage-pushed inflation.

1. Initial Results of the Reform in the Distribution System

In the traditional model of a planned economic system, the interests of the enterprise's members were not linked to profit. Profit was not a significant objective or goal of enterprise management. This situation, along with the absence of a conduit for market signals, made it unlikely that enterprises would be managed efficiently.

The establishment of the enterprise profit retention system, which links up the interests of the producer with its profits, represents a major reform. In the 429 enterprises covered by the current investigation, the ratio of retained profits to gross profits rose to 21.59 percent in 1984 against 19.36 percent in 1983, and the ratio of bonus payments to retained profits went up from 25.43 percent to 36.70 percent. The absolute amount of retained profits, as within regular budget, by

The following participated in preparing this report: Wang Xiaoqiang, Diao Xin-sheng, Zhang Shaojie, Shi Xiaomin, Chen Xiaolong, Bai Nanfeng, Huang Xiaojing, Zhang Weijing, Song Guoqing, Deng Yuanhong, Yu Huabin, and Zhang Xinhua.

state-owned industrial enterprises in sixteen cities increased 66 percent in 1984 over 1982, with the share of bonus in retained profits growing from 25 percent to 39.5 percent.

The rate of increase of retained profits was closely related to the growth rate of realized profit. The correlation coefficient between the two from January through June 1985 in the enterprises studied was 0.57, and the correlation coefficient between the growth rate of average per capita bonuses and the growth rate of retained profits was 0.29. This clearly indicates that both the collective welfare and the personal income of workers and staff are now closely linked to profits. This change in the distribution system prompted the enterprises to shift from fulfillment of production plans for output or output values, to improvement of efficiency and realization of higher profits. In the 359 questionnaires to factory directors, among fourteen operational goals, "improvement of efficiency" was ranked first; "increase profits" ranked fifth, and "fulfillment of production plans" occupied eleventh place, whereas "doubling of output value" came last. The profit motive stimulates the enterprise to raise the management level and increase economic efficiency, which necessarily requires appropriate responses to changing market signals. A strong mechanism for economic growth is thus established.

Enterprises that make more profit have an easier access to external funding for investment. For 259 enterprises, external investment funding was highly correlated with realized profits tax. The correlation coefficient of fixed capital investment and the profit growth rate was 0.1393. Investment was not correlated with other plan targets. This implies that, with the continued reform in the investment system, which emphasizes more effective utilization of capital, financial institutions, banks, and other sources of capital are more willing to invest in enterprises that make more profit. This is an additional factor strengthening the profit motive for enterprises.

Implementation of the profit retention system and of various contract responsibility systems has touched off a wave of reform that takes different forms in different enterprises. The old unitary wage system based on egalitarianism is beginning to crack. In 429 enterprises, the share of the basic wage in total wage payments dropped from 72 percent in 1983 to 63 percent in 1984, while the "variable" part of the wage (bonuses, subsidies, etc.) rose from 28 percent to 37 percent. The expansion of the "variable" part of the wage has forged a better link between rewards and work, mobilizing the enthusiasm of the workers and stimulating production.

2. Consumption Fund Expansion

Concurrent with the reform of the distribution system, a new problem has arisen—the problem of consumption fund expansion. During the Sixth Five-Year Plan period, the overdistribution of national income gradually worsened, owing to the expansion of both consumption and accumulation. In 1983, aggregate demand (purchasing power) exceeded aggregate supply of final goods by RMB 102.5 billion, and that figure went up to RMB 153.5 billion in 1984. This contradiction is becoming increasingly prominent. In 1984, national income increased in nominal terms by RMB 25.8 billion. The bulk of this went to consumption spending, or in other words, arose from the expansion of consumption funds.

The growth rate of consumption funds has been higher than the growth rate of national income in every year since 1979. The expansion of consumption funds has accelerated and shows signs of peaking. Labor productivity increased by 7.8 percent in 1984; the national income increased by 12 percent; but the increase in the wage earnings portion of the income of city and town dwellers was 22.3 percent. The nominal income of the entire people, including the rural population, rose by 25.3 percent. Looking at consumption funds of social units, there was an increase of 38 percent in administrative expense. The increase of consumption funds in the cities studied was above the national average.

This simultaneous large expansion in the consumption funds of the urban and rural population and of social units as well is something rarely seen since the founding of the People's Republic. The consumption funds of the three blocs are estimated to have increased by RMB 80 billion in 1985 over 1984. What we are confronted with is an overall expansion of consumption funds.

Another salient feature of the consumption expansion is irrational distribution (or outside-the-system distribution), which has increased sharply and may well become uncontrolled. It has been found that irrational distribution in some cities, in the form of excessive bonuses, reckless payments in kind, increased subsidies, expansion of floating wage scales and wage increases, etc., could account for as much as 20 percent of overall wage payments.

The consumption fund expansion, reflected in these statistics, reveals only part of the problem. Even more serious is the hidden part of the problem, the so-called off-the-books leakage. As efforts were made in 1985 to control the expansion of consumption funds, some restraint was shown in the open violations of policy, but in disguised ways such distribution is just as rampant as before. Underground channels of distribution grow. The principal forms of "off-the-books" payments are: fraudulent drawing of cash; private-account deposit of public funds; unmerited drawing of income; turning bonuses into wages; using "labor service" companies as "mini-treasuries"; workshops contracting for outside projects and dividing the proceeds among individuals; distributing management expenses to staff and workers for personal consumption; expansion of the self-marketed share of output above allowed levels to earn profit from price differentials; raising product prices to make false profits and enlarge the wage base; using production development funds for bonuses; selling shares to individuals with secured principal and high dividends; and barter exchange of goods in short supply for consumer products, as a way to evade taxes. In addition to the

Table 6.1

Bank Statistics on Consumption Fund Increases in Eighteen Cities*

	1984 (I,II) over 1983 (I,II)	1984 over 1983	1985 (I,II) over 1984 (I,II)	1985 (I,II) over 1993 (I,II)
I. Wages and other payments to individuals including:	13.1	23.8	35.2	52.8
1. State wages	12.1	16.0	20.2	34.7
2. Bonuses	2.7	57.4	89.7	94.7
3. Other payments to individuals	21.5	37.6	63.2	98.8
4. Wage and other payments to indivduals (1 + 2 + 3)	13.0	25.1	36.1	53.9
5. Wages of collectives in cities and towns	13.0	22.43	33.8	51.2
II. Administrative and enterprise overhead expenses	19.3	40.4	72.5	105.7

*The eighteen cities are Guangzhou, Hangzhou, Kunming, Nanchang, Tianjin, Fuzhou, Xiamen, Nanjing, Xian, Lanzhou, Hefei, Shashi, Shijinzhuang, Wanzhou, Weifang, Jinan, Shenyang, and Harbin.

above, distribution also takes the form of subsidies or allowances under many new names. In our investigations alone, some forty to fifty such channels of consumption funds leakage have been discovered, and the funds leaked are roughly estimated at RMB 20 billion per year for the whole country.

The consumption fund expansion has another easily overlooked aspect, that is, the even more rapid increase of state funds for welfare, subsidies, and other transfer payments to workers and staff. This is what we call the ''hidden'' expansion of consumption funds. China has adopted a labor system in which employment, welfare, and security go hand in hand. Social welfare (medical care, housing, etc.) and social security (retirement benefits and relief), which fall within the category of the secondary distribution of national income, are all obtained at the place of employment. As a result, the expenditures on social welfare and social security naturally are integrated into labor cost. Loosened control over labor costs, therefore, necessarily produces a simultaneous upward movement in the other two categories. And compared with wages, the budgetary constraints on welfare and social security are far less rigid, and so their rate of increase far exceeds that of wages. Take state workers and staff as an example. The average annual increase of wages was 11 percent in the period 1978–1984, while the increase in labor protection and welfare expenses was 22 percent. Expenditures on price subsidies (exclusive of the part directly distributed to workers and staff) increased by much more: 36 percent per annum from 1978 to 1983. Housing subsidies also expanded continually, with an annual sum already

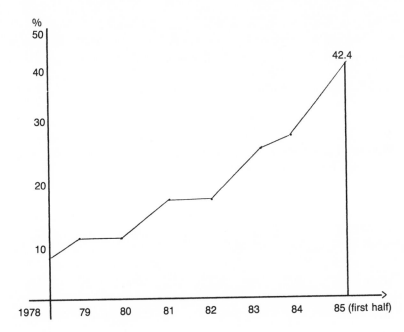

Figure 6.1

Gross Wage Bill: Actual Bank Expenditures vs. SSB Statistics

exceeding RMB 10 billion. The annual rates of increase in spending for culture, education, and health and in administration spending to benefit individuals have both overtaken the rate of wage increase. The various forms of transfer payments by the state to workers and staff equaled 85 percent of gross wages in 1983, reaching an average of more than RMB 600 per person. This level rose further in 1984 and 1985.

Such serious off-the-books leakage as well as the hidden consumption fund expansion clearly indicate that the expansion of consumption funds is abnormal and unprecedented. The prevailing statistical approach can no longer capture the true situation in consumption fund expansion and can lead to unrealistic judgments of the national situation.

Different approaches to statistics can lead to considerably different results. For instance, the difference between the gross wage bill as compiled by the State Statistics Bureau (SSB) and the expenditures by banks on cash wages is getting larger every year. Figure 6.1 shows the percentage by which the bank statistics surpass the SSB statistics. The bank statistics are based on the actual amount of cash distributed and are therefore a more accurate and comprehensive reflection of consumption fund expansion. Even so, they cannot reflect off-the books leakages.

Owing to the situation mentioned above, the real wage cost—"the price of the labor force''—has gone up rapidly in recent years. While the total wage bill on the books is less than 10 percent of gross cost, the real cost of labor, with welfare, social security, and subsidies added, is over 15 percent, exceeding the corresponding figures of 13 percent in Japan and 15 percent in the Soviet Union.

Moreover, in calculating the real cost of wages, account has to be taken of the presence of large numbers of redundant personnel in China's enterprises. Particularly in recent years, redundancy of personnel has become an even more serious phenomenon, with the full-employment policy and the ''family succession'' mode of employment. According to our study, redundant personnel currently account for 15-20 percent of workers and staff in enterprises, and even reach 20-30 percent in capital-intensive enterprises. If this element is included in labor cost calculations, the unit price of labor moves even higher. Using this method of calculation, the true cost of each urban worker more than doubled in the period 1979-1984, while national income generated by them during the same period increased only by 9.28 percent.

These facts suggest that our advantage as a country with cheap labor is being weakened by consumption expansion. On the one hand, there is an ''unlimited supply'' of labor—a serious surplus, in fact; on the other hand, there is no cheap labor to be bought. This absurd reality threatens the nation's modernization.

3. Consumption Expansion and Macroeconomic Imbalance

Consumption expansion is one major cause of the expansion of aggregate demand and the overdistribution of the national income. The gravity of the matter does not merely lie in the consumption fund expansion in the narrow sense, but also in the consequent expansion of the share of consumption-oriented investment in total investment. The overall expansion of consumer demand has led to ''premature consumption'' by urban dwellers and to a rapid expansion of surplus purchasing power. It has also exerted a tremendous pull on the pattern of production and investment, skewing them toward consumer goods (especially consumer durables) and away from producer goods. These four problems are explored in this section.

3.1. Premature Consumption

At present, although the consumption level of the Chinese people is of course much lower than that of the developed countries, it is far beyond the level warranted by our level of per capita national income. This is often referred to as ''premature consumption.'' For example, the per capita national income for the Chinese population was only RMB 579 in 1984, but the rate of possession by urban families of such consumer durables as TV sets, electric fans, tape recorders, and sewing machines has already reached the level of Japan when its per

Table 6.2

Surplus Purchasing Power vs. National Income

Year	a. National Income Spent (Y100m.)	b. Surplus Purchasing Power (¥ 100m.)	b/a × 100%
1976	2,424	423.8	17.5
1977	2,573	436.4	17.0
1978	2,975	480.7	16.2
1979	3,356	585.2	17.4
1980	3,686	790.5	21.5
1981	3,887	980.5	25.2
1982	4,256	1,179.0	27.7
1983	4,731	1,450.7	30.7
1984	5,542	1,994.0	36.0
1985 (estimate)	6,700	2,600.0	39.0

capita income was more than U.S. $1,000. Take housing as another example. The present floor space for city and town dwellers is, on average, close to 7 square meters per person, which is almost the same as the average floor space of Japanese (7.1 sq. m.) when their per capita national income was two times that of ours. If the current momentum in housing construction holds, China will achieve, in another two or three years, the goal of an average floor space of 8 square meters per person, which was originally the target for the year 2000.

3.2. Rapid Expansion of Surplus Purchasing Power

As a result of the consumption fund expansion, and despite premature consumption, surplus purchasing power is rapidly expanding (table 6.2).

Of course, part of the ever growing surplus purchasing power is voluntarily deposited in savings accounts. But it cannot be denied that involuntary savings also occupy a growing proportion, owing to supply shortages. In 1983 and 1984, the gap between effective demand and available supply of retail commodities stood at RMB 5.63 billion and RMB 39.8 billion respectively; and the surplus purchasing power increased correspondingly by RMB 27.1 billion and RMB 52.8 billion. This gap was expected to widen to RMB 58 billion in 1985, with a further corresponding increase of surplus purchasing power to approximately RMB 70 billion. Our economy is now characterized by a striking excess of demand and oversupply.

The ratio of the annual increase of surplus purchasing power to the annual increase of the cash income of the residents is also growing by leaps and bounds. As shown in table 6.3, an increasing part of the annual increase in cash income

Table 6.3

Increase of Surplus Purchasing Power (SPP)

Year	a. Annual Growth Rate of Cash Income (¥ 100m)	b. Growth of SPP (¥ 100m)	b/a × 100%
1976	51	19.6	36.7
1977	77	16.3	21.2
1978	117	41.1	35.1
1979	268	111.1	41.5
1980	378	177.9	47.1
1981	191	178.2	93.3
1982	215	198.7	92.4
1983	333	303.7	91.2
1984	668		

has turned into surplus purchasing power. This also shows that the readjustment of the state distribution policy has increased the people's incomes beyond the level of production, and to that extent it has failed to play its intended role of raising consumption levels.

The rapid expansion of surplus purchasing power has generated tremendous pressure on the consumer goods market. It is estimated that, by the end of 1985, the surplus purchasing power of the country came to more than RMB 260 billion, which is approximately 60 percent more than 1985 gross retail sales. We conducted an investigation last March for the purposes for which 2,060 households were saving. Some 18.8 percent said they were saving for high-cost consumer goods. This suggests that there is now, across the country, a surplus purchasing power of approximately RMB 50–60 billion directed at the consumer durables market.

The highly expanded surplus purchasing power is also exerting an extremely strong pull on the rate of production development. Calculated on the basis of 2.03, which is the ratio of total output to consumption output in 1983, to absorb the existing surplus purchasing power would take an approximately RMB 500 billion increase in industrial and agricultural output. The increase in surplus purchasing power in 1984 was RMB 52.36 billion. Just to absorb this amount, the gross output value of industry and agriculture would have had to grow by 9.85 percent in 1985.

3.3. Consumption Fund Expansion and Investment Expansion

Normally, 30 percent of fixed capital investment (some say the figure is 40 percent for recent years, but this is yet to be confirmed) will turn into expanded consumption funds through the multiplier effect. It seems as if the problem of

Table 6.4

**Wages, Residents' Income, and Capital Investment
(Annual % Increase)**

Year	Gross Wages	Cash Income of Residents	Capital Investment
1978	10.4	10.2	25.5
1979	13.7	21.4	4.5
1980	19.5	24.8	6.76
1981	6.2	10.0	−10.5
1982	7.5	10.3	26.6
1983	5.9	14.4	7.0
1984	21.3	25.3	25.0

consumption funds expansion could be solved by simply reducing fixed capital investment. Particularly starting from this year, this view has been strengthened when statistics have shown an upward move of the accumulation rate. But in recent years, the increase has been less closely related to the scale of the fixed capital investment. It is now oversimplistic to explain consumption fund expansion only by applying the multiplier to fixed capital investment. For example, in 1985, even though fixed capital investment fell, the consumption funds still rose steeply, as if unaffected, and by a much bigger margin than in 1984. The obvious conclusion is that the rapid expansion of consumption funds has its independent mechanism and is not merely triggered by larger fixed capital investment.

Table 6.4 shows that whether investment registers a big increase or negative growth, the consumption funds increase irreversibly. There is no close relation between the two.

Increased accumulation in nominal terms and a "nominal decrease but real increase" of consumption have led to an overestimate of China's accumulation rate. The nominal increase in accumulation is higher than the nominal increase in consumption. But this principally reflects the fact that in recent years, the prices for investment goods (building materials in particular) have gone up twice as much as the prices for consumer goods: In 1984 alone, the prices for building equipment and materials jumped 11–13 percent. The increase in construction cost alone accounts for a nominal increase in investment of over RMB 10 billion per year. In the supply of building materials, the ratio of commodities supplied at negotiated price is constantly growing. For such commodities, prices no longer show a 30 percent increase, but double or redouble. Consumption funds, protected by "off-the-books" leakage, show a nominal decrease but real increase. This part of the consumption funds is not included in national statistics. Hence the corollary: overestimate of the accumulation rate.

3.4. Expansion of Consumption-Oriented Investment

The expansion of consumption funds of surplus purchasing power documented above has produced tremendous pressures on the market. This has created a very bright environment for investment activity. Particularly striking is the expansion of nonproductive investment. This reflects current emphasis on accelerating urban construction and the development of the service sector (a debt long overdue). It is also due the integrated system of employment and welfare, under which housing and other welfare facilities are considered part of wages, and are important measures through which an enterprise can stabilize and attract its labor force.

The share of nonproductive investment, approximately 70 percent of which was in housing, has grown considerably during the Sixth Five-Year Plan period. Given this change, even if the rate of accumulation has risen, one can hardly say that accumulation has encroached on consumption. On the contrary, the steep increase in nonproductive investment, especially in housing, is an important indicator of rising consumption levels. The demand for this part of total investment is closely linked to consumption expansion. Nonproductive investment demand is rigid, analogously to wage rigidity. Macrocontrol policies have but a weak restraining effect on such investment. If the situation is allowed to develop unchecked, the development of the national economy will in the long run be seriously impeded by a shortage of investment in productive capacity.

The expansion of consumption-oriented investment and the softening of bank credit controls suggest that the present investment expansion has its own mechanism. Enterprises and the local governments are only weakly motivated to increase production-oriented investment while their urge for consumption and consumption-oriented investment is strong. More and more of their resources are flowing into consumption-oriented investment, leaving productive investment increasingly dependent on bank loans. The danger of such a process is this: it will make the expansion of bank credit a basic precondition for the preservation of a reasonable level of productive investment. But this expansion will accommodate not just investment but also consumption at all levels. The inevitable result is the expansion of aggregate demand, and sustained inflation. The experience of Yugoslavia has already shown the serious impact of such a mechanism.

4. The Mechanism of Consumption Funds Expansion

The new characteristics of the expansion of consumption funds, as discussed above, clearly indicate that the traditional methods of macro control (i.e., equating the wage bill with retail sales and other sorts of central government calculations) are insufficient. In response to the rampant expansion of consumption funds, the central government, the State Council, and other organs have issued more than a hundred documents in the first nine months of 1985, but the results were not satisfactory. Although the overall examination of finance and taxation which began in late 1985 may serve as a temporary brake to the expansion, it cannot solve the problem at its roots. Instead, we must understand the inherent causes of consumption funds expansion and adopt corresponding mechanisms to battle this expansion.

Consumption fund expansion is a phenomenon associated with the process of restructuring the economic system of any socialist country. Since the 1960s, the Soviet Union and the Eastern European countries have all experienced different degrees of consumption fund expansion in their reforms. For instance, during 1975–78, the average annual growth rate of Yugoslavia's national income was only 3 percent, and its per capita gross social product only grew by 2.5 percent. But the average annual growth rate of wages was 16–23 percent. This common phenomenon indicates that consumption fund expansion is not caused solely by a particular policy and by mismanagement at a particular time in a particular place. Rather, it is determined by something inherent in the economic mechanism.

Insofar as China's current economic mechanism is concerned, the soft budget constraint arising from the relationship of "paternal love" of the state for the enterprise has freed the latter from any fear of losses or bankruptcy. This is the basis for the reckless distribution of bonuses by the enterprises; the "upward emulation" among the enterprises exacerbated by the unequal external conditions and immobility of the labor force is the triggering mechanism of the expansion of consumption funds in the enterprises. The consequence of the mechanism is that in the process of reforming the distribution system, following the partial liberalization of wage-setting powers, structural wage inflation has emerged.

As reform proceeds, the enterprise budget constraints tends to be tight. But the pressure for consumption fund expansion also gradually intensifies. Here, the intensified and distorted "upward emulation" plays an important part. A desire to "keep up with the Joneses" is a normal sociopsychological phenomenon. In a market economy where the factors of production can move freely from one use to another, profits are mainly determined by the efforts of labor and management, and emulating other peoples' high incomes is achieved first and foremost through emulating their labor productivity or economic efficiency. What is seen here is a normal mechanism of economic growth. But in China's enterprises, where controls are soft, where productive factors cannot move freely, and where the external environment is irrational and operational conditions are unequal, a higher income has nothing to do with economic efficiency. "Emulation" plays an irrational role as a result.

Why is effort divorced from reward in China's enterprises? Because profit does not depend solely on effort; because retained profit does not depend solely on profit; and because rewards can diverge from retained profit. We explore each of these three "decouplings" of the effort-reward mechanism in turn.

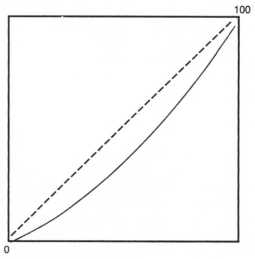

Figure 6.2

Lorenz Curve for Fixed Capital per Capita

4.1. Profits Are Not Mainly Determined by Efforts

It is true that in recent years, the autonomous power of enterprises over production, management, and distribution has been considerably enlarged. But due to the continued immobility of key production factors, the enterprises face an external environment imposed by the old system of planned allocation, and there is extreme inequality in operating conditions between enterprises. In the enterprises we investigated, those with more fixed capital per capita enjoyed a higher rate of profit than those with less. And the amount of fixed capital per capita varies greatly from enterprise to enterprise, as shown in figure 6.2.

This Lorenz curve is drawn on the basis of investigations of 429 enterprises. Within the sample range, the maximum value and the minimum value differ by as much as a factor of 200. In the 429 enterprises, the per capita load of expenses for the retired also differs by a factor of over 10. Many enterprises even go into the red as a result of increased retirement subsidies. The decisive influence of price factors on the profits of an enterprise need not be mentioned here. In short, the influence of external factors on profits can easily offset even the most industrious labor force or efficient management.

Labor productivity—a synthetic index of work quantity and quality—is one of the important indices of the quality of operation of an enterprise. Data on 308 enterprises show that a rapid rise in labor productivity does not ensure a high growth rate of profit. As shown in figure 6.3, the enterprises with the highest rates of profit increase could point to only a middling rate of increase of labor productivity while enterprises with the most rapid increase in labor productivity

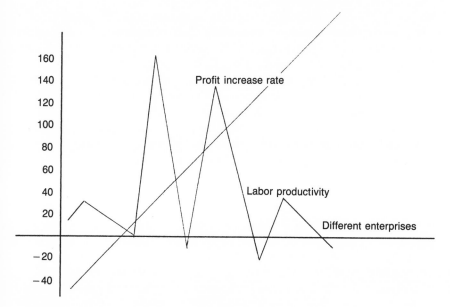

Figure 6.3
Profit Increase Rate and Labor Productivity Rise of 308 Enterprises

had a rate of increase profit averaging almost zero. In seven iron and steel plants we investigated, output only grew 10 percent in 1984 compared with 1983. But due to increases in the share of self-marketed products and in their prices, their profits jumped approximately 30 percent. Under such circumstances, the principle of "to each according to his work" or equal pay for equal work cannot be realized through the method of pegging the wage bill to the size of the tax component of profits (hereafter called tax-profit).

4.2. Asymmetry of Profit Retention to Profits

The second stage of the change of profit into tax was designed to redress the inequalities created by external conditions through the establishment of a regulatory tax. But such inequalities can hardly be redressed through a regulation *post factum*, and if anything, they might even be aggravated through redistribution of production factors. This is because: (1) the regulatory tax is levied on state enterprises only; collective enterprises are exempted; (2) the level of the regulatory tax is subject to "negotiation" between the state and individual enterprises: if an enterprise is in an advantageous position in the negotiation (i.e., good personal relations or network, strong bargaining power, etc.), the level of the profits tax will be lower; (3) as a fixed regulation, the regulatory tax cannot suit the rapidly changing situation. It will at best be rational only at the time it is set.

Meanwhile, the provision for a reduction of the regulatory tax on the incremental part of profits constitutes a de facto preferential treatment to those enterprises that have a fast rate of profit increase. Take the seven iron and steel plants for example. While they registered a substantial increase of profits in 1984 as against 1983, the ratio of the regulatory tax to the total profits fell to 18.6 percent from 27 percent, and their retained profits rose by 27 percent as a result. For another example: a certain jewelry factory turned out a great amount of gold and silver jewelry this year. Because the products are selling well, and with the price rise factor also considered, the profits of the factory are almost doubled. Its tax-to-profit ratio dropped from 53 percent to 8 percent with an increase of 2.5 times in retained profits.

4.3. Discrepancy Between Rewards and Retained Profits

The rules and regulations in different enterprises, industries, and regions over the level of retained profits and provisions for their use vary greatly. This has created a situation in which large differences may exist in bonus ratios even though the level of retained profits is the same.

As a result of the separation of the three links mentioned above, there have appeared a group of high-income enterprises and individuals, whose contribution does not match actual economic gains. Other enterprises see only that the difference in rewards far exceeds the difference in the labor itself, and thus a strong feeling of ''inequality'' is aroused. Because of the immobility of the labor force, the fortunate workers face no competition. So long as income is, to a great extent, determined by external conditions which the less fortunate enterprise is powerless to change, the enterprise is likely to seek various ways of evading regulations as a way to boost the workers' incomes, instead of trying to raise efficiency or output. At the same time, the high-income enterprises wish to preserve the ''interested rigidity'' of the existing income gap.

This upward emulation mechanism has produced in recent years a spiral movement of wage hikes, granted in turn to different industries and sectors. For example, many public bus drivers, whose wages were much lower than the wages of taxi drivers, asked to be transferred. When the competent body at a higher level refused permission, the bus drivers countered by going slow. The result was a substantial increase of wages in the public transportation sector, without producing any economic results whatsoever. In the meantime, a small number of enterprises have emerged that have both a high level of profit retention and a high level of bonuses. But for the majority of enterprise, the difference in income among workers remains irrationally small. Egalitarianism still persists and even increases, as figure 6.4 shows, despite the fact that retained profit and workers' incomes have both increased considerably.

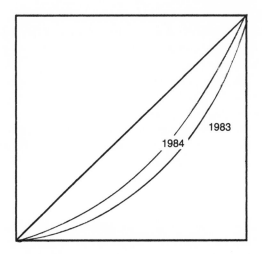

Figure 6.4

Lorenz Curve for Showing per Person Retained Profits in 308 Enterprises 1983–1984

Calculated using the statistics underlying figure 3.4, the Gini coefficient for 1983 was 0.208, but it went down to 0.182 in 1984. This shows that the distribution of retained profits is increasingly equal, as a result of upward emulation among enterprises and their bargaining with the state. The distribution of bonuses per person within enterprises shows a similar trend, as seen in figure 6.5.

The Gini coefficient was 0.192, slightly higher than that for the retained profits, also pointing to a relatively equal distribution. The sample of 308 enterprises has a disproportionately large share of general processing enterprises, and consequently the sectors that benefit most from preferential state treatment are underrepresented.

Owing to the lack of necessary elasticity in the employment system, relative wages cannot rise and fall with changes in supply and demand. It is true that the wages for those types of labor force in short supply have gone up as a result of the floating wage system, but it is also true that the wages for unskilled labor have gone up at the same time as a result of upward emulation. Meanwhile, the large surplus labor force in the rural areas finds it difficult to enter the urban labor market because of the barriers between city and countryside and among enterprises. This has already caused problems in some cities, where newly established enterprises or institutions face a shortage of labor and thus the wages even for unskilled labor have to be raised. In Beijing, for example, companies vie to employ new entrants to the labor force with a starting wage at around RMB 100. This will inevitably stimulate other workers to ask for a wage hike, thus pushing up the overall level of wages.

If the labor market were opened, the structural wage inflation would be restrained in at least the following ways: First, the supply and demand of labor will be adjusted. When the demand in a particular occupation exceeds the supply, higher wages will attract more labor in this direction, thus creating competition for jobs, which will, in turn, lower the temporarily high level of wages. This effect is strongest in an economy where a large surplus labor force exists. Second, national flows of labor and competition in job choice will eventually help to establish a rational relative wage structure, by which each will be paid according to the amount of work he does and the importance of the job he holds. Third, conditioned by the relations between supply and demand, a low-income person will set an income target commensurate with his actual competence. This may help weaken the abnormal mentality of "blind" upward emulation.

While the most fundamental cause of the consumption fund expansion lies in the mechanisms of the economic system, the guiding ideology and policy slogans have also played an important part. In the initial stage of the reforms, the prevailing emphasis on rewards and incentives and the widespread slogan about "paying overdue debts" and achieving a high level of consumption created the false impression that "reform equals more personal gain." Even today, in most regions and enterprises, reforms still means restructuring the internal distribution system to increase rewards and incentives, thus weakening control of the consumption fund. Second, an inadequate wage reform program, which was implemented out of step with other reforms, raised people's wage expectations and engendered many loopholes in distribution. Third, unequal sharing of the tax burden under the new taxation policies means that things are difficult for some enterprises and easy for others. This arbitrariness evokes wide-spread complaints of "unfair distribution" and the blind upward emulation mentality.

Insofar as control methods are concerned, first, the unidirectional and partial macro controls no longer suit the reality of highly scattered and diversified economic units and forms of operations. Second, there are many loopholes in control and administration. In the process of opening and invigorating the economy, such means of control as economic legislation, supervision, and taxation have failed to keep up. In addition, because of the inadequate strength of the comprehensive economic control bodies and their inability to coordinate with one another, several "vacuum areas" have appeared in the field of control. Third, the intensified tendency of local governments and authorities to promote their own interests leads to the weakening of the control systems. Since the upward emulation is itself a result of the current economic mechanisms, some extralegal wage increases in the enterprises have won the tacit understanding and acquiescence of the local governments and competent organs, as well as of banks and tax departments. Worse, the local governments and responsible organs at different levels even stand by the enterprises within their jurisdiction and undertake bargaining with the state. This change in the behavior of the local governments supports the unreasonable conduct of the enterprises and weakens central control, which depends on local government support.

5. Consumption Expansion Must Be Checked by a Joint Approach: Change the Mechanisms, Tighten Controls

In recent years, a consumer psychology has been created by the premature consumption, and a high-level consumption drive has been touched off by the "demonstration effect" of opening to the outside world. It is necessary, on the one hand, to raise rapidly the living standards of the people and satisfy their psychological needs, and, on the other hand, to curb consumption expansion. This is one of the key issues in reform and development during the Seventh Five-Year Plan. Given the rigidity of the interests, consumption expansion also presents difficult problems for macro control.

The present situation clearly shows that a precise description of the micro mechanism of consumption expansion is not yet possible, and mechanisms to curb consumption expansion are not yet developed. If the power of distribution continues to be decentralized and delegated in a simplistic way, the continuation of consumption expansion is unavoidable. Before the present loss of control over the macro situation can be reversed, it will be necessary to strengthen administrative constraints on consumption funds. But this is not our long-term aim. From the medium- and long-term point of view, reform should seek the following goals: to free wage-determination from the yoke of rigid planning so that the labor market will be opened and the potential of an unlimited supply of labor will be fully tapped. Let the market mechanism—the relation between labor supply and demand—determine relative wage levels. This will check the rising trend of wages and will free the state from the tedious work of setting specific wage scales, to concentrate its energy on controlling macro distribution policy and total wage funds.

The control of the consumption fund is a very complicated project. There is as yet no accurate picture of the macro and micro mechanisms of consumption expansion. This report cannot fulfill the purpose of designing a detailed and adequate policy system to deal with it. Still, we suggest the following guidelines for further policy research on this subject.

1. Seek symmetry in distributional reform between rewards and incentives and controls. Since the reform was launched, more attention has been devoted to economic stimuli, and not enough effort has been made to tightening budgetary constraints, preventing overdistribution, and eliminating the enterprise mentality of blind reliance on the state. This asymmetrical development needs to be corrected by perfecting the taxation system, strengthening the comprehensive control organs, and accelerating the formulation of economic laws and regulations. In distribution policy, macrocontrol targets should be established concerning the ratio between consumption and accumulation and the ratio between productive accumulation and nonproductive accumulation. The growth of the consumption

fund should not exceed the growth of national income or labor productivity. In managing the wage fund, the state should control the gross fund and the local governments should control the funds at different levels, to simplify the equational controls and reduce direct intervention by the central government in specific wage scales of grass-roots units. Thus, enterprises would be given the right to determine wage scales at their own discretion, subject to a limit on total wages paid. But in a short period of time the rate of increase or gross wages in each enterprise should still be determined and controlled by the central government, and adjustments made where necessary.

2. Continue the reform of the distribution system by separating the incentive function of wage payments from the equity function. The experience of other countries shows that the primary function of income distribution is to solve the question of efficiency (incentives); the secondary function is to solve the question of equity. But in China, these two functions are comingled at the enterprise level. During the Seventh Five-Year Plan period, we suggest dividing these two functions. To achieve this, it is necessary first to separate the employment system from the system of welfare and social security (see 3). Second, it is necessary to separate wage policy from income distribution policy. The state can adopt a "sliding-scale wage policy" in different industries in the light of state development goals. Wages should be increased and rewards should be given, so long as they are warranted on efficiency grounds. But at the same time taxes, including a personal income tax, should be levied wherever warranted, to reduce unreasonable disparities in the distribution of income.

3. Remove the barriers to labor mobility by separating employment from welfare and social security. Why is China's employment system so rigid? In part because we have maintained that socialism must guarantee the employment of every person. But the rigidity also originates in the overlap of employment, social welfare, and social security. The wages and salaries, relief funds, pensions, housing, medical care, and various subsidies of the workers and staff are all bound up with the employment relationship with sharp differences in these benefits between different enterprises and institutions, and between different forms of ownership. If a worker changes his work unit, he may lose many of the benefits he is enjoying. This constitutes a big barrier to the free flow of labor. During the Seventh Five-Year Plan period, reforms can be launched to disconnect welfare and social security from employment. The central task is to establish unemployment protection and to transform the "covert compensation" of job-linked welfare benefits into overt compensation.

4. To exploit the advantages of an unlimited labor supply, create wage competition by opening the labor market. To introduce the market mechanisms into wage determination will in the end be the only path open to us. At present, the entire wage structure is prepared by the state. However painstaking and meticulous our work, this program will never be considered fair and reasonable by all employees. Everyone will always want more. But if wages are regulated by the

supply and demand in the market, where an employee will have to submit his ability or competence to the objective test of the market, the wage-wage spiral will be subdued.

5. Create necessary preconditions through the reform of the labor employment system for the strengthening of controls over the enterprises and correcting their behavior. Through these years of implementing reforms, particularly after the peaking of the consumption fund expansion since the end of 1984, the comrades studying the reforms have increasingly come to emphasize the importance of establishing an enterprise bankruptcy system. But without employment reform paving the way and specifically without a change from ''employment guarantee'' to ''unemployment compensation,'' the ''bowl'' is still an ''iron bowl,'' and it is still impossible to smash the ''big public pot.'' When workers can never be permitted to lose their jobs, there is no way to make the enterprise face a real risk of bankruptcy.

The opening of the labor market will not by itself eliminate consumption expansion. We do not deny the significance of strengthening controls. We also believe that weakening the consumption urge of the enterprise by strengthening its desire to invest and expand is of great importance in controlling consumption expansion. But opening the labor market is a necessary first step.

Because of short-run inelasticity of labor supply and demand, opening the labor market will, in the short run, cause further wage increases. Therefore, reform in this area should be carried out very cautiously. But the emergence of a normal economic mechanism is clearly in sight, a mechanism that will bring into full play the most active factor in the productive forces—the human factor. When people are placed where they can do their best and are paid what is their due, we will see a sharp increase in labor productivity and efficiency, and in innovation and creativity, and we will find ourselves on a development path with unlimited vitality.

7

Investment: Initial Changes in the Mechanism and Preliminary Ideas About Reform

Zhang Shaojie, Cui Heming,
Xu Gang, and Ji Xiaoming

One characteristic of the very rapid economic growth since 1984 is the sharp expansion of investment by local authorities and enterprises, using funds from dispersed sources. As economic reform brings about changes in China's investment mechanism, the traditional means for achieving readjustment and control cease to be effective, while the new control methods of a mature commodity economy are not yet available. The key to carrying out reform of the mechanism of macroeconomic control is not to establish and improve macrocontrol machinery per se, but rather to reform even further the specific operational micro mechanisms, so as to smooth the way for macro control. As a summary of the results of this stage of our research, this report does not attempt to clarify all the problems that we face. Instead, we shall here discuss a few aspects of the investment mechanism and some ideas for further reform.

1. Impact of Decentralizing Investment Authority

Some of the reforms during the Sixth Five-Year Plan period involved the investment mechanism (e.g., the expansion of enterprises' investment decision-making authority and the replacement of appropriations by bank loans). Others affected the incentive to invest in various areas (the most important of these measures were separation of the financial from the administrative departments, two-phased implementation of imposing taxes to replace the old practice of handing over all profits to the state, and reform of the commodity circulation system of planned-materials prices). These reforms changed the sources of investment funds, improved the signals guiding investment activities, strengthened the enterprise's profit motive, and changed the investment motives of government at all levels.

The overall effect was to strengthen the position of enterprises in China's investment system.

At present, investment decision-making in China involves two distinct systems. On the one hand, the system under which investment decisions are made by administrative authorities at different levels, which was the norm before 1979, still plays an important role. On the other hand, the position of enterprises in making investment decisions has been considerably strengthened. When one investigates the concrete procedures for investment decision-making now prevailing, most investment activities in China's economy appear to emerge from a process in which enterprises, governments at various levels, and banks depend on and simultaneously interfere with one another. Consequently, it is very difficult empirically to establish who makes investments and for what purpose. But our investigation shows clearly that China's investment mechanism is now undergoing a profound change in which decision-making authority has been greatly decentralized and the pattern of investment has greatly shifted.

Decision-making authority has been decentralized in two respects: the authority to invest is now more decentralized, and the funding for investment now comes from many dispersed sources. The latter change has gone much further than the first. This obviously results from one specific feature of China's urban economic reform: the reform began with the distribution link. Equally important, the scattered nature of investment funds has in turn effectively changed the pattern of investment decision-making. The results of these two aspects of reform are reflected in the changed pattern of investment in fixed assets in recent years, in particular, in the rapid growth of extrabudgetary investment (see table 7.1).

In recent years, as local governments gained new powers over investment, local investment has been used increasingly for nonproductive projects (see table 7.2). Local governments have rapidly increased the share of their direct investment in fixed assets invested in nonproductive projects such as urban renovation, housing construction, and scientific, educational, cultural, and public health undertakings. This tendency may continue. "Building a beautiful city" has become a major objective of local governments. Moreover, the lower the level of government, the larger the proportion of investment in nonproductive projects. In Jiangsu province, the share of nonproductive investment in total public-sector capital construction in 1984 was 21 percent for central government ministries, 56.4 percent for the province, 67.8 percent for cities, and 64 percent for counties. In the cities covered in this study, nonproductive investment accounted for 60 percent of the gross investment in capital construction, well above the national average of 40 percent. When investment in fixed assets was sharply cut in 1985, some city leaders even declared, "We must maintain nonproductive investment, even if this can only be achieved at the expense of investment in productive projects."

There are two reasons for this characteristic of provincial-level investment. (1) Provincial authorities play a big role in the current planning system in China.

Table 7.1

Changes in the Pattern of Investment in Fixed Assets in the Cities Investigated

	1983	1984	1985 Jan-June
Capital investment/gross investment	61%	64%	74%
Investment for equipment renewal and technological transformation/gross investment	39	35	26
Productive investment/capital investment	40	41	40
Nonproductive investment/capital investment	60	59	60
Budgetary investment/ capital investment	45	40	28
Extrabudgetary investment/capital investment	55	60	72
State investment/budgetary investment	62	61	57
Local investment/budgetary investment	38	39	43

For the factories under investigation, of all the mandatory production plans (excluding those for armaments production) received by the factories, those from provincial authorities account for 37.84 percent, which amounts to about 72.92 percent of the mandatory plans received from the central authorities, or 368.7 percent of those received from city governments. (2) The situation is linked to a large extent with the restrictions placed on the economic development of the provinces by the present underdeveloped and imperfect state of the market system in China and the lack of coordination between various sectors of the provincial economic structure.

With the gradual change in the function of local governments with regard to investment, enterprises have become the major investors in productive projects, and they have already taken a lion's share of extrabudgetary investment. In the cities we studied, the share (for both capital construction and technological development) of enterprises and their upper-level administrative departments exceeded 80 percent of gross extrabudgetary investment (see table 7.3).

This is alarming, because enterprise investment is shifting toward welfare (especially housing construction) and short time-horizon projects. Factory directors' questionnaire responses identified "improving economic performance" as their most important objective and gave "technological transformation" fourth place, with "enlarging market shares" and "and expanding the size of the enterprise" eighth and twelfth place respectively, whereas "doubling gross output value" came last (fourteenth). The poll demonstrates, first, that at present the desire for quicker speed occupies a rather less significant position in factory operation and in investment decision-making, and the primary motive for investment is no longer the traditional one of increasing production value. Second, since the enterprises' desire to increase staff and worker fringe benefits can only

Table 7.2

Pattern of Capital Investment Financed by State, Province, and Cities in 1984

Item	A. Total Investment (%)			Item	B. Industrial Investment (%)		
	State	Province	Cities		State	Province	Cities
Industry	48.26	28.7	11.1	Metallurgy	14.29	6.2	5.8
Agriculture, forestry, water conservancy, and meteorology	6.2	6.7	4.25	Coal	16.3	19.1	8.3
Transport, post, and telecommunications	15.6	11.2	2.1	Electricity	12.21	22.5	27.0
Commerce and foreign trade	4.15	2.3	4.9	Building materials	4.3	6.2	10.7
Finance	0.45	1.02	0.33	Textiles	4.5	8.0	10.2
Scientific research	0.42	0.5	0.44	Machine building	2.28	1.8	2.4
Culture and education	6.09	16.3	22.76	Light industry	4.7	10.0	21.0
Urban development	6.03	7.52	22.45	Electronics industry	1.7	2.6	1.7
Others	2.74	20.6	32.25	Others	6.5	12.66	6.5

Table 7.3

Sources of Extrabudgetary Funds and Investment Spending in Twenty-three Cities

	1983		1984	
	amount (10,000 yuan)	%	amount (10,000 yuan)	%
Gross extrabudgetary funds	1,123,808.8	100	1,432,758.6	100
Local financial income	97,563.8	8.68	114,383.6	7.98
State enterprise and upper-level organs	899,928.1	80.08	1,084,872.8	75.72
Gross extrabudgetary capital investment	112,216.4	100	120,553.8	100
Local capital investment	16,248.1	14.48	3,809.9	3.16
State enterprise and upper-level organs	82,732.7	73.73	101,538.7	84.23
Gross extrabudgetary investment in equipment renewal and technological transformation	452,844.8	100	480,729.3	100
Local financial spending	20,403.0	4.51	17,056.5	3.5
State enterprise and upper-level organs	410,077.6	90.56	432,630.8	88.86

be satisfied through increased profits, enterprises attach great importance to economic performance and technological transformation in their production and investment decision-making. This does not mean, however, that the "profit comes first" motive has not been firmly established in Chinese enterprises, and in particular not in investment decision-making, because enterprises still invest heavily in consumption and worker welfare. Also, the profit motive is still constrained by provisions governing the use of self-raised funds, and the allowable proportion of self-owned funds in gross investment when negotiating loans. Third, the enterprise's long-term development should be decisive in investment decision-making. But the reform so far has not established an incentive structure that ensures that priority. As a consequence, enterprises make investments first of all for welfare purposes, thus forming a tendency to "build housing with self-owned funds and invest in technological transformation with loans." At the same time, they are biased toward projects which "make easy profits" in a short span of time, and lack enthusiasm for long-term projects of a technologically revolutionary nature.

It should be noted that large enterprises and some advanced medium and small-sized enterprises have an incentive structure conspicuously different from that of the ordinary run of enterprises. A breakdown of the answers to our questionnaires shows that "technological transformation" ranks second on the list of objectives among the directors of enterprises directly under central government ministries or under provincial authorities, much higher than the ranking of directors of other types of factories. As all of these factories are key national or provincial enterprises enjoying a fairly stable position in the market and maintaining close ties with the international market, they give more consideration to long-term investment and attach great importance in their respective industrial sectors. In making investments in technological transformation, they seek long-term transformation and try hard to catch up with advanced international technological levels. In executing the plans for technological transformation, they adopt without exception measures to "break down the whole into parts" and "conduct technological transformation in a section-by-section process" for the purpose of fulfilling the plans.

Bank loans have become a major intervention mechanism. At the present stage, investment by enterprise is still subject to government intervention. The pattern of enterprise investment emerges jointly from enterprise decisions and government intervention. The government intervenes both through the administrative procedure of examining and approving investment plans and through control over the supply of funds and materials. The supply of funds, particularly loans, has become the major form of intervention.

At present the portion of profits retained by Chinese enterprises is very small. Although state enterprises and upper-level departments (mainly the former) already control 80 percent of extrabudgetary funds, these funds are widely dispersed. In 1984, the profits retained by the enterprises under study amounted to

Table 7.4

**Distribution of Enterprises by Profit Retention
(computed as a ratio to fixed capital)**

Retained Profits per 10,000 Yuan of Fixed Assets (Original Value)	Number of Factories	Percent
Less than 500 yuan	190	45.67
500–1,000 yuan	108	25.96
1,000–1,500 yuan	57	13.7
1,500 yuan or above	61	14.66
Total	416	100

only 950 yuan per 10,000 yuan of original value of fixed assets, while the Gini coefficient showing the inequality of the distribution of profits retained by enterprises (as a ratio to fixed assets) was only 0.22. All this indicates that the amount of retained profits (as compared with asset value) of different enterprises is by and large quite similar, and small (see table 7.4).

Because profits retained by enterprises are small and widely dispersed in distribution, enterprises have become dependent to a large extent on outside funds for investment. In current circumstances, where local authorities use most of their funds on nonproductive projects, bank loans have become the most important source of funds for enterprise investment (see table 7.5).

As the banks' share in total enterprise investment loans increased rapidly, this change seems to affect the division of investment between productive and nonproductive purposes, and the allocation of investment among enterprises. A correlation analysis of gross investment, appropriations, loans, and self-raised funds, in relation to the original value of fixed assets in the enterprises under study, shows that the correlation between the distribution of bank loans and that of gross investment is lower than the correlation between self-raised funds and gross investments ($r=0.5862$ for the former, $r=0.7407$ for the latter), and both are clearly higher than the correlation between appropriations and gross investments ($r=0.3890$). One may conclude that not only do bank loans for investment constitute an important force supporting current investment activities in enterprises, but the orientation of bank loans granted also strongly influences the orientation of enterprise investment and the capacity of enterprises for future development.

The increasing influence of bank loans on enterprise investment activities and the decreasing share of funds granted directly by planning organs in the gross productive investment have markedly strengthened the position of banks in investment decision-making. For instance, in Jiangsu province, the provincial Industrial and Commercial Bank eliminated 50 percent of the projects planned

Table 7.5

Sources of Funds for Investment in Fixed Assets by Enterprises (1984)

Sources	Percent	
1. Gross appropriations	18.26	
State appropriations		12.5
Appropriations from a higher organ		5.76
2. Gross bank loans	31.84	
Construction Bank loans		12.92
Industrial & Commercial Bank loans		19.82
3. Funds raised by enterprises	45.59	
Funds owned by enterprises		29.1
4. Other funds	3.53	
Total	100%	

and requested by various provincial departments for 1985. Undoubtedly, the shift of investment decision-making authority to banks is an important achievement of the reform over the past few years and is also an important indication of the progress made in the monetization of the entire national economy.

To summarize, the current investment mechanism displays an increased tendency of local authorities to invest in nonproductive projects, an expansion of the investment decision-making authority of enterprises, and a gradual growth of the banks' central role in investment decision-making. In the field of investment in productive projects, the market mechanism has already started to play an important regulatory role. Price signals, and in particular profit increase rates, now effectively regulate the allocation of investment funds. Analysis of the enterprises under study shows that investment (computed against the original value of fixed assets) is not correlated with the growth rate of output value, but is to a certain extent correlated with the rate of growth of the profits/fixed assets ratio. (For 244 sample cases, $r = 0.1939$.) This new role for a market signal is one of the most important achievements of our reform program in recent years.

2. Some Characteristics of Current Investment Activities in China

Development and reform, the two major objectives, generate conflicts that merge in the investment process. The macroeconomic instability that emerged during reform requires that we limit the overall scale investment. But the Seventh Five-Year Plan, with its historic task of laying a foundation for economic takeoff in the 1990s plus its drastic changes in current consumer demand, implies a new investment boom. Since 1984, we can see this conflict manifested in three aspects

Table 7.6

Distribution of Authority to Examine and Approve Investment after Delegation of Such Authority to Lower Levels

Unit: 10,000 yuan

	Capital Construction Projects	Projects for Equipment Renewal & Technological Transformation
County	100–500 (a few exceeding 1,000)	50–100
County group (under comprehensive structural reform plan)	500–1,000	50–200
Prefecture, city, and provincial departments	500–3,000 (some exceeding 3,000)	50–500 (some exceeding 1,000)
City under direct provincial administration	1,000–3,000	1,000
City with provincial status	above 3,000	above 1,000

of investment activity in China: (1) overall investment expands as soon as decision-making authority is delegated to a lower level; (2) reform creates a tendency toward more projects of smaller size; and (3) it also generates a tendency toward investing in light industrial and nonproductive projects. These three features all underscore the fact that the present investment mechanism in China is not adequate to accomplish effectively both development and reform.

Investment expansion since 1984 is directly linked to the delegation of authority to lower administrative levels and to enlarged enterprise decision-making power. Expansion can also be traced, indirectly, to the decentralized sources of funds, mainly extrabudgetary funds and bank loans. The direct cause of investment expansion since 1984 is the ''delegation of authority to lower levels.'' This includes the decision to place quite a few state enterprises under the administration of cities, and to allow lower levels of authority to examine and approve investment. This delegation of authority took place mainly in the second half of 1984. Table 7.6 summarizes the distribution of authority to examine and approve investments in the twenty-seven cities investigated.

As far as local governments and functional departments are concerned, since enlargement of investment authority, the authority to examine and approve is no longer a binding restriction because now few projects are big enough to require approval of the central government departments, and even projects needing such approval can be divided up into smaller items to be separately examined and approved on an individual basis, which places them under local investment decision-making authority.

Harbin was the only city investigated where authority of examination and approval was not enlarged in 1984. Consequently, this city did not exceed the planned level of investment in that year. From 1985, the city began to draft its own plan, and authority to examine and approve investments was expanded, in money terms, to some 30 million yuan. The investment level also rose by a big margin. This shows the link between the delegation of authority to examine and approve, and the higher level of investment since 1984.

The reasons why the level of investment expanded immediately following the delegation of authority to lower levels are mainly the following. First, in the prereform circumstances, where investment activities had to be reported for approval, for a long period of time investors at lower levels, though attracted by many investment opportunities, could not make use of them. Now, with the power delegated to them, they immediately grabbed these opportunities. Investment increase in this category is in a way a vacuum-filling expansion aimed at satisfying the accumulated demands for investment long suppressed in the past. This is a unique and inevitable phenomenon in the process of reforming the investment mechanism. Second, encouraged by the "upward emulation" for higher real wages, competition among enterprises to have the best welfare and housing facilities has become one important aspect of consumption expansion. Now, enterprises and institutions use housing benefits as an important means to compete against one another on the labor market. This part of the demand for investment follows the law of the fluctuation in consumption demand and constitutes an integral part of the current expansion of consumption for which there are no internal constraints. Therefore, it is inevitable that the investment scale should expand once authority is delegated to lower levels. Third, the impulse of the investment in productive projects, spurred on by the desire for rural employment, the demand for enterprise welfare, and the boom in short-term undertakings, stimulates the rapid expansion of investment. Moreover, investment activities of these sorts create a generalized investment boom, with rosy prospects and high-growth signals, which feeds upon itself.

The expansion in investment consequent to the delegation of authority does not in itself undermine overall balance. The previous rounds of expansion of investment scale experienced in China resulted not in imbalance, but in raising the investment rate and reducing the supply of consumer goods. The simultaneous expansion of investment scale and consumption in 1984 led to overall demand far surpassing supply. This unprecedented phenomenon was linked with the historic change of banks becoming a principal fund supplier for investment activities, in particular for investment in productive projects.

Investment in fixed assets financed by banks has been a major stimulus to the expansion of investment since 1984. National investment financed by domestic loans in fixed assets in 1984 increased 47.3 percent over 1983, further increasing by 129.8 percent in the period January-August 1985 over the corresponding period of the preceding year. This latter increase was 2.6 times as fast as the increase (49.6 percent) of investment in fixed assets financed by self-raised funds. The proportions of investment in fixed assets financed by domestic loans were 18.7 percent and 29.3 percent, respectively, of the overall investment in extrabudgetary capital construction and in equipment renewal and technological transformation; 20.5 percent and 35 percent, respectively, in 1984; jumping to 29.5 percent and 44.3 percent, respectively, during the first half of 1985. What deserves special notice is that at the same time that overall credit is being refused, banks tend to cut down on working capital loans and to increase loans for investment in fixed assets. The summarized data on bank loans in eighteen cities show that the proportion of investment in fixed assets financed with bank loans was 6.3 percent in 1983, rising to 6.8 percent by the end of June 1984, 7.7 percent by the end of 1984, and 8.9 percent by the end of June 1985.

Also meriting serious attention is the tendency among banks to relax funding constraints on enterprises. When appraising the constraints on enterprise operation, the factory directors questioned ranked ''inadequate funds'' second on the list of sixteen choices. In choosing sources for funds, they placed ''borrowing from banks'' above ''relying on the higher-level administration for funds'' and other choices (see table 7.7). Furthermore, this ranking holds for all fourteen categories on enterprises under study, regardless of scale or form of ownership. The predilections of the directors for particular sources of funds correlate with the availability of the funds and the strictness of economic responsibility that has to be undertaken to obtain the loans. Thus it appears that at the very time that reform is strengthening constraints over administrative funding, banks may be relaxing their constraints. According to the Construction Banks in seven cities, the balance of overdue loans by the end of 1984 increased by 6.6 percent over the preceding year, and it grew in June 1985 by 44.7 percent over the corresponding period of 1984. Meanwhile, the balance of overdue loans that the borrowers were unable to repay to the Construction Banks in eighteen cities has grown steadily over the years, growing from 24.26 percent in June 1983 to 41.9 percent in June 1984, and to 51.8 percent in June 1985. This development is another manifestation of the aforementioned tendency.

It is necessary to conduct a close study of specific cases before we can clarify the present state of relaxation of bank credit. Nevertheless, available data show that the mechanism through which investment expands in China has assumed a new nature. To wit: enterprises have a bias against productive investment and in favor of investing in consumption projects; more and more self-owned funds are used for consumption or investment in consumption projects; and investment in productive projects is financed in the main by bank loans. The expansion of consumption and investment in consumption projects generates an economic boom that offers an excellent investment environment at all levels. This exerts tremendous pressure on individual banks to provide more loans for investment in fixed assets, and the shortage of investment in productive projects creates in broad terms a strong impetus to increase the supply of funds from banks. The

Table 7.7

Enterprise Directors' Preferred Funding Sources

Order of Preference	Source	Grade
1	Loans from banks	4.1246
2	Raised within enterprises	2.5552
3	Requested from higher-level administration	2.0680
4	Sale of redundant assets	1.6587
5	Reduction of redundant personnel	1.4476
6	Raised in society	1.3626
7	Borrowed from other enterprises	1.0567
8	Reduction of real wages	0.2890

danger of this mechanism is that it makes the expansion of bank credit a basic condition for maintaining an appropriate rate of productive investment. This mechanism may seemingly restore the rate of accumulation to its original levels, but this is achieved at the cost of expansion of overall demand and continued inflation.

The experience of Yugoslavia shows the possible grave consequences of such a mechanism. Yugoslavian factories, after becoming responsible for loss or profit on their own, used large sums for consumption purposes without leaving enough for accumulation for production. But Yugoslavia still kept up a very high rate of accumulation. As compared with 1970, the personal consumption rate in Yugoslavia in 1976 increased by 273 percent, collective consumption by 330 percent, and investment in fixed assets by 290 percent. The accumulation rate remained as high as 40 percent. This rate of accumulation caused excessive supply of money and huge foreign debts. Some Yugoslav economists estimated that 46 percent of the gross investment in that country in 1973 was from foreign debts and the percentage increased to 61 percent in 1975, and only 12 percent of the gross social product was actually used for investment. Clearly, this is one of the main reasons why the Yugoslav economy has deteriorated in recent years.

While the scale of overall investment expands, the tendency toward more investment in smaller-sized units has become a problem worthy of concern. In 1984, among 3,212 urban capital construction projects investigated, projects worth more than 10 million yuan accounted for only 5.5 percent of the total, while those worth less than 500,000 yuan each accounted for 52.6 percent, with an average of 237,000 yuan. The average size of projects worth less than 10 million yuan each was in money terms only 1.18 million yuan. If we consider the fact that China's township-run enterprises are only worth 35,000 each on average, the problem is all the more salient. (Figure 7.1 shows the situation in Sichuan province.) The problem of small scale of investment per project is reflected especially clearly in some industries and trades. For instance, there are in Jiangsu province 361 factories that refit automobiles, with an aggregate refitting capacity of 15,000 vehicles annually—each factory only refitting 42 vehicles on average. This province has now instituted a "thermopower generation" craze, and cities, counties, and townships plan to install 45 small power-generating plants with an aggregate generating capacity of 518,200 kw. But the average generating capacity per plant is 12,000 kw, with the smallest capacity being only 1,500 kw. In Shanxi province, over 1,000 small blast furnaces were built with an average capacity of 30 cubic meters. These furnaces were nicknamed "one-kick furnaces," meaning that they can be toppled with one kick. These projects hardly have the potential for future renovation and development, because they have inherent deficiencies, very poor cost-benefit economic returns, and backward technology. Their existence shows that the efficiency of investment quality has dropped very seriously as the aggregate investment in China continues to expand.

The unduly small scale of investment per project may be caused in part by parcelization of the products market. For instance, the scale of investment in electricity generation is subject to a very large extent to the quota constraints of the electricity supply networks. In general, however, the tendency toward a small scale of investment is mainly caused by the imperfection of the factor market, in particular the funds market, rather than by the imperfections of the product market.

1. The portion of profits retained by Chinese enterprises is very small, not sufficient for reinvestment in large-scale projects. Large and medium-sized enterprises account for 57 percent of all enterprises we investigated, a percentage much higher than the national average. If the average portion of retained profits in these enterprises is 21.59 percent of gross profits, the retained profits are in money terms only 1.53 million yuan per enterprise, of which funds for production are less than 0.5 million yuan. This amounts to only some 300 yuan of production funds per 10,000 yuan of the original value of fixed assets. This amount, plus the depreciation fund used every year for reinvestment in fixed assets, is only 7–8 percent of the original value of the fixed assets, a percentage even smaller than the ratio of depreciation funds in the developed countries of the West.

2. The low mobility of the labor force, in particular the employment barriers between different cities, between city and town, and between different rural areas, results in very great differences in employment pressure on different regions. In those areas where unemployment is high, capital investment is made mainly with an eye to creating job opportunities, reducing the scale of investment per project in such areas. In addition, the same pressure compelled governments at various levels to allocate investment disproportionately to high-unemployment areas, causing a shortage of funds for investment activities that mainly produce profits rather than job opportunities. For example, farmers in Shazou county, Jiangsu province, set up with their own funds a glass factory capable of producing

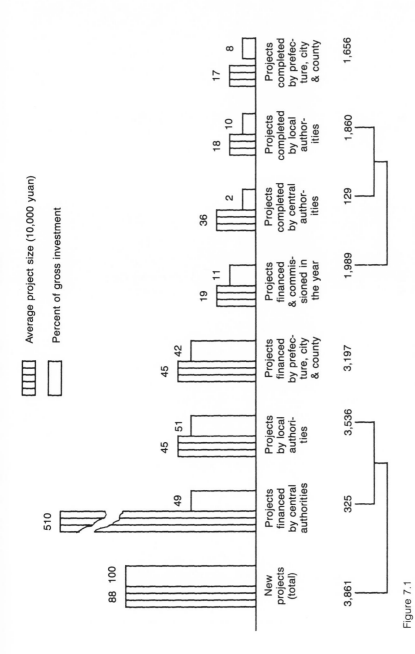

Figure 7.1

Average Size of Newly Launched Public Capital Construction Projects in Sichuan Province, 1984

annually 1.3 million standard crates of plate glass, and they needed only 20 million yuan of floating loans to put the factory into operation. However, this loan was unavailable for a long time because senior provincial leaders repeatedly hinted to the Agricultural Bank that the bank should bear in mind how many smaller projects they could finance with that sum of money.

3. The traditional mechanism for funds concentration, that is, investment by central financial organs, is weakened. But the new mechanism has not yet come into its own. There is no mechanism through which enterprise-retained profits can be pooled and directed horizontally to larger-scale projects—despite the fact that enterprise-retained profits represent 80 percent of extrabudgetary funds. Some new methods of fund accumulation, such as combined investment by different investors, compensation trade, and trust investment, have been developed in recent years but are not being used on an extensive scale and fall far short of forming an adequate mechanism.

4. Enterprises that have no long-term perspective in making investment decisions and are mainly interested in short-term and quick-profit projects can hardly accomplish the immense task of investing in large-scale projects. During the reform period, relevant policies cannot remain completely stable and the policy decision-making environment is not absolutely certain; all these factors contribute to make investment in long-term, large-scale projects, which are already rather risky, even more so. For example, Zhejiang province invested in coal production in the form of compensation trade with Shanxi province and the Ministry of Coal Mining Industry, but the province's economic returns on its investment have been seriously undermined as a result of the introduction of the two-tier coal pricing regulations and the rise in coal haulage costs in July 1985.

The tendency toward smaller scale of investment per project poses a challenge to our ideas about reform. One set objective of the reform is progressively to weaken the functions of government with regard to investment so that economic organizations responsible on their own for loss and profit and for the risks involved will behave in this fashion regarding investment in productive projects. However, at present, where enterprises lack far-sightedness in making investments, the factors market is not yet fully developed, and the mechanisms of funds accumulation and funds concentration still need improvement, the delegation of authority to lower levels will result only in decentralizing possession and use of funds, and this sweeping decentralization of funds use is obviously not very helpful to long-term economic growth. If we cannot create a new fund-accumulating mechanism in China to replace the government's role in fund accumulation for investment purposes, it will be very difficult to advance the reform program.

The third characteristic of investment activities in China is the tendency toward investing in light industry. An important aspect of economic reform in China since 1979 is that we criticized the traditional development strategy of overemphasis on accumulation and the self-sustaining mechanism of recycling accumulation within heavy industry, and instead established the principle of giving priority to the development of consumer goods production. Doubtlessly, the principle has played a very important role in bringing about a fundamental turn for the better in the national economy and social stability. Nevertheless, if light industry dominates the industrial structure for a long period of time, it will be extremely detrimental to the economic growth of a big country like China. There is no precedent in history for a big country achieving economic prosperity by relying on an industrial structure composed mainly of light industry.

At present, light and heavy industries in China are about on a par with each other. However, the pattern of China's industrial investment differs greatly from the average pattern of investment of the United States, Japan, France, Great Britain, and West Germany at the time when their per capita national income was U.S. $1,000. The coefficient of the differences between the two is as high as 0.2256, the Chinese pattern having a large share for light industry. In 1965, when the chemical and metallurgical industries of Japan accounted for 30 percent of the gross value of industrial output, investment in these industries was still 26 percent of gross industrial investment, whereas in China in 1984, when the two industries only accounted for 20 percent of gross output value, investment in the two industries was only 20 percent of gross industrial investment. It is obvious that this difference between investment patterns may continue to expand. At present, the investment in ordinary projects has increased much faster than that in such priority expansion sectors as energy and transport. The proportion of investment exclusively in the energy industry between January and June 1985 was 19.7 percent of gross investment, a sharp drop from 23.8 percent in the corresponding period in 1984, and the proportion of investment in the transport, post, and communications sectors dropped from 15.1 percent of total investment in the same period in 1984 to 13.9 percent in 1985.

The tendency toward increasing the share of light industrial investment will certainly expand the share of light industry in the overall industrial structure. During the Sixth Five-Year Plan period, the increments in production capacity in the highway, railway, steel-making, and power-generating sectors declined by varying degrees as compared with the Fifth Five-Year Plan period. The development of basic industries is far from adequate for the needs of the growing economy. In the first half of 1985 gross industrial product grew by 23.1 percent while investment in the metallurgical industry in the same period was only 3.384 billion yuan. The annual average between 1980 and 1984 of the consumption coefficient of the production value of the metallurgical industry against the gross industrial product is 0.084, and the rate of investment output in the metallurgical industry is 0.66. Computed according to this formula, the metallurgical industry needs an investment worth 10.4 billion yuan to support its growth, but the investment actually made is only 32.4 percent of this figure. Clearly, the inadequate investment in the metallurgical industry is an important cause of the increased import of foreign metallurgical products in recent years to maintain China's economic growth.

With the delegation of investment-making authority to lower levels, the tendency toward increasing light industry's share of investment may further intensify, and this should arouse our serious concern. The pattern of investment in industry financed by locally raised funds differs greatly from the national pattern of industrial investment. The coefficient of the difference between the pattern of investment financed by provinces with local funds and that of state investments is 0.3112, and that between the pattern financed by cities with their own funds and the national investment pattern is as high as 0.524. The proportion of investment in light and textile industries financed by cities with their own funds is much larger than that of the national average, and in heavy and chemical industries, city investments that are proportionally above the national average are mainly in electricity and construction materials.

The causes of this pattern are extremely complex. First, the rapid expansion of consumer demand over the past few years in China is undoubtedly an important cause. The expansion of consumption demand and the change in the pattern of the demand exert a very strong influence on the pattern of production and investment. Second, logically speaking, price signals should have a tremendous influence on the investment pattern. However, the price system has been considerably improved over the years, thanks to the introduction of the two-tier price system for producer goods. Thus one hesitates to blame the influence of prices for a light industry bias in the investment activities of local authorities.

Among the numerous factors affecting investment decision-making, the conditions in factors markets may be more important than those in the product market. First, widespread employment pressure has compelled local governments to invest in labor-intensive projects. The light, textile, and construction materials industries have therefore become priority sectors for investment. Second, the small size of projects consequent upon the overdispersion of investment bars the way to investing in the heavy and chemical industries, where an average project is larger in scale and requires a capital-intensive technology, to say nothing of complex additional investments in auxiliary facilities. Small projects, such as those in the light, machine-building, and textile sectors, are less subject to the influence of overall investment policy, in particular a policy decision to reduce the total amount of investment. Therefore, growth in these sectors is fairly steady. But investment in the raw and semi-finished materials industry, where large projects are the rule, is to a much higher degree affected by fluctuations in the overall level of investment (see table 7.8). We can explain the rise over time in the share of light industry in total investment chiefly with reference to the above factors.

This bias toward light industry shows that abandoning the old development strategy of recycling profits into heavy industry does not necessarily lead to a benign cycle of consumption-production-investment. To transmit the market demand for final products to the interior sectors of the economy is an extremely complex process. This not only requires a rational and flexible price system and

Table 7.8

Annual Growth Rate of Capital Investment in the Sixth Five-Year Plan Period

Year	Gross Capital Investment	Capital Investment in Raw and Semi-Finished Materials Industry	Capital Investment in Energy Industry
1981	−20.75	−18.5	−20.7
1982	25.43	44.1	11.7
1983	6.95	4.4	24.8
1984	25.06	12.3	28.6

investor behavior that can respond positively to market demand—improvement in the two aspects has already been made—but also a flexible and effective factors market and competent and far-sighted investment decision-makers. In the absence of the two latter conditions, excess supply in some industries may coexist with shortage of supply in others. Even when the investment side can respond to a certain extent, this response may be low in quality and uneconomical. The boom in "one-kick" small blast furnaces in Shanxi province is a case in point.

3. Policy Recommendations: Develop Enterprise Groups and Improve the Investment Mechanism

The three major characteristics of investment activities in China at present show that although important progress has been made in the reform of China's investment mechanism, the present investment mechanism is still inadequate for the complex tasks posed by the Seventh Five-Year Plan. The question of whether we will be able to improve investment performance has a bearing on the smooth economic growth during the current five-year plan period and will have a profound impact on the economic growth of China within this century. Therefore, further reform of the investment system demands urgent attention.

The investment mechanism affects many aspects of the national economy. Therefore, reforms should also start in many areas at the same time and proceed as an integral whole. Improvement should proceed on two fronts: (1) We must change the financial system through which investment funds are channeled, and the incentives guiding enterprise investment decisions; and (2) we must encourage the formation of large industrial groups.

The reform of the financial system is of vital importance. To strengthen the budgetary constraints on enterprises so as to eliminate investment hunger, improve the cost-benefit results of investment, and accelerate the readjustment of industrial structure all require profound change in the financial system. However, this cannot be achieved with one stroke. It is far more difficult than reform in other areas, and it requires very careful coordination. Furthermore, any large reform effort here incurs a great deal of risk. It will be very difficult to complete a comprehensive reform of the financial system during the Seventh Five-Year Plan period. The following ideas may be feasible: (1) Promote and guide the development of nongovernmental credits (including commercial credit between enterprises, investment financed by multiple fund sources, mutual-aid financial organizations among enterprises, and locally invested development companies) and thus launch and promote a "two-track" financial system; (2) readjust the relationship between the government financial administration and the banks, and change the two "big pot" practices, namely, the financial departments depending on overdrafts from the "big pot" of the banks, and relying on the "big pot" of the financial departments by demanding and receiving repayment for debts out of the tax on investment in fixed assets; (3) strengthen mandatory administrative control by the central bank over the gross money supply, pursue a tight financial policy, and set strict limits on borrowing from state banks, to ensure room for nonbank financial organizations to develop. At the same time, introduce new controls over such financial activities, including reserve funds, deposit insurance, and licensing. It may be possible to make fewer waves and run fewer risks if we start the present banking system only after the emergence of a financial market.

It is the task of the subreport on the financial question to analyze and discuss in detail the reform of the financial structure. The present report deals primarily with the other aspect of reforming the investment mechanism, that is, allowing enterprises to be the investors.

The traditional investment mechanism, with government as the sole investor, must be changed. This system is at the root of the recurring cycles of investment expansion and low economic returns that have plagued China ever since the founding of the People's Republic over thirty-five years ago. The mechanism leaves only a meager portion of profits with the enterprises and ensures the continued existence of all enterprises irrespective of their performance. Such a mechanism neither stimulates nor constrains enterprises to respond actively to the market.

However, to reform the traditional investment system does not simply mean to expand the share of profits retained by enterprises and to enlarge their authority to make investments. Small enterprises in China account for 98 percent of the total number of enterprises. They are technically weak, unable to follow closely developments in science and technology and respond quickly to market changes. Although in recent years small enterprises have been subjected to a greater degree than medium-sized and large enterprises to the stresses of a commodity economy and have gained valuable experience and shown great adaptability to commodity production, we cannot afford to overlook their limitations in management capability and vision. On the other hand, large and medium-sized enterprises in China are not yet playing their full role in guiding and determining shifts in the pattern of investment and production. It is true that compared with small enterprises, their investments are in large-scale and long-term projects, where short-term, profit-oriented motives are less important than such considerations as market share, technological standards, and keeping pace with domestic and foreign competition. But the present system has made it less likely that enterprises will have a long-term development motive. And even if they do. it is often difficult for them to translate their plans into action.

Therefore, an improved investment mechanism should encourage enterprises to focus on long-term development, and to become sophisticated investors. Recent examples (Capital Iron and Steel Works, No. 2 Motor Works, Mindong Electric Motor Company, and other medium-sized enterprises) show that once enterprises are given a chance to seek development relying on their own efforts, a fairly strong urge for development may be generated, which will in turn stimulate the expansion of internal accumulation and investment in long-term projects.

Experience in some advanced countries shows that if antitrust measures are properly applied, merged enterprises can give a powerful impetus to development. Japanese industry has a high degree of concentration. The largest 1 percent of Japanese enterprises account for 41.9 percent of corporate assets and 35.7 percent of gross sales. These groups play an extremely important role in implementing the government's production policies and development plans, and in promoting technological progress and foreign trade.

Therefore, at the time of streamlining administrative departments and delegating power to lower levels, it is of great importance to China's future reform and development to develop and organize groups without delay. The experience of Japan and other countries tells us that a funds market that directly accumulates and concentrates funds takes a rather long historical period of time to develop. In China this process may turn out to be even longer. The formation of group enterprises will make it possible to correct for the immature funds market and to concentrate and employ investment funds on a collective basis. This will make it possible for the government to transfer to enterprises its functions of concentrating funds for investment in large-scale, long-term projects while avoiding the fragmentized investment and the bias toward light industry that would otherwise emerge. Enterprise groups will constitute a new organizational structure that will play a major role in investment and in technological progress. These structures will attract many medium and small-sized enterprises to take part in a division of labor within the group, thus greatly improving China's industrial organization and creating conditions for the "showcase guidance" of enterprises by government.

At present, conditions already exist for setting up enterprise groups. The emerging market environment over the past few years has made enterprises keenly aware of the need for association. Answers to the question on association by 351 factory directors show that 88 percent were in favor of association with other enterprises in one form or another. Of these, 34 percent would like to form joint enterprises with others, 8 percent opted for mergers, and 37 percent favored pooling. There exists strong tendency toward association in one form or another.

The enterprises' motive for association clearly reflects the desire to benefit from economies of scale. Factory directors were asked the question, ''Why do you need association?'' The directors were to choose five answers out of fourteen choices. They gave most consideration to seeking scale economies (including improvement of economic performance, expansion of production scale, formation of new product series, and reduction of cost). Of secondary importance was a desire to improve the input situation (including the improvement of raw and semifinished materials supply, access to advanced technology, and increase of funds).

The conditions for the formation of enterprise groups already exist to a great extent. For example, the economic efforts by enterprises to control cost, guarantee quality of processed parts, and ensure raw and semifinished materials supply and sale of products will promote in a comprehensive way the vertical association of enterprises. The division of large enterprises into small business accounting units will help to extend their feelers more deeply into all aspects and directions of the economy, thus promoting lateral economic association. And financial mutual aid among enterprises may also help to unite medium-sized and small enterprises to form ''groves of stunted trees,'' so to speak each, with an internal ''bank'' at its center.

The formation of enterprise groups and creation of new ''enterprise investors'' require active intervention by central and local authorities, along the following lines.

1. Experimentation with a system of share-holding by legal persons. In this experiment, ownership of enterprise shares will be restricted to the enterprise level. Different enterprises may become one another's share-holders, and the share-holding enterprise will have the right to participate in the production and management decision-making in the enterprises whose shares it holds. This structure helps to form a common interest among some enterprises. Damage to one is damage to all, prosperity of one is prosperity of all, so that they concern themselves about and safeguard the interests of the group as a whole, strongly checking the tendency of any member enterprise to expand consumption or to use up reserves. The interests of factory operators become closely lined with the long-term interests of the enterprises.

2. As the share of profits retained by enterprises enlarges in the Seventh Five-Year Plan period, some retained profits can be earmarked for an industrywide fund, and loans will be granted from this fund to advance enterprises on a selective basis. Or several enterprises (those capable of forming an association) may bid for loans, or such funds may be used to purchase stocks or bonds of enterprise groups.

3. In granting loans, group enterprises can be given preferential terms, espe-

cially in industries where the minimum economic scale is clear. Bank loans could be granted only to those new projects that are above a certain scale. Enterprise groups will enjoy more power in production, management, and foreign trade. Tax policy should encourage enterprise associations. In particular, progressive taxation, which is harmful to the expansion of enterprises, should be abolished. In short, after the past several years of reform, conditions already exist for us to introduce new forms of economic organization, and it is now possible for us to make a variety of choices. While the government continues to expand the power of enterprises and weaken administrative intervention in production, management, and investment activities, it should carry out active administrative and economic intervention in some other aspects of the economy, such as economic organization. This should be the basic orientation of further reform efforts during the Seventh Five-Year Plan period.

Based on its importance and complexity, the subject of investment is one of the most difficult problems in economic reform in socialist countries. A new investment mechanism has begun to take shape after several years of reform. The basic orientation of the reform should undoubtedly be acclaimed and confirmed. However, great attention should be paid to the deficiencies of the new mechanisms, which have already been noted. We should not be too critical of every detail, nor should we ignore these deficiencies. We should gradually improve the mechanism during the historic process of reform. This should be the basic idea and approach for pushing forward reform in this field.

8

Management of Extrabudgetary Funds

Zhao Yujiang

Highlight: Excessive growth of extrabudgetary investment (that is, fiscal departments' direct raising of state-owned enterprises' funds) has become a widespread policy in recent years. Local banks, enterprises, and governments have played an important role in investment expansion.

Microeconomically, the soft budget constraint imposed on enterprises is the most important factor contributing to swollen investment in the past few years. The role of local governments, however, is not a factor that should be ignored. Also, enterprises use their own money to increase consumption funds rather than to increase investment. Lastly, a major problem in investment is the miniaturization of scale of investment.

The key to solving the problem of management of extrabudgetary funds is to rationalize the behavior of local governments. The ideal system would be a triangular set of restrictions: horizontal restrictions between enterprises, local government restrictions on enterprises through policies, and enterprise restrictions on local governments through economic performance.

Promoting a horizontal flow of funds between enterprises and between non-bank financial organizations, depriving local governments of their power to control enterprises' funds directly, is the principle to be followed in arranging extrabudgetary funds in a rational and effective way. As things stand right now, this principle is completely feasible.

As investment and consumption funds swell, extrabudgetary funds have become a matter of common concern, and the cry for tight control of them has become louder and louder.

However, there is a lack of accurate analysis with regard to such problems as what responsibilities extrabudgetary funds assume and what role each component of the funds plays. Without accurate analysis, there can be no accurate policies.

1. Analysis of the Situation

1.1. The Soft Budget Constraint Plays a Paramount Role in Investment Expansion

Extrabudgetary investment, as it is popularly understood, includes that portion of extrabudgetary funds that is used for investment by state-owned enterprises, local fiscal departments, administrative organizations, and institutions; investment by collective-owned enterprises and by individuals; and bank loans for investment. For the sake of analysis, we will analyze the role of each part.

Economic restructuring in the past few years has brought about great changes in the supply of investment funds. Although years ago funds were granted gratis and now must be repaid, one still cannot say that economic restrictions have not yet been established among the state, banks, and enterprises. In the past, enterprises, departments, and localities contended for funds allocations; now they vie for loans. They bargained for fund allocation in the past and now bargain for loans. In the past, the fiscal constraint was soft. Now it is the bank loans constraint that is soft. The softened constraint of loans over microeconomic activities is the major reason why too much money was issued and why credit funds ran out of control. It is also the most important contributor to the swelling of investment as a whole in the past couple of years.

Table 8.1 shows that investment in fixed assets from extrabudgetary funds has grown more slowly than aggregate investment in fixed assets. If it is popularly understood that budgeted investment grows far slower than extrabudgetary investment, then the accelerated growth of aggregate investment has resulted from the growth of investment by urban collective-owned enterprises and individuals and the growth of investment through bank loans. Table 8.1 also indicates that investment in fixed assets from extrabudgetary funds has grown much more slowly than investment through bank loans, and that bank loans granted to rural enterprises and urban collective-owned enterprises have grown at the fastest rate of all.

Therefore, it can be said that bank loans have assumed more responsibility than extrabudgetary funds in the supply of investment funds and in the swelling of investment as well.

1.2. The Role Played by Local Governments in Investment Expansion Should Not Be Ignored

With bank loans separated from extrabudgetary funds, we should further separate enterprises from local governments in their use of extrabudgetary funds for investment.

Of the extrabudgetary funds, a small proportion (less than 10 percent) is controlled by local fiscal departments. As shown by history and by the present

Table 8.1

Growth of Investment in Fixed Assets in Twenty-three Cities

	Growth Rate, 1983–84 (%)
Extrabudgetary investment in fixed assets	7.4
Aggregate investment in fixed assets	20.42
Investment in fixed assets of state-owned enterprises by bank loans	52.79
*Loans granted to rural enterprises	75.3
*Loans granted to urban collective-owned enterprises	52.9

*These statistics come from eleven cities, and about half of the loans granted to rural enterprises are used for investment in fixed assets.

situation, local governments have a strong desire to expand investment and a great ability to arrange and control funds, in at least the following three ways.

1. Requiring banks to grant loans through administrative orders. This is a prevailing phenomenon all over the country. Individual enterprises have much less ability to apply for extra loans than local governments. Almost no large-scale unplanned investment projects can be conducted without the support of local governments. Banks are required to grant loans and preferential credits, or to change repayment terms. These are the major ways of dealing with funds shortage. Therefore, the softened constraint of bank loans, which has played a paramount role in investment expansion, has resulted in part from local governments' direct interference in banking (as well as from an inadequate bank system and loose monetary policies).

2. Miscellaneous exactions (ad hoc taxes) upon enterprises and mandatory collection of various funds. A sample survey of twenty-three cities indicates the amount of exactions from 100 enterprises in 1984 (see table 8.2).

About 20 percent of miscellaneous apportionments were put into production costs or nonbusiness expenditure, about 10 percent were seen as after-tax welfare funds and about 70 percent were seen as after-tax expenditure for technical transformation. However, there was no trace at all in local governments' accounts of this extrabudgetary revenue and expenditure. Looking at the accounts, one would conclude that enterprises themselves used more extrabudgetary funds for investment. In fact, however, local governments funded this activity using enterprises' money. Local governments invaded enterprises' funds for technical transformation to build such nonproductive projects as public infrastructure and cultural facilities. Local governments' ability to expand investment was strengthened, while enterprises, hard pressed by funds shortage, pressured banks to grant loans.

3. Expanding in disguised form their capital construction quotas and vying

Table 8.2

Ad Hoc Taxes on 100 Enterprises in 1984
Unit: 10,000 yuan

Amount of apportionments by local governments, provincial and city departments	872.35
Amount of profits retained by enterprises	11,392.78
Average $\dfrac{\text{amount of apportionments}}{\text{amount of profits retained}}$	7.65%
of which $\dfrac{\text{maximum rate}}{\text{minimum rate}}$	81.60%
	0.95%

for more projects. This is a malady that has existed for years. One disguised form is to use maintenance funds for capital construction. According to a 1983 investigation of a branch of the Construction Bank of China into capital construction in the city where it is located, above-quota expenditure amounted to more than 30 million yuan, of which about 10.03 million, or more than 30 percent, was used for capital construction in the disguised form of maintaining municipal facilities; about 3.68 million was used by various companies for capital construction; about 7.93 million was retained by the city government. The three portions amounted to 21.64 million yuan, accounting for 72 percent of the total above-quota expenditure. This case illustrates that local governments have played a leading role in expanding the scope of investment with self-raised funds. Every year when the central government arranges the country's key projects, local governments arrange their own, too. The trend still continues to show that the number of local key projects is rising. According to the Ministry of Finance, local governments want to build more than 3,000 large and medium-sized projects during the Seventh Five-Year Plan period (1980–1985). This increase may lead to an increase in the pressure brought to bear upon banks for loans.

When local governments have much to do and many projects to build at the highest possible speed, they directly or indirectly compel banks to grant more loans. Investment aided by bank loans has widened the gap between the amount of money in circulation and the amount of materials available, and between the supply of investment materials and the demand for them. Although local governments are not the sole factor contributing to the drawn-out scope of investment and to the overissuance of bank loans, one certainly cannot find local governments blameless for investment swelling.

1.3. Enterprises' Role in Investment Expansion and Consumption Funds Expansion

The extrabudgetary funds owned by enterprises make up 70 percent of the total extrabudgetary funds. Therefore, it is mainly enterprises that should be blamed

Table 8.3

Expenditure of Extrabudgetary Funds by State-Owned Enterprises in Twenty-three Cities (%)

	1983	1984
Total amount of investment in fixed assets/total extrabudgetary income	54.6	49.2
Total expenditure on fringe benefits and bonus/total extrabudgetary income	23.62	27.30

Table 8.4

Expenditure of Twenty-three Cities on Fringe Benefits and Bonuses by Using Extrabudgetary Funds

	Growth Rate 1983–84 (%)
State-owned industrial enterprises	29
State-owned enterprises	39
Administrative organizations and institutions	90

for the behavior of the funds. If the aforementioned discussion that bank loans are more responsible than other factors for the investment expansion and local governments have more investment potential than enterprises is true, then what role do enterprise funds play in both investment expansion and consumption funds expansion?

Table 8.3 shows that state-owned enterprises' spending on fringe benefits and bonuses grew faster than their investment in fixed assets. If their consumption funds were added to their ''off-account'' actual expenditures upon fringe benefits and bonus, and if local governments' miscellaneous apportionments were deducted from their investment, then a new proportion would prove all the more clearly that enterprises tended to spend their own funds more on increasing consumption funds than on increasing investment.

The following is a more detailed account of the consumption funds swelling. The extrabudgetary funds of the twenty-three cities' administrative organizations and institutions increased by 84.8 percent from 1983 to 1984, and they spent more money on fringe benefits and bonuses than enterprises. Therefore, they constitute a factor that should not be ignored when it comes to discussing how to control consumption funds (see table 8.4).

The fact that state-owned enterprises use their funds to increase consumption

Table 8.5

Size of Industrial Enterprises

Size Grade (No. of Workers)	China 1982	Britain 1979	U.S.A. 1977	Korea 1981	Japan 1972	India 1976–77	Yugoslavia 1981	Hungary 1981
5–33	59.2	65.2	56.4	70.6	80.2	51.7	6.6	2.2
33–75	19.5	15.7	20.3	14.4	10.7	85.3	15.8	4.8
75–189	12.2	10.8	12.4	9.2	6.1	7.8	32.1	18.7
189–243	8.5	1.4	3.8	1.5	0.8	0.8	12.0	9.2
243 +	0.6	6.9	7.1	4.3	2.2	4.4	33.5	65.1

funds does not mean that their investment behavior is completely reasonable. According to the survey of twenty-three cities, a serious problem in investment is that enterprises spend money on small projects. The World Bank China Economic Inspection Delegation once made a comparison between the size of China's industrial enterprises and that of other countries (see table 8.5). In terms of size, China's industrial enterprises rank as the smallest in the world.

Compared with most East European countries, China's large enterprises make up only a small proportion; whereas compared with most market economies, China lacks a sound capital market and cooperative activities among enterprises. Our country lacks both these methods of concentrating investment for economic growth. Of the randomly sampled 429 enterprises in the twenty-three cities, large and medium-sized ones make up 57 percent, a percentage far higher than the national average. However, the profits they retained were, on the average, only 1.53 million yuan, of which the portion they retained for production came to only 500,000 yuan on the average. Allowing for the portion retained by the large and medium-sized enterprises, the profits retained by the small enterprises was, on the average, 260,000 yuan, of which the portion they kept for production was only 100,000 yuan on the average. In aggregate, extrabudgetary funds are matching budgeted funds. Individually speaking, most enterprises find themselves short of production funds. They often have no money for needed technical renovation, much less to build new projects or make big expansions. As a result, they can only afford to do small things with limited money, which leads to fragmented investment.

2. Countermeasures

The above analysis of the present situation shows that a wide range of countermeasures is necessary, such as strictly controlling the scope of credit, hardening the enterprises' constraint of loan repayment, curbing local governments from conducting investment and raising funds, controlling the growth of enterprises' consumption funds, and solving the problem of fragmented investment by enterprises. However, in the past two cycles of investment expansion, local governments have been one of the major contributors. Therefore, this discussion of countermeasures will center on the problem of how to rationalize the behavior of local governments.

2.1. Innate Characteristics of Local Governments' Behavior

Western economists advocate that in a multilayer governmental organization, the power of overall balance will naturally decline from the top to the bottom, while economic restrictions should become stronger and stronger. The same is true of China's multilayer economic management. Needless to say, ours has its own peculiarities because of its system of ownership and economic management. To simplify the issue, we only make a horizontal comparison between the behavior of local governments, on the one side, and the behavior of the central government and enterprises, on the other.

Local governments have advantages in both economic restriction and overall balance. In comparison with the central government, local governments must closely heed the economic demands of their localities and the interests of their people in building projects, raising funds, and conducting other activities. They must more closely follow the principle of "from the people, to the people." They must seriously consider their localities' economic benefits and thus are all the more closely supervised from every quarter in their localities. Local governments are superior to the central government in monitoring economic performance. The economic reform aimed at delegating the central government's financial power to its local counterparts is intended to cancel the system of centralized management, and yet local governments have more power to monitor their economic performance. At the same time, in comparison with enterprises, local governments have the power to concentrate their localities' human and financial resources for special construction and other public facilities. Our enterprises have less experience in the market, and there is a distorted picture of price and other economic relations. Therefore, enterprises are all the more liable to develop blindly. At the same time, the central government's macroeconomic policies have to be implemented by local governments; there would be no way to develop the product market, capital market, and labor market. Local governments should strengthen, not weaken, their advantages shown in overall balance.

On the other hand, local governments have disadvantages in both economic restriction and overall balance. Compared with enterprises, a management organization at the lower level, local governments are less subject to the restriction of economic efficiency, a drawback shared by the central government. Their activities are hardly influenced by any change in price, labor force, the cost of raw and semifinished materials, or the interest rate. To fulfill their purpose, they can use their political might to go beyond the law of the market. This peculiar behavior, if allowed to go unchecked, may lead local governments to ignore the market economy and eventually to violate completely the laws of economic development. At the same time, local governments are apt to go after their own development without considering the general picture of the country as a whole, culminating in a regional separation. Also, they are apt to contend for more projects and more funds out of consideration for their own politicoeconomic interests, which might be brought about by high speed development. As a result, macroeconomic activities might become unbalanced. In comparison with the central government, local governments share the same drawbacks as enterprises.

This characteristic of local government behavior did not suddenly appear in the current economic reform. It is a built-in characteristic of our country's multilayer economic management, merely changing form or degree as time goes on. A good grasp of this peculiarity will enable us to avoid deviation when making countermeasures.

2.2. How To Form Triangular Restriction Relations

Between two parties, the most stable and rational relationships will exist when one party restricts and is restricted by the other. Among three parties, the most stable and rational relation requires that each restricts and is restricted by the other two. An ideal pattern in this case is to establish a triangular relationship of restrictions between local governments, as shown below.

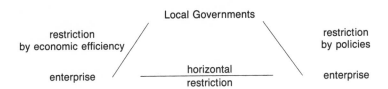

In this triangular structure, there are the following aspects.

Horizontal restriction between enterprises. There have been few horizontal connections between enterprises in our country's economic activities. Therefore, there has been almost no horizontal restriction between them for quite a long time. The economic reform in recent years has brought about an increase in activity between enterprises, and the appearance of various forms of cooperation, in commercial credits, credit investment, stock investment, and in labor, equipment, and technology. As a result, horizontal restriction caused by horizontal connections has been strengthened at a time when the fiscal constraint and credit constraint still remain soft. Compared with vertical restriction, this horizontal restriction is notable for adherence to contracts, repaying loans, raising efficiency, and distributing benefits. When the "father and son" aspect of the relationship between the state and enterprises dominates and the vertical restriction fails to be appropriately strict, the development of horizontal restriction helps improve enterprises' behavior. More importantly, horizontal connections may help collect small sums of money for some big projects. When the power to make decisions about investment remains scattered in the hands of enterprises or others, horizontal connections may help eliminate the side effects brought about by transforming the old defect-fraught economic system of centralized management and contribute to the invigoration of the economy.

Local governments' restriction to enterprises through policies. The development of horizontal connections between enterprises provides a venue for local governments to exercise indirect management. Local governments can make the most of their strong points to encourage, assist, guide, or control horizontal activities between enterprises through industrial policies, tax and subsidy policies, and laws and regulations. Many localities have accumulated experiences in guiding horizontal connections between enterprises. However, governments at various levels have had a perfect command of direct management over the past several decades. When policies were made, it was quite natural to follow the formula that excessive growth of extrabudgetary investment precipitates control of extrabudgetary funds, which precipitates local governments' direct control of enterprises' funds. It is inconceivable to change direct management of the funds into indirect management overnight. However, it would be even more absurd to curb the development of indirect management. "Now on and then off" will never make any progress in economic reform.

Horizontal investments have opened up vast prospects for enterprises. Rising prices for imports and raw materials, and the increased cost of funds, have caused an increase in enterprises' investment cost, which may indirectly curb enterprises from increasing their consumption funds. Of all the factors contributing to the swelling of consumption funds, local governments should not only eliminate those irrational factors shown in primary distribution, but should also exert themselves with regard to how to use consumption funds in the field of redistribution. Such measures as levying taxes, encouraging bank savings, and establishing social security will help cut off the present links between consumption funds and current consumption, so that wage hikes will not change into consumption expansion overnight. In particular, the establishment of a social security system will create conditions for a freely flowing labor force and for a rational mechanism in which surplus labor will curtail a rise in the price of labor.

Enterprises' economic restriction to local government. In the old economic system, local governments, as agents of the central government, directly controlled the management of enterprises. Under the economic reform, they have become economically even more powerful, getting money from both unbudgeted and budgeted funds as well as from various apportionments and fund-raising efforts. Therefore, it is now necessary to foster a force restricting local governments and improving their behavior.

Horizontal activities or organizations among enterprises are a collective force. They can establish a dialogue relationship with local governments. Local governments are not given the power to transfer enterprises' funds directly, and they do not have the need to provide funds to enterprises gratis or at low interest. The only means they can use to bring pressure to bear upon enterprises is through policies. Alliances among enterprises based on common economic interests will contribute to gradually improving the old functions of local governments.

In short, local governments should develop and strengthen their restriction to enterprises through policies, support horizontal activities between enterprises, and gradually promote the concentration of enterprises' funds on investment. They should not be given the power to control directly the unbudgeted income of enterprises so that their ability boundlessly to expand the scope of investment will be curbed. As for enterprises, they should be made to improve gradually their behavior through horizontal restriction and through policy restriction by local governments, and they should continue as a restriction force toward local governments while maintaining and developing their own interests.

2.3. Local Governments' Role in NonBank Funding

The so-called management of extrabudgetary funds should be conducted in two areas. First, we should straighten up prices and taxation and follow hard-and-fast regulations in enterprise accounting, so as to squeeze out these sources of extrabudgetary funds and beef up the state budget. Second, let local governments play their proper role in arranging the funding for the fulfillment of the economic plan. This subreport will discuss the second aspect.

Directly concentrate and use enterprises' funds. Fiscal departments of some provinces and municipalities have set up special accounts for enterprises' extrabudgetary funds, so that local governments can directly use them or grant them as low-interest capital of "trust and investment companies" to other organizations. In addition, local governments across the country have made many apportionments and conducted rigid fund-raising drives, as discussed earlier. Money is collected mandatorily, gratis or at low interest, by the administrative decree of local governments. Local governments do not need to consider the economic results of the money. The same is true of their use of budgeted funds. This mandatory behavior creates financial conditions for local governments to expand their investment. On the other hand, local governments are money-hungry for the construction of public, cultural, educational, and other service facilities. Therefore, the way to solve the problem is to put budgeted and extrabudgetary funds into unified use and divide taxes with the central government according to each related function. Efforts should be made to standardize measures for the recovery of extrabudgetary funds, such as to match up the funds of energy and transportation with the funds apportioned or mandatorily raised for the construction of power stations and roads and to match up the funds of urban construction with the funds apportioned or mandatorily raised for that purpose. Apart from the procedures of budgeted funds that local governments should be responsible for, they should not be given the power directly to control enterprises' funds. To keep a clear account can restrict local governments from expanding investment and reduce the burden of enterprises.

Directly participate in the high-price funds market. The "high-price funds market" refers to those nonbank funds exchanged at an interest rate higher than that of banks, but not to the black funds market in which the interest rate is more than 100 percent. Some local governments absorb enterprises' and individuals' funds through such means as setting up joint-stock companies to handle commercial housing, establishing development companies to grant loans at high interest rates, or issuing local debentures for the construction of some projects. In this market, money is collected voluntarily and at high interest by the direct administration of local governments. When the supply of funds falls short of the demand for them and the bank system still remains fossilized, the upshot is that local government directly collects some funds at high interest rates to build some profitable projects with quick economic returns. A feasible future plan is gradually to establish a local bank system and to integrate it into the macrocredit control system as soon as possible.

Indirectly support the high-interest funds market. At present, the flow of funds among enterprises is very active, in the form of commercial credit, or enterprise debenture, compensatory management, or profit sharing. The horizontal flow of funds has become a major way to maintain enterprise alliances or amalgamations. But the support of government is called for with regard to matching up enterprises for that purpose. The support is also called for in signing contracts, in avoiding double taxation, in defining principles for profit and dividend sharing, and in providing industrial policies as well. Apart from directly participating in the funds flow, many localities have set up intermediate, nongovernmental, nonbank organizations that run any risk to pool funds scattered in the hands of small collectives and individuals—funds that banks find hard to collect. No doubt, these nongovernmental organizations should also be integrated into the macrocredit control system, for example, by setting a ceiling on the interest rate and stipulating bankruptcy regulations. In comparison with the former two activities, in this case, the money is collected voluntarily and at high interest rates by the indirect regulation of local governments.

Of course, our country's major financial channels are still its fiscal and banking systems. If the reform of these two systems fails, macrocredit control will not be achieved. Unless the poor efficiency of our low-interest official funds is changed for the better, it will be difficult to equilibrate the supply and demand for funds. But it should be noted that right now there is already a double-track interest rate system for funds, and an active high-price funds market, and local governments have already participated in the high-price funds market directly or indirectly. Therefore, the only thing we can do is to face the situation squarely and strengthen our management. If the management works, a rational and effective way will be found for the use of extrabudgetary funds.

These three kinds of behavior of local governments in nonbank funding should be evaluated from two angles: overall balance and economic restriction. It often happens that when overall balance is emphasized, the horizontal flow of funds is hindered and local governments' vertical control is restored. On the other hand, when economic restriction is needed, local governments' rational behavior is ignored. This way of thinking, like ''refusing food for fear of choking,'' does great harm to our economic policy-making. Therefore, it can be said that the principle for managing extrabudgetary funds should be to free ourselves from the narrower concept of managing extrabudgetary funds.

IV
SOLUTIONS

Opening the Labor
and Capital Markets

The reform wing represented by the Chinese Economic System Reform Research Institute strongly believes that the inflationary pressures chronicled in part III have one underlying solution: opening up markets in China for factors of production. In agriculture, the market for land would be important. In urban China, two other factors of production are paramount: labor and capital. Other Chinese economists argue that China should first complete the process of moving to a market system in the allocation of consumer and producer goods. But the members of CESRRI recommend a swift and decisive transition to markets in labor and capital. Their analysis, in rough form, goes as follows. The underlying source of wage inflation is not labor shortage—on the contrary, China is a labor-surplus economy. But under the iron ricebowl system of complete job security and zero labor mobility, steel workers envious of rising wages in the coal industry are prevented from moving in that direction (a movement which, in addition to benefitting workers who move, would also dampen the wage inflation in coal). When they turn to their own enterprise for matching wage hikes, their demands would be easier to resist if managers could say, "You're free to pursue a higher wage in coal." Thus the basic instrument for controlling wage inflation must be labor competition.

The other main source of inflationary pressure, according to this analysis, is inefficient use of capital. Managers use existing capital stock in unproductive ways. Local governments undertake irresponsible investment projects, with low or negative rates of return. The necessary instrument to correct that situation is the threat of bankruptcy. Managers and workers must recognize the link between their use of enterprise assets and their own fortunes. Those whose enthusiasm for investment pushes China's budget into the red must temper that enthusiasm with the need to break even. But bankruptcy presupposes a mechanism for valuing capital assets: a capital market, which would apply a "market test" to the effectiveness with which a particular enterprise's assets are being used.

The first two chapters in part IV ask: how would Chinese citizens react to a move to a free labor market? The first chapter is based on a five-city survey of worker attitudes. The survey responses show that younger Chinese workers would like very much to have the freedom to find their initial or subsequent jobs on their own, that is, they would welcome the creation of a free labor market. But at the same time, they value the security provided by the present system. The authors argue that creation of labor markets, labor mobility, and "right to fire" must be accompanied by a variety of social security, welfare, and unemployment provisions.

In the second chapter, Bai Nanfeng presents in detail and crosstabulates responses to a questionnaire distributed to the readers of *China Youth*. Ninety-one percent of the respondents were aged 16–30; 70 percent were male; 20 percent were college graduates. Bai's most important finding is that these respondents' career aspirations hinge more on idealism than on avarice.

For example, respondents placed "self-employment" first in a ranking of career alternatives based on anticipated income, and high school teaching tenth. But when asked about their own job preferences, they placed high school teaching fifth and self-employment eighth. The reason: high school teaching would satisfy the respondents' other, more altruistic needs.

In perhaps the most poignant question in this survey, respondents were asked: "Imagine a place where wages are high and people have more of a chance to give full play to their ability and enhance their social status, but the work is extremely unstable and very demanding, competition is cutthroat, and prices fluctuate from time to time. Would you wish to live there?" The response: "yes" from 64 percent; "no" from 13 percent; 23 percent "uncertain." The author shows the correlation between these responses and age, sex, and education.

In the final chapter, we move to the capital market. The authors identify two aspects of the investment dilemma: a problem of investment pattern and a problem of aggregate level of investment. Too much is being invested in the consumer goods industry rather than producer goods and key infrastructure, and the typical investment project is of an inefficiently small scale. In addition, excessive aggregate investment—due to soft budget constraints on enterprises and excessive credit expansion—is generating inflationary pressure. Hoping to resolve these problems while preserving reform measures, the authors propose a two-track financial system. The national banking system would retain or even strengthen planned control over credit and pursue a tight money policy; but a nonbank loanable funds market would be developed, through which enterprises and local governments could pool funds. (This sort of market has in fact begun to develop in China already.) This would permit an increase in the scale of locally initiated investment projects. Section 3 presents twelve pages of cogent policy proposals.

The proper functioning of a capital market presupposes that ownership of capital is clarified. But in fact, it is not at all clear who owns China's industrial capital stock (or financial capital, for that matter). That ambiguity lies at the root of the motivational problems that have made urban reform so much more difficult than rural reform. This core problem—not addressed by these authors—will continue to play the part of Banquo's ghost in the ongoing drama of economic reform in China.

From Iron Ricebowls to Labor Markets: Reforming the Social Security System

Huang Xiaojing and Yang Xiao

Abstract: China's current social security system works, in essence, through an employment security system. The goals of social welfare and security are achieved to a large degree through the instrument of employment. This type of social security system inevitably transforms the welfare and security provided through redistribution of the national income into part of the cost of labor. When consumption funds expand because of excessive wage increases, this three-in-one system causes an additional swelling of consumption.

Another consequence of the three-in-one system is its guarantee of lifetime employment with the same enterprise. This cuts the link between supply and demand for labor. It leads to the "structural unemployment among the employed" (meaning jobholders who have no work to do because of the defective employment structure).

We maintain that social security reform should separate employment from welfare and security. On the one hand, we must break down all barriers and introduce the market mechanism to regulate wage levels and labor flows. At the same time, we must repackage welfare benefits by exchanging employment security for an income floor and/or "unemployment security." That is, such social programs as retirement pay, medical care, and unemployment compensation should be worked out and implemented through redistributing national income, so as to avoid the widening of income disparities that might occur when labor market regulation is introduced.

1. The Employment Security System and Consumption

The employment security system is inherently related to swelling consumption. If this interrelationship between them is overlooked and our policy is only aimed at

This study is a collective work. Wang Xiaoqiang and Yang Guansan of this institute took part in the work from beginning to end. During its actual writing, Bai Nanfeng generously shared with us his invaluable ideas. Sociologists and many others at Beijing University and Nankai University participated in conducting this survey. We also wish to express our sincere thanks to the leading comrades and others of Beijing and Shashi for their kind help in our work.

controlling total consumption, a breakaway from the old model will be impossible.

1.1. Background

China's social security system is actually not a "social" system. There is no national system covering retirement pensions or medical care. Instead, China's social security system is largely realized by means of employment. Anyone will have welfare benefits and security so long as he or she gets a job. Peasants fall completely outside this welfare net. In addition, collective enterprises offer fewer benefits than state enterprises. Tight employment barriers in all areas of the urban economic structure bar outsiders while guaranteeing employed urban residents a sort of "professional rent." By our rough estimate, urban workers' income from wages and benefits in 1984 totalled 160 billion yuan, of which wages accounted for 63 percent and the income from other sources 37 percent. In the United States the workers' income in addition to their wages accounts for only 27 percent of their total earnings; 20 percent in Britain; 13 percent in Japan; and 28 percent in Hungary. From 1979 to 1983, government spending on various welfare programs and subsidies to the workers increased by 21 percent annually, far exceeding the 11 percent increase in wages. If all welfare expenses are counted in labor cost, the labor cost in our country is by far higher than most people think, since such expenses make up 13 percent of the total labor cost. (For details see part II, Xia Xiaojun et al.)

Our survey, "Public Reaction to Reform of the Social Security System," shows an increasingly strong desire on the part of the people to earn a large income. Among five goals—reputation, income, welfare, security, and freedom—most people chose income. (Income scored 1.98, welfare 1.37, security 0.87, reputation 0.81, and freedom 0.78.) Yet the current employment system does not allow people to satisfy their desire for a good income by competing for good jobs or displaying excellent working ability. They can realize their expectations only by pressing their employer for additional wage increases and bonuses.

The most serious problem in the area of welfare and insurance today is that enterprises have overspent on workers' retirement pensions and medical care fees. Retirees in China now number 14 million, or about 15 percent of the country's total employed population. The total amount of the retirement pension in 1984 exceeded 10 billion yuan, or 10 percent of the country's total payroll, and the figure is as high as 30 percent for some regions and industries. With more and more workers preparing to retire, the present pension system, which requires that pensions be calculated as an item outside the business expenses of the enterprises, will increasingly become a heavy burden on the enterprises. It will also cause friction between the retired workers and those still employed.

China's population will be rapidly aging in the next fifteen years. According to some projections, by the year 2000 as many as forty million workers will retire on a pension totalling forty billion yuan. The problem will grow increasingly acute if the retirement pension or insurance system is not reformed and insurance funds are not set up before the employees reach their retiring age. So, to solve this problem, it is necessary to change the ineffective insurance system, siphon off part of consumption, and establish social security funds.

One result of economic reform and readjustment in industrial structure was a disharmony in the employment structure, reflected in the redundant personnel in some industries or trades. Under the impact of structural change, technological advance, and other factors, some industries or trades are overstaffed while others are understaffed. Our survey of factory directors suggests that there are more understaffed industries than overstaffed ones. For these 400 enterprises, while there was a severe shortage of skilled workers, there was a surplus of auxiliary employees. According to our investigations, in some cities, redundant personnel make up approximately 15–20 percent of the total number of employees. If this holds true for other cities, then at least an estimated fifteen million workers in the whole country need to switch jobs. This is a very serious problem, yet it has not attracted as much public attention as the unemployment issue in the 1970s, simply because it is an "employment problem." The "unemployment crisis" that threatens social stability causes more widespread concern than redundant enterprise personnel, which debilitates the vigor and efficiency of enterprises.

Some enterprises are short of manpower, while others have redundant personnel. The contradiction is reflected mainly in the disproportionate numbers of employees of different sexes, of skilled and unskilled workers, and of frontline and secondary workers. The practice of "son succeeding to father's job" has led and is still leading to gross disproportion in the number of employees of different sexes. Take the city of Chongqing for example. Female workers make up 38.7 percent of the city's total employed population and 40 percent of the entire industrial work force. The Chongqing Water Transport Company had 100 women workers in 1966, but now it has 1,108, a tenfold increase, and most of them are redundant.

The disproportion is also striking with respect to the different technical qualifications of the workers. Because job training has been overlooked for years in the country, there are now far fewer professional or skilled workers than ordinary laborers with educational attainments at or below the junior middle school level. An investigation into 550 enterprises in Beijing found that they have a mere 9 percent professional or skilled workers, while the figure for ordinary workers is as high as 62 percent. Correspondingly, low-grade (grades 1–3) workers account for 58 percent of the total and high-grade workers, 5 percent. Facts prove that the job security system does not stimulate workers to try to improve their skill level. They are far more likely to pressure the enterprise for higher wages and more welfare benefits.

As to the problem that some industries or trades go shorthanded while others have redundant people, the main cause lies in the employment barriers that interrupt the flow of labor between different industries, or between enterprises of different ownerships. Generally speaking, China is short of technical personnel, but the shortage has been aggravated by the long-standing practice of assigning jobs to all college graduates and technical personnel by the government. This practice has resulted in departmental barriers that block the transfer or flow of technical personnel. A survey revealed that 64 percent of the technical personnel asked about their attitude toward the flow of labor said they would like to have vocational and occupational choice, and that the majority of factory directors listed technicians as their most needed people. Some industries even suffer serious shortage of unskilled laborers, while actually there is an almost inexhaustible supply of them in the country. For instance, in Beijing such industries or trades as construction, coal mining, textiles, slaughtering, vegetable growing, and public transport have found it increasingly difficult to recruit workers in recent years. Obviously, the tight job security system has created a very peculiar phenomenon—scarce labor is not a rare commodity, and the labor that has an abundant source is in short supply. Facts show that the centralized assignment system cannot regulate supply and demand for labor; it only leads to a waste of labor instead.

2. Solving the Problems of the Urban Employment Structure

In solving the problems of the urban employment structure, two alternatives are open: Adjust the pattern of employment within each enterprise or via mergers, or do so through labor markets. The reform requires us to make a choice between these two.

Most enterprises have already shown a strong inclination to eliminate surplus employees. But they are pursuing this goal by moving employees around within the corporation, rather than by firing and hiring. This internal corporate readjustment not only fails to resolve the overemployment problem, but also cannot reduce the tendency toward wage inflation and excessive consumption. If enterprises rely instead on labor markets, it is highly likely that overemployment will disappear and overconsumption will come under control.

Most enterprises now permit individual employees to leave their jobs to pursue other businesses, "with their salaries suspended and their posts kept for them." The enterprises also transfer groups of workers to their subsidiary factories or service companies. These are the two main forms of labor transfer in China today. But these forms of labor transfer cannot solve the dilemma.

In our survey of the attitudes of workers and managers toward this issue, we found that 52.1 percent of the 1,341 people sampled said they would prefer choosing jobs by themselves, even at the risk of being unemployed, while 48 percent said they were in favor of being assigned jobs by the authorities, even though they were low-paying jobs, and did not want to run the risk of being unemployed. When they were asked to examine a hypothetical case—that a factory has 1,200 men but needs only 1,000, and that the employees (if they are to be laid off) and their dependents will be given some subsidies—78 percent of them said they would support the factory laying off the redundant workers. The figure was 82 percent for managers and 66 percent for workers.[1]

It can be seen clearly from the study that the majority of people, whether factory executives or workers, favor paring down the factory's work force by dismissing redundant personnel. This wish, however, is seldom translated into action. What most factories are now doing is to divert, through internal readjustments, their surplus labor to other businesses they own and run, mostly commerce and service trades. (According to a study, of the more than 1,000 enterprises set up by factories in Beijing since June 1984, 70 percent are tertiary industries, ranging from chicken raising to hotels.)

This sort of labor-force reorganization is a phenomenon that appeared only in recent years, as enterprises were given greater decision-making power. In some regards, it is similar to the household-based reorganization of agricultural production factors that occurred during the rural reform. By channeling their funds, idle equipment, and redundant personnel to the production of goods or services in great market demand, some enterprises did achieve some microeconomic efficiencies. For example, the Chongqing Water Transport Company, which had run at a loss for years, began making money in 1984 when it made efforts to diversify its operations. That year the company reduced its loss by 550,000 yuan, 40 percent of which—220,000 yuan—came from the income of the newly set up businesses. Under the stimulus of the market—rising energy prices, sluggish water transport business, and falling transport charges, for instance—such reorganization and diversification does help.

But these actions are sporadic. The same contradiction seen in the rural reform, the contradiction between the enlivened microeconomic activities and an imperfect macroeconomic regulating device, is now emerging in the urban reform. Therefore, the internal readjustment of labor structure by enterprises, which aims at guaranteeing employment to all people, has only limited effects. It cannot substitute for employment competition coupled with unemployment security.

2.1. Promote Employment Competition Among Unskilled Workers by Allowing Peasant Labor to Flow into Cities

The most salient feature of China's employment policy over the past thirty years is that, under the job security system, cities have always shut their doors to rural farm laborers. Now, when some city enterprises are trying to break down the wall separating cities from countryside, many people have come forward to sound a historic warning against any such attempts. But if a reform is to be introduced in the current employment system, it is necessary—and feasible and profitable—for cities to open their doors and create a unified labor market comprising both cities and countryside.

First, by opening their doors, cities can make full use of the inexhaustible supply of unskilled labor provided by the countryside, thereby enlarging the pool of job-seekers available to their enterprises. The state can also exploit the peasants' competition for employment to curb excessive consumption. In 1984, the average annual wage of an employee of rural enterprises was 620 yuan, 35 percent lower than those of an urban worker. This wage discrepancy is big enough to draw peasants to cities, even if the city enterprises do not guarantee them all the welfare benefits or job security enjoyed by current workers. So it is a practical proposition to let peasants obtain jobs in cities, to raise their wage income to an appropriate level, and to create a new social security and welfare program.

Second, allowing free urban-rural labor flows will also assist employment. The current employment strategy, which allows peasants to "leave their land but not their hometowns," may not be the best strategy for long-term rural development. By rough estimate, there will be 110 million peasants looking for nonagricultural jobs in the next fifteen years, and in the same period there will be 70 million more new laborers in the countryside waiting for jobs. This means there will be 12 million newly idle laborers in the rural areas each year. If the town and town enterprises are asked to employ all these laborers, it would be tantamount to asking them recklessly to increase investment and enlarge employment.

To open up a labor market should mean to create a nationwide, unified market. Already, urban technicians are drifting off to rural towns to help develop nonagricultural industries there, while farmers are flocking to cities to find jobs in construction, transport, and other industries. If the government can seize the opportunity provided by these new developments to abolish the job security system currently in force in cities and establish a social security system that promotes the flow of labor, then both urban and rural economies will be invigorated and will grow harmoniously.

2.2. Promote Employment Competition Among Highly Educated Workers

Comparatively speaking, in China those who have acquired higher education form only a very small proportion of the total work force. The 1982 census revealed that such people made up only 0.87 percent of the country's economically active population, while those with an education below junior middle school level accounted for 60 percent. By contrast, in the United States, the 1971 statistics showed that 23.3 percent of its adult population (beyond the age of twenty-five years) had received higher education. In Japan the figure was 5.5 percent in 1970, and in West Germany, 8.5 percent in 1970.

Scarce workers such as technicians should receive higher remuneration than ordinary workers, thus providing a stimulus to the latter to improve their ability. Under the equal pay system that exists in conjunction with the job security system, however, there is little if any difference between the wages of technicians and average workers. As our survey shows, most people recognize the defects of the wage system and consider it logical to raise technicians' wages.

Question 1: Who do you reckon will have a wage increase?

	Rank Order	*Synthetic Points*
Technicians	1	2.03
Managing personnel	2	1.57
Technical workers	3	0.93
Political workers	4	0.48
Nontechnical workers	5	0.12

Question 2: Who do you think will get higher pay?

	Rank Order	*Synthetic Points*
Technicians	1	1.97
Managing personnel	2	1.17
Technical workers	3	1.44
Nontechnical workers	4	0.31
Political workers	5	0.25

Labor mobility for highly educated persons should include skilled workers, both current and retired. A survey of thirty-eight enterprises in Chongqing reveals that 20 percent of their retired workers now have been "reemployed" in various trades throughout the city, forming "a stratum of high-priced elders," (so-called because these people are usually handsomely paid for their services). The free flow of these retired workers, who are actually not very old because of the low retiring age limits and who are well versed in their trades, has solved the shortage of skilled workers in some industries. Enterprises should rely on competitive pay to keep or attract people and should not intervene in the flow of labor by administrative means.

In short, only by encouraging employment competition and promoting the flow of labor through the creation of a labor market can the undesirable tendency among the people to compete for additional wage increases and bonuses be checked, the soaring consumption level arrested, the structural contradictions between labor supply and demand resolved, and surplus employment eliminated. Therefore, to create a labor market should be the guiding ideology of the employment security system reform; it should be our choice.

2.3. To Separate Employment from Welfare and Job Security, Build on Existing Precedents

Lifelong employment is the concrete embodiment of the principle of job security in China. Over 95 percent of the country's total employed population have permanent jobs. Once one is employed, he is free from worries that he might someday lose his job or be dismissed, and he is entitled to many welfare benefits. Lifelong employment had ruinous effects not only on enterprises' efforts to raise economic efficiency, but also on the incentive mechanism. In the extreme, welfare nurses lazy persons, making it extremely difficult for companies to stop some employees from going slow in their work.

Recent years have seen a contract labor system introduced in some places alongside the lifelong employment system. In 1984 there were more than 700,000 contract workers in the country. The contract labor system works through consultation among enterprises, labor service firms, and job hunters. The labor service firms assume the function of an employment agency, acting as an "intermediary" between labor supply and demand. The city of Shashi, Hubei province, had 3,000 contract workers at the end of 1984, 50 percent of whom were employed by the textile industry. These workers have made up for the industry's once serious labor shortage.

A labor contract may cover one year to twenty years, and during the term workers can quit their jobs and enterprises can dismiss them. The provisions for welfare and social security usually differ from those for lifetime workers. For instance, in Shashi, the employer must appropriate a sum of money equal to 18 percent of the total of the contract worker's wages to fund the worker's retirement pension, to match 2 percent contributed by the contract workers. This shows that the divorce of the employment mechanism from the welfare security mechanism can build on existing precedents.

Because the job security system and especially the lifelong employment policy remains unchanged, the "dual-track" employment experiment has met with many difficulties. In most cases, contract workers are asked to do the most taxing jobs, but their salaries and welfare are not much better than those of other workers doing less taxing work. The result is that many of them quit their jobs before their contracts expire. Some enterprises even transfer their redundant employees to their subsidiary enterprises through internal labor readjustments and then hire contract workers to fill up the vacancies created by the transfer. This practice has sharpened the contradiction between the two groups of workers. Moreover, urban labor departments still have doubts as to whether contract labor can serve as a fixed and universal form of employment. They fear that the "dual-track" system may someday be changed back to the "single-track" system, or that contract workers today may become permanent employees tomorrow (something that has happened before). Unless unemployment and dismissing workers by enterprises are no longer regarded as something forbidden, there can be little hope that contract labor will grow into a stable and standard practice.

3. Public Opinion Supports Such a Reform

Will the reform win the people's understanding and support? Does the society have the capacity to endure the reform? To find out we organized the "Survey of the Public Reactions to the Social Security System Reform."

The survey was conducted in Beijing, Shanghai, Chongqing, Xiamen, Shashi, and Harbin, using a random sample of 1,341 people of different occupations, ages, and family backgrounds. Questionnaires were sent to the sample population. The questions were formulated to find out their assessment of the current employment, welfare, and social security systems, their inclinations, and their attitudes toward risks involved in the reform. Our findings show that as reform goes deeper, public attitudes are undergoing tremendous changes. Most people, and especially young people and technicians, expressed understanding and support for the reform.

3.1. The Desire to Change Jobs

The survey found that workers of various types all expressed a strong desire for a change of job, or for free job choice. This can be seen clearly in their responses to the question, "Do you want to change your work?"

	Yes	Don't Care	No
Question 3: Do you want to change your work?	48.2%	27.7%	24.1%
Question 4: Do you want to change your place of work?	52.2%	26.3%	23.5%

The "guaranteed job" system has ensured everyone an equal opportunity to be employed, but it has failed to encourage people to make progress and bring their ability or special talents into full play. It does not offer people an equal opportunity for "super pay for super service."

A developing trend in many cities today is that large numbers of workers are drifting from the textile industries and public transport companies to jobs in the service sector. Obstruction of the flow by administrative measures has resulted in a slowdown staged by these workers. Some workers even have purposely stayed away from work without leave in order to get dismissed. All this stresses the need for a reasonable industrial policy to regulate and direct the flow of labor.

3.2. People's Openness to Bearing the Risks of Reform

To many people, the reform means a change from lifelong employment to impermanent employment under contracts, a change from riskless employment to possible unemployment. However, the majority of people have adopted a positive attitude toward this change, and their capacity to accept the risk of possible unemployment is much greater than many imagined.

Question 5: Alternative Answers

I would rather keep the "iron bowl" (a permanent job) than
have a wage increase.   36.5%
If I could get better pay, I'd like to be a contract worker.   52.6%
If my wages were to quadruple, I would accept the risk of
being out of a job.   11.7%

People know that it is not realistic for them to hope to have a wage increase without running a risk, or to get a benefit without paying a price. They are prepared to accept the risk involved in the reform.

Unemployment is almost unavoidable when a labor market is opened up. Unemployment may result from an enterprise's move to eliminate surplus employees, or simply from its bankruptcy. Whatever the case, unemployment will become a social problem. The success or failure of reform will largely hinge on how the masses view this development. Our survey revealed that most people supported enterprises firing redundant personnel and showed a positive attitude toward unemployment resulting from bankruptcy.

Question 6: Suppose a factory needs 1,000 people, but it has 1,200. Should it lay off the 200 surplus persons? (Condition: Relief aid will be given to the dismissed workers and their dependents.)

> It should.   71.8%
> It should not.   28.1

When the question was reformulated to include "you yourself" in the ranks of those who would be dismissed, 77 percent of the respondents said they would go and try to find work elsewhere, or open an individual business and become a self-employed laborer. Only 16.5 percent replied that they would "go to the leadership" for a settlement. Eighty-two percent of managers and 79 percent of technicians who were asked question 6 said they would approve the factory's move to lay off surplus employees. Sixty-nine percent of managers said they would go and try to find jobs elsewhere (question 7).

Question 7: If you were included in the 200 people, what would you do?

Go the the leadership for a settlement of the problem.	16.5%
Try to find employment elsewhere.	64.3
Leave the factory and open an individual business.	13.3
Would like to receive unemployment compensation.	5.8

Needless to say, only some enterprises in China are overstaffed, and society as a whole does not have an overemployment problem. The fact that so many people said they would seek employment elsewhere demonstrates that there exist other job opportunities in the country. Unemployment is but a means by which the labor force adjusts its structure. If rationally disposed, the entire labor force can be employed, or the goal of full employment can be attained. And, with a complementary social security program, there will be "secure unemployment."

Because there is not a "security mechanism"—unemployment insurance established for workers thrown out of employment by enterprises going bankrupt—how to handle enterprise bankruptcy remains a problem. In China today, if a factory closes down, all its people, from the director down to the workers, will continue to draw the same pay as usual from the factory, and all of them will be transferred to other enterprises by departments concerned. Such a "close-down" will not impose a true penalty on the bankrupt factory. No one will be held responsible for the bankruptcy. Rather, the punishment will fall on society at large or on other enterprises.

A sound policy toward bankruptcy should call for the establishment of a bankruptcy relief fund and ask the employees to find employment elsewhere after they draw a certain proportion from the fund as compensation. Our survey showed that the majority of people supported this idea. About 87 percent of the sample population said they would leave and seek jobs elsewhere, or try to open an individual business and become self-employed.

Question 8: What would you do if your factory closed down or declared bankruptcy?

Go to the leadership for a settlement of the problem.	10.0%
Seek employment elsewhere.	51.8
Try to open an individual business.	35.0
Do nothing but wait for the state to provide relief.	3.0

3.3. Attitudes Toward the Present Welfare System and Possible Reforms

Although it appears to embody the equality principle, China's current welfare system has actually caused low efficiency and inequality. The enormous amount of retirement pensions, the shocking wastefulness of the free medical service, and the associated problem of "welfare nursing lazy people" all have lowered the economic efficiency of the enterprises and increased the financial burden on the state.

The government's and enterprises' heavy spending on medical insurance funds and the serious waste of the funds already have aroused widespread dissatisfaction among the people. Fifty percent of the survey sample said the free medical service should be reformed, and 4 percent even went so far as to call for its abolition. Of the factory directors or managers who were asked the same question, 52 percent said they would accept a reform of the medical system. These general attitudes conform to the medical insurance reforms now going on in selected organizations.

A package of social security programs covering retirement, medical care, and unemployment insurance has to be drawn up before employment and welfare can be disconnected from one another. With respect to unemployment insurance, our survey showed that the great majority—74.8 percent—do not want to depend entirely on the state; instead, they said they would like to participate in new social security programs. A new social security system should, through a reform of the fiscal and financial structures, combine social programs financed by the government and insurance funds established by enterprises (and individuals). That is, the state offers basic social security to a large section of the citizens, thereby realizing the principle of equality, while enterprises (and individuals) set up their insurance funds and attract talented people so as to raise their efficiency. Such a social security system will win the approval of the people.

Question 9: How can unemployment insurance best be implemented?

Both enterprises and individual employees make contributions to an insurance fund.	48.2%
People insure themselves against unemployment (on condition that their income increase).	26.2
The state provides the insurance.	24.7

3.4. The Progressive Attitudes of Younger Respondents

One basic fact of China's labor force is that while it is aging as a whole, it has a large group of relatively young members. As the 1982 census showed, members of the 16–35 age group accounted for approximately 60 percent of the nation's economically active population. A question thus arises: Should the job security system be oriented to the needs of the 14 million older workers who are going to retire soon, or the needs of the young people who are going to be the main labor force in the future? Our survey showed that youths, more than any other group of the population, tend to support establishing a labor market and carrying out the welfare system reform. Their ideas are far in advance of the times.

More than 50 percent of the young people surveyed expressed their willingness to choose jobs by themselves at their own risk, a percentage much higher than other age groups. The survey finding also showed that people over forty tended to be more conservative in this respect, and the more advanced their age, the more conservative their attitude.

Such being the case, the government must adopt a phased approach to reforming the employment and welfare systems, trying to avoid hurting too much those people who have a "vested interest" in the existing economic arrangements. There should be a "transitional period" of fifteen to twenty years. During this period, first the young people and then the older people (over forty) are given the freedom to choose their job at their own risk, while their wages increase substantially and social insurance funds are established. The important thing is to seize the opportunity and start the transition right now.

4. Core Recommendation: Create Unemployment Compensation and an Income Floor

The employment security system is the cause of swelling consumption and over-employment. The object of reforming the system that incorporates employment, welfare, and security is to rationalize the employment structure and to rid the nation of the plague that consumption funds inflate the moment administrative controls are lifted.

To achieve this object, we have to resolve many difficult issues, including a decision on what form and content the labor market should have. But the most important thing is to select a proper point at which a breakthrough can be made, thereby pushing forward the whole reform.

On the basis of the above analysis, we believe that to replace employment security with unemployment security (implying an income floor and temporary unemployment benefits) will be a breakthrough point in reform of the whole employment system.

If the employment system is to be made more elastic, then some unemployment will be unavoidable. It is imperative to create a labor market to regulate supply and demand for labor by competition, allowing casual unemployment among some unemployed reserve. Such a breakthrough will not necessarily create an enormous unemployed reserve. On the contrary, it will create more job opportunities as improvements in industrial structure are gradually made.

If at the same time we assure social security, it is possible to reduce the shock that might be caused by unemployment. If unemployment compensation funds are established and if there are special organizations to help those who have been thrown out of work find new jobs, then the now "abnormal" practice of enterprises paring down their work force will be viewed as "normal." Up to now the

Table 9.1

Answers Chosen to Various Questions, by Age Group

Answer	Age		
	20–35	36–40	41–45 +
1. I want to choose my job and am not afraid of being unemployed.	61	16.4	7
2. The factory should lay off surplus employees.	56.5	18.3	8.8
3. If dismissed, I would find work elsewhere.	57.5	26.9	15.8
4. Both enterprises and individual employees should make contributions to an unemployment fund.	53.6	27.8	18.3
5. Because lifelong employment is defective, it should be reformed.	55.5	28.6	15.4
6. If my wages were to quadruple, I would accept the risk of being unemployed.	66.5	25.0	8.6

social security system reform going on in the country has not gone beyond the limits of the old models. As a result, the entire reform has one link missing. Considering the demand of the ongoing reform, we think that only by introducing a new social security system along with a labor market can the missing link be found and the reform be made complete.

We recommend: During the period of the Seventh Five-Year Plan (1986–1990), the social security system reform should focus on the establishment of unemployment compensation funds and an ''unemployment security'' system. Retirement insurance and medical care should be considered and designed in the context of the labor market.

To fulfill this task, social security legislation, including a law on unemployment compensation, should be enacted as soon as possible. These laws should be enforced on a trial basis in some cities, and then, after they are perfected, enforced throughout the country. This reform, like the reform in the area of bankruptcy, will be of overall importance to both the present and future development.

10

Young People's Attitudes and Aspirations: Will They Welcome Reform?

Bai Nanfeng

Reform will bring changes to our social and economic lives. Some things that people have taken for granted will disappear gradually, giving way to those that are strange to people. What attitude will people, in particular youth, take toward these changes? To find the answers we designed a simple questionnaire, which was published in *China Youth*, no. 6 (1985).

Questionnaires returned totaled 76,000, more than we anticipated. To shorten the time needed to process them, we took samples from various provinces, municipalities, and autonomous regions, carefully stratified in accordance with the proportion of their population in the national population. This sample totaled 3,340.

Regional Distribution. Questionnaires were returned from 29 provinces, municipalities, and autonomous regions. Among them, 28.2 percent came from the countryside, 41.6 percent from small cities, 9.2 percent from medium-sized cities each with a population of 500,000–1 million, and 21 percent from large cities each with a population of more than 1 million.

Occupation. Of the people who returned the questionnaire, workers account for 21.7 percent; peasants, 4.5 percent; people involved in commerce and service trades, 5.7 percent; cadres from administrations and institutions, 21.8 percent, nongovernmental enterprises, 12 percent; middle and primary school teachers, 8.1 percent; people involved in other special fields (such as culture and education, science and technology, and hygiene), 7.3 percent; university and graduate students, 6.6 percent; individual laborers for 0.5 percent; and unemployed youths and middle school students, 9.8 percent.

This report is the result of the investigation we conducted with China Youth magazine. People involved in the work include Bai Nanfeng and Huang Xiaojing from the China Economic System Reform Research Institute, Zhang Fan from China People's University, and Cui Weide from China Youth. Throughout the investigation, we received energetic support and help from Yan Yonggong of China People's University.

Age. People 15 and below account for 1.2 percent; 16–20, 23.1 percent; 21–25, 49.7 percent; 26–30, 18.5 percent; 31–35, 4.6 percent, and 36 and above, 2.9 percent. Among them, those who are between 18 and 28 account for 80.1 percent. The youngest is 13 years old, the oldest is 70 years old, and the average age is 23.6.

Sex. Males account for 69.6 percent and females for 30.4 percent.

Education. People with primary school education account for 0.6 percent; middle school education, 17.7 percent; senior middle school or special or technical secondary school education, 61.2 percent; and college or university education, 20.4 percent. Not one of them is illiterate.

Two further points must be explained: First, army members are not included in the occupations analysis, out of technical considerations. For the same reason, university students, graduate students, youth waiting for jobs, and middle school students are included in "Occupations." Second, as the questionnaire was published in a youth magazine and not according to a sampling scheme worked out beforehand in the light of, among others, residential places, occupations, ages, sexes, and educational level, samples taken are unavoidably not impartial. For example, 91.3 percent of the people who returned the questionnaire are between 16 and 30 years old, and their educational level is much higher than the average of the society. Moreover, the bulk of them are readers of *China Youth* magazine, who hold a comparatively positive attitude toward life. Therefore, strictly speaking, our analysis of the results applies only to this group and should not be extended to the whole society. For convenience in writing, however, we use the term "society" or "whole society" occasionally when explaining the general situation in the following analysis.

1. Ranking Different Occupations

1.1. Assessment of Occupations' Economic Rewards

What is the economic status of various occupations in the mind of the public? In the questionnaire, we asked people to arrange various occupations in order of economic rewards. Table 10.1 shows the results. The individual laborers come out first, and middle and primary school teachers are placed second from the bottom, with the young job-waiters (waiting for job assignments) bringing up the rear.

As table 10.2 shows, a ranking based on perceived social status of the occupation is very different. University and graduate students come out first and individual laborers take ninth place, followed by peasants. The young job-waiters still bring up the rear.

Tables 10.3 and 10.4 show the way in which people in each occupation ranked their own and others' economic and social positions. Table 10.3 shows that most people believe that their own economic position is low. Except for individual laborers, personnel in special fields, middle and primary school teachers, and

Table 10.1
Prospective Occupations Ranked by Economic Rewards

Occupation	Comprehensive Class	Order
Individual laborers (IL)	10.10	1
Enterprise cadres and technical personnel (ECATP)	7.01	2
Commercial and service trade people (CASTP)	6.89	3
Nongovernmental enterprise people (NGEP)	6.31	4
Peasants (P)	6.27	5
Workers (W)	6.00	6
Administration and institution cadres (AAIC)	5.91	7
People in special fields (PISF)	5.86	8
University and graduate students (UAGS)	4.95	9
Middle and primary school teachers (MAPST)	4.38	10
Young job-waiters (YJW)	1.87	11

Table 10.2
Prospective Occupations Ranked by Social Status

Occupations	Comprehensive Class	Order
University and graduate students	10.31	1
Administration and institution cadres	8.68	2
People in special fields	8.55	3
Enterprise cadres and technical personnel	8.01	4
Middle and primary school teachers	7.15	5
Commercial and service trade people	5.32	6
Workers	5.24	7
Nongovernmental enterprise people	4.28	8
Individual laborers	4.05	9
Peasants	2.56	10
Young job-waiters	1.51	11

young job-waiters, the other seven occupations' self- evaluation is lower than the ranking given by society as a whole. In general, individual laborers take first place and the young job-waiters bring up the rear.

Unlike the evaluation of the economic status, table 10.4 shows that various occupations' evaluation of their own social status is either equal to or close to the social evaluation (with a difference of only one class), including seven that equal the social evaluation, one that is higher, and three that are lower. Compared with table 10.2, the self-evaluation of various occupations is generally relatively high.

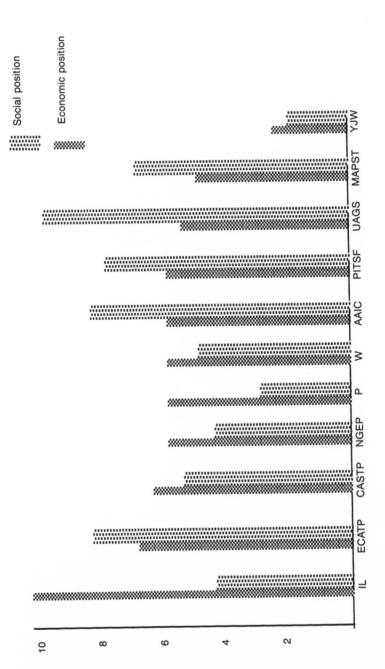

Figure 10.1

Economic and Social Position

Table 10.3

Economic Ranking (Breakdown by Evaluator Occupation)

Evaluator Occupation	IL	ECATP	CASTP	NGEP	P	W	AAIC	PITSF	UAGS	MAPST	YJW
IL	1	1	1	1	1	1	1	1	1	1	1
ECATP	3	8	2	2	2	2	2	4	2	2	2
CASTP	2	2	10	4	3	4	3	2	3	3	5
NGEP	5	3	6	8	6	7	4	5	5	5	8
P	10	4	3	10	9	3	7	6	7	8	3
W	8	7	7	6	5	10	5	3	4	4	6
AAIC	4	5	4	3	4	5	10	7	6	6	4
PISF	6	6	5	5	7	6	6	8	8	7	7
UAGS	9	10	8	7	8	8	8	10	10	9	9
MAPST	7	9	9	9	10	9	9	9	9	10	10
YJW	11	11	11	11	11	11	11	11	11	11	11

Table 10.4

Social Position (Breakdown by Evaluator Occupation)

Evaluator Occupation	UAGS	AAIC	PITSF	ECATP	MAPST	CASRP	W	NGEP	IL	P	WJW
UAGS	1	1	1	1	1	1	1	1	1	1	1
AAIC	2	3	3	2	2	2	2	2	2	2	2
PISF	3	2	2	3	4	3	3	4	3	3	4
ECATP	4	4	4	4	3	4	4	3	4	4	3
MAPST	5	5	5	5	5	5	5	5	5	5	5
CASTP	7	7	6	7	9	7	6	6	6	6	6
W	6	6	7	6	6	6	7	7	7	7	7
NGEP	8	8	8	8	8	8	8	9	8	8	8
IL	9	9	9	9	7	9	9	8	9	9	9
P	10	10	10	10	10	10	10	10	10	10	10
YJW	11	11	11	11	11	11	11	11	11	11	11

Table 10.5
Kendall Harmonic Coefficient Analysis of Responses

Variable	Kendall Harmonic Coefficient	P
11 kinds of evaluations in table 10.3	0.7572	P 0.005
11 kinds of evaluations in table 10.4	0.9784	P 0.005

Table 10.6
Overall Preference Ranking of Prospective Occupations

Occupation	Comprehensive Class	Order
University and graduate students	3.27	1
People in the special fields	2.76	2
Administration and institution cadres	2.61	3
Enterprise cadres and technical personnel	2.36	4
Middle and primary school teachers	1.43	5
Workers	0.87	6
Commercial and service trades	0.69	7
Individual laborers	0.56	8
Nongovernmental enterprise people	0.27	9
Peasants	0.13	10
Young job-waiters	0.03	11

Which table is more consistent internally could be determined with a Kendall harmonic coefficient (which indicates the multiseries correlation level). The result of the computation is shown in table 10.5.

There exists a clear correlation in both tables, but the correlation is stronger for table 10.3. In other words, a person's own occupation does not affect his ranking of the social status of various occupations, but it does affect the ranking of economic status.

1.2. Respondents' Own Choice of Occupations

How do young people select their own occupations? We asked two questions: what is your own job preference, and what aspects of the job are important to you? We asked respondents to suppose that they could freely choose their own occupation. Their choices are shown in table 10.6.

Compared with tables 10.1 and 10.2, it is obvious that when considering choice of occupations, people pay more attention to social status. Although in the minds of the public "individual laborer" is the most lucrative occupation, it is

Table 10.7
Correlation Analysis of Occupational Preferences

Variables	Spearman Series Correlation Coefficient	P
X_1 and X_2	−0.1727	Not evident
X_1 and X_0	−0.1818	Not evident
X_2 and X_0	0.9727	$P < 0.001$

put only at the eighth place. Although "university and graduate student" (whether they should be taken as an occupation is not considered here) ranks ninth in terms of income, here it beats all to take the first place. The pay of "middle and primary school teachers" is generally acknowledged to be low, and hence it takes tenth place there, followed only by "young job-waiters," who receive almost no pay at all. However, when people choose occupations, it is put in fifth place (and its social status is fifth place, too).

One method to see whether people pay more attention to economic status or social status in choosing an occupation is to undertake a correlation analysis. Let X_0, X_1, and X_2, respectively, represent choice of occupation, economic status of occupation, and social status of occupation. Results of the analysis are shown in table 10.7.

The results show that there exists no significant interrelationship between economic position and social position or between economic position and choice of occupation. The social position of an occupation and choice of occupation, however, are closely associated with each other. This shows that when selecting their own occupations people stress first and foremost the social position of the occupation, instead of its economic position.

The results on another question, designed to find people's basis for choosing an occupation, confirm this finding. (See table 10.8.)

From this we learn that first and foremost people pay attention to noneconomic issues such as whether they can give full play to their ability, whether they will be offered chances to further their education, and whether the job enjoys a prestigious social position. For the sake of convenience, we will refer to these noneconomic rewards as individual social demand. Rate of pay, which we will refer to as economic demand, takes fifth place among the selection standards, higher only than the lightness of the work, but lower than stability. On the one hand, reform will bring more people a chance for higher pay and social position; on the other hand, people are required to make more effort and take greater risks.

This prompts us to ponder the question from two angles: First, what motivates people to take part in daily economic and social activity? Second, how able are people to cope with changing social and economic life? In particular, can they adapt to the new lifestyle that will come into existence during the reform?

Table 10.8
What People Look For in an Occupation

Selection Basis	Comprehensive Class	Order
One can give full play to one's skill.	4.66	1
It will provide chances for further education.	4.42	2
It enjoys high social position.	3.80	3
It is stable.	3.25	4
It pays decently.	2.92	5
It is light work.	1.91	6

Both the reform and the new system that is the ultimate aim of the reform take the people as the main force. How to better integrate the design and implementation of the reform scheme with the quality of the people is a key to reform. Therefore, we included an "Attitude" form into the questionnaire. The form is composed of four parts: Attitudes toward money income (or economic demand), toward individual social demand, toward risk, and toward effort. The first two parts measure motivation, and the remainder measure ability to adapt.

2. Attitudes Toward Risk, Effort, and Reward

For society, reform means the establishment of an economic system that is vital and able to rationally organize the effective use of resources. For individuals, it means at least two kinds of changes.

2.1. Attitude Toward Money Income (Economic Demand)

The first six questions in the Attitude form concern attitudes toward income. The results are shown in table 10.9.

The table shows that, on the one hand, most people are not satisfied with their present level of income and hope they will be able to make more money after the reform. This is shown in the answers to the fifth and second questions. On the other hand, most people had reservations about money, holding that pay should not be the only standard in selecting jobs, and people should not go after money only. This is shown in responses to the first, fourth, and sixth questions. Eighty-five percent of the people said no to the first question, and about 30 percent expressed strong disagreement. About 60 percent of the people agreed with the fourth question. In addition, most people hoped to see a narrowing of the wage gap.

Table 10.9
Attitudes Toward Money Income

Questions	Strongly Agree	Agree	Disagree	Strongly Disagree	Agree (Total)	Disagree (Total)
1. I will do any work so long as it is well-paid	2.1	12.5	55.2	29.8	14.6	85.0
2. I hope to earn more after reform.	10.4	48.4	31.9	8.7	58.8	40.6
3. The income gap should be narrowed.	10.4	42.3	38.2	8.4	52.7	46.6
4. One can't be too greedy for money.	9.6	50.1	31.6	8.2	59.7	39.8
5. I'm satisfied with my present income.	2.6	26.2	44.6	25.0	28.8	69.6
6. As for money, the more the better.	8.7	37.8	37.2	15.4	46.5	52.6

2.2. Importance of Noneconomic Rewards (NER)

We explored people's attitudes toward these issues with questions 7 to 12. The answers to the six questions are summarized in table 10.10

The table shows that most people strongly emphasize the noneconomic rewards of work. About 95 percent yearn to satisfy their ideals and to use the full range of their abilities. The figure in the seventh question—64.4 percent—shows how idealistic the young people are.

2.3. Attitude Toward Risk

People's attitude toward risk and stability were probed with questions 13–18 (table 10.11).The respondents show a positive attitude toward risk. In answering the fifteenth and seventeenth questions, which are relatively abstract, the overwhelming majority hold a positive attitude. Answers to question 15 show that 91.9 percent of the people hold a positive attitude, 32.7 percent of them marking "strongly agree." On the other hand, people's attitude toward risk is not unambiguous. Take, for example, answers to questions 14 and 16. The number of people who said yes and no is about the same.

Furthermore, the responses are inconsistent, showing a weak understanding. In answering question 18, close to 90 percent said no, with 40.7 percent standing in strong opposition to it. This shows most of the people have a strong aversion to the old system of "everyone eating from the same big pot." However, 65.6 percent of the people agreed with question 13, an indication of the influence of decades of egalitarianism in the distribution system.

Table 10.10

Responses Dealing with Noneconomic Rewards

Questions	Agree Strongly	Agree	Disagree	Disagree Strongly	Agree Total	Disagree Total
7. Ideals are more important than money.	64.4	30.2	3.9	1.0	94.6	4.9
8. I want to have a decent job even if it is low paid.	11.3	51.3	31.7	4.5	62.6	30.2
9. I wish to accomplish something no matter how much I'll be paid.	39.9	48.4	10.1	1.1	88.3	11.2
10. I hope to be interested in my job.	34.9	50.6	13.3	0.8	85.5	14.1
11. I'm very much concerned whether I can use what I've learned.	46.9	48.7	3.7	0.4	95.6	4.1
12. I hope to be able to improve my cultural level through work. I pay comparatively less attention to the pay.	41.8	47.8	9.0	1.0	89.6	10.0

Table 10.11

Responses Showing Attitudes Toward Risk

Questions	Agree Strongly	Agree	Disagree	Disagree Strongly	Agree Total	Disagree Total
13. The government should take care of everything with regard to people's life.	22.3	43.3	28.6	5.2	65.6	33.8
14. If people have more chance to earn more and enhance their social position, it doesn't matter if life is less stable.	11.3	39.6	37.8	10.8	50.0	48.6
15. I'll strive for achievement even if I might suffer failure.	32.7	59.9	7.1	0.9	91.9	8.0
16. I'm not accustomed to change with regard to prices and wages. It's better to have less change.	11.2	35.2	41.8	11.3	46.4	53.1
17. A too peaceful life would be lackluster.	19.9	49.6	23.1	6.8	69.5	29.9
18. The "eating from the same pot" system has its own strong points. For example, it guarantees the stability of life.	1.0	9.7	48.1	40.7	10.7	88.8

Table 10.12

Responses Showing Attitudes Toward Effort

Question	Agree Strongly	Agree	Disagree	Disagree Strongly	Agree Total	Disagree Total
19. I prefer a relaxed job to a tense one.	4.8	32.9	50.3	11.6	37.7	61.9
20. I'm willing to do my best to complete my assignment.	28.7	45.8	20.1	4.6	74.5	24.7
21. I don't like an environment with sharp competition.	4.3	28.4	50.6	16.4	32.7	67.0
22. One should know one's place.	11.0	39.2	35.0	14.4	50.2	49.4
23. One's situation can be bettered if one makes an effort.	37.9	48.4	9.9	3.2	86.3	13.1
24. Better trust to luck.	3.1	8.5	33.0	54.9	11.6	87.9

2.4. Attitude Toward Effort

People's attitude toward effort is explored in questions 19 to 24 (table 10.12). Like answers to the questions concerning people's individual social demand, answers to the six questions in table 10.12 are all positive. First of all, the overwhelming majority trust their own ability instead of fate. More than 86 percent of the answers to questions 23 and 24 show this positive attitude. In particular, 54.9 percent expressed strong opposition to question 24. Second, most people are willing to accept a tense and competitive job and make efforts and sacrifice. For example, 60 percent of the answers to questions 19, 20, and 21 show people hold this attitude. Finally people split 50–50 on whether people should "know their own place."

2.5. Comparison Between Various Attitudes and Their Interrelationship

The basic unit used to measure people's attitudes is comprehensive point. The answers to various questions listed above are conducive for our making concrete analysis of attitudes. But if an attitude is measured with single questions, its reliability and effectiveness are certainly questionable. This is why we have to make further analysis in accordance with comprehensive point.

Each attitude is measured with six questions. Answers to these questions are graded in the light of a predesigned standard, with the total points (comprehensive points) representing the intensity of an attitude. The higher the points, the higher the intensity of attitude; this means people have a more positive attitude.

Table 10.13
Intensity and Variance of Attitudes

Attitude	Comprehensive Points	Deviation
Attitude toward money income	17.43	3.867
Attitude toward individual social demand (personal needs)	24.66	3.096
Attitude toward risks.	20.47	3.486
Attitude toward efforts.	21.89	3.804
Comprehensive attitude.	84.45	8.550

For each attitude, the lowest point is 6 and the highest 30, with the middle-level point being 18. When the comprehensive points of the four kinds of attitudes are brought together, we get the general attitude (or comprehensive attitude) of people who fill in the forms toward social and economic life.

Table 10.13 shows the average intensity of the public's attitude. Here, the "average value of comprehensive points" refers to the average points of attitudes of people investigated; the "standard discrepancy" is used to measure differences. A big standard discrepancy would mean greater difference between the high and low points of people's attitudes; in other words, it means less unanimity of attitudes.

Obviously, people have a more unanimous attitude toward individual social demand and have the greatest difference in attitude toward economic (or money) income. As different attitude forms were used to measure different attitudes, we should not make simple comparisons between the high and low comprehensive points of various attitudes. However, it still gives us the impression that people's attitude toward noneconomic or personal needs is more positive than their attitude toward economic demand, as shown in the world of difference between the comprehensive points of the two. We may have some understanding of this from answers to questions in the previously listed "Attitude" forms.

What kind of correlation exists between various attitudes? Table 10.14 is the result of the relative analysis of the comprehensive points of various attitudes.

The r in table 10.14 represents the Pearson correlative coefficient and the P of all the six correlative coefficients in the table is more than 0.000, indicating that there exists a highly obvious correlation between them. Interestingly, within the motive force, people's attitude toward money income and people's attitude toward individual social demand are strongly negatively related, showing that people with strong demand for income will have a weaker demand for noneconomic benefits and vice versa. Within the range of ability, people's attitude toward risks and efforts are highly related, showing the close relationship between the two—people who dare to take risks are often more willing to make an effort. Now let us take a look at the relationship between the composition of motivation and

Table 10.14

Simple Correlation (r) Among Attitudes

Individual Attitude	Social Demand	Risks	Effort
Economic income	−0.2161	0.1922	0.1176
Individual social demand		0.1017	0.1727
Risks			0.4633

P < 0.000

the composition of adaptability. The correlation coefficient between the attitude toward money income and the attitude toward risk stands at 0.1922, higher than the correlation coefficient between the attitude toward individual social demand and the attitude toward risk. The correlaton coefficient between the attitude toward individual social demand and the attitude toward effort is 0.1721, higher than the correlation coefficient between the attitude toward money income and the attitude toward effort (but the gap is smaller). This shows economic demand has strong influence on adventurist spirit; one cherishing stronger demand for economic benefit will be more adventurous. And individual social demand has strong influence on attitude toward effort; the stronger the individual social demand, the stronger the attitude toward effort. The above-mentioned relationship between various attitudes is shown in figure 10.2.

2.6. Factors Influencing Attitudes

One person may hold an attitude different from another's. Moreover, they will differ with regard to age, sex, education, and standard of living. What relationship exists between these individual factors and attitudes? What influence will they exert on attitudes? If there is any, which one is more influential? These are questions we are going to discuss here.

We reanalyzed the correlation between these factors and various attitudes, with the results shown in table 10.15. To save space and to make the table more understandable, we have omitted the measuring coefficient, which could be used to judge the influence of various factors, and list only their order, beginning with the most influential ones. By the way, because it is a reanalysis of the correlation, we have ruled out influence of the other factors when measuring the influence of a factor on various attitudes.

Obviously, living standard has the greatest influence on the attitude toward economic income and the attitude toward risks; age has the greatest influence on the attitude toward individual needs; and the length of service has the greatest influence on the attitude toward effort. As regards the comprehensive attitude, the most influential ones are, respectively, length of service, utilization of mass media, and the flow frequency.

Length of Service. According to statistics, the investigated have 36.0 years'

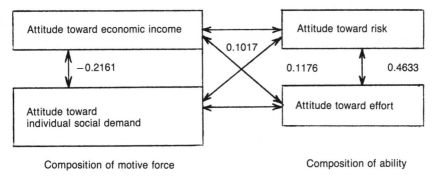

Figure 10.2

standing, averaging 4.8 years. Table 10.15 shows that the length of service has the greatest influence on the comprehensive attitude. Its influence on attitude toward effort ranks first; its influence on attitude toward risks takes sixth place; and its influence on attitude toward economic income and attitude toward individual social demand is not impressive. This means people with longer service will have poor adaptability—less adventurous and less positive in their attitudes toward effort. Among them, the influence of length of service on the attitude toward effort is more pronounced. (See table 10.16.)

The length of service is calculated only among workers and staff of state-owned enterprises and township collective enterprises. The above table shows the influence of the distribution system of "everyone eating from the same big pot" on people.

Table 10.15

Attitude Relative Order Factors	Comprehensive Attitude	Attitude toward Economic Income	Attitude toward Individual Needs	Attitude toward Risks	Attitude toward Effort
Length of service	1	Not Clear	Not Clear	6	1
Mass media	2	Not Clear	Not Clear	2	2
Flow frequency	3	Not Clear	Not Clear	4	3
Changes in living standard	4	1	2	1	4
Education	5	Not Clear	Not Clear	3	7
Flow distance	6	4	Not Clear	7	6
Sex	7	2	3	5	5
Age	Not Clear	Not Clear	1	Not Clear	Not Clear
Residential	Not Clear	3	Not Clear	Not Clear	Not Clear

Table 10.16
Impact of Length of Service

Length of Service (Year)	Average Value of Comprehensive Attitude Points	Order	Average Value of Attitude Toward Effort Points	Order
0	86.22	1	22.67	1
1–5	85.02	2	22.03	1
9–10	83.37	3	21.45	3
11–15	81.31	4	21.02	5
16–20	80.59	5	20.53	6
21 and over	79.56	6	11.23	4

P=0.0000

Table 10.17
Impact of Use of Mass Media

Utilization of Mass Media	Average Value of Comprehensive Attitude Points	Order	Average Value of Attitude toward Effort Points	Order
Often	84.89	1	22.07	1
Sometimes	83.94	2	21.75	2
Occasionally	81.89	3	20.60	3
Never	80.33	4	20.14	4

P=0.0000

Mass Media. Results of the investigation on public utilization of the mass media, including newspaper, radio, and TV news programs, are: 67.2 percent of the people—often (almost everyday); 27.2 percent—sometimes (no less than once a week); 4.8 percent—occasionally (no less than once a month); and 0.8 percent—never.

Utilization of mass media ranks second among various factors that influence people's comprehensive attitude as well as their attitude toward effort and toward risks; but it does not exert much influence on people's attitude toward money income and their attitude toward individual social demand. In other words, the more mass media (news programs) are used, the more effort people will make and the more adventurous people will become. However, it does not have much influence on people's economic demand and the individual social demand (see table 10.17).

Frequency of Circulation. Circulation frequency means whether people often

Table 10.18
Impact of Frequency of Travel

Circulation Frequency	Average Value of Comprehensive Attitude Points	Order	Average Value of Attitude toward Effort Points	Order
Often	89.26	1	22.70	1
Sometimes	84.54	2	21.96	2
Never	83.06	3	21.17	3

P=0.0000

go out to travel. The result of the investigation is: Often—8.7 percent; sometimes—75.5 percent; never—15.8 percent.

Out of the relationships between circulation frequency and various factors, the relationship between circulation frequency and comprehensive attitude ranks third; the relationship between circulation frequency and attitude toward effort also ranks third; the relationship between circulation frequency and attitude toward risks takes fourth place. However, circulation frequency has no outstanding relation with money income and individual social demand. This shows that when circulation frequency is high, people will become more adventurous and more willing to make an effort, but circulation frequency has no way of influencing economic demand and noneconomic demand (see table 10.18).

Perception of Rising Living Standard. From the answers to questions concerning change of living standard, we see 18.3 percent of people think their life has been improved a lot, 69.4 percent think their life has bettered slightly, 7.2 percent think their life has undergone no change at all, 4.4 percent think their life has gone down a little bit, and 0.7 percent think their standard of living has lowered a lot.

Out of the influence of the change of living standard on various factors, that on comprehensive attitude ranks fourth, on attitude toward economic or money income and attitude toward risks ranks first, on individual social demand (noneconomic personal needs) ranks second, and on attitude toward effort ranks fourth also. When the standard of living has been improved only a little or has gone down significantly, people will have strong economic demand; meanwhile, people will become less adventurous and their attitude toward individual social demand and effort becomes weaker too. The reason for this is that the interrelationship between the latter three and the comprehensive attitude, on the one hand, and changes of economic income, on the other hand, is in the negative (see table 10.19).

Table 10.19
Impact of Perceived Change in Living Standards

Change of Living Standard	Average Value of Attitude toward Economic Income Points	Order	Average Value of Attitude toward Risks Points	Order
Improved a lot	16.71	5	20.91	1
Improved slightly	17.47	4	20.53	2
No changes	18.15	2	19.64	3
Lowered slightly	18.14	3	19.27	4
Lowered a lot	19.42	1	18.42	5

$P = 0.0000$

Table 10.20
Impact of Educational Level

Educational Level	Average Value of Attitude toward Economic Income Points	Order	Average Value of Attitude toward Risks Points	Order
Primary school	82.30	4	19.00	4
Middle school	82.56	3	19.30	3
High school or secondary technical school	84.11	2	20.36	2
College and university	87.20	1	21.81	1

$P = 0.0000$

This result is very interesting. The slow increase or drop of income has fueled people's economic demand, but failed to reinforce correspondingly people's attitude toward risks and toward effort, causing separation of the two.

Educational Level. Educational level takes fifth place among various factors in terms of influence on comprehensive attitude. Its influence on the attitude toward risks ranks third, and its influence on the attitude toward effort ranks seventh. But it exerts no significant influence on the attitude toward economic income and the attitude toward individual social demand. People with higher educational level tend to be more adventurous and more willing to make effort. However, higher educational level has no influence on one's economic and noneconomic demand (see Table 10.20).

Circulation Distance. Circulation distance implies how far people will go. Statistics show that the circulation distance of the public averages 1,234.4 kilometers.

The relation of circulation distance to comprehensive attitude ranks sixth; the

Table 10.21
Impact of Average Distance of Travel

Circulation Distance (km)	Average Value of Attitude toward Economic Income Points	Order	Average Value of of Attitude toward Effort Points	Order
0	16.72	5	21.00	5
1–200	17.17	4	21.75	4
201–1,000	17.42	2	21.84	3
1,001–2,000	17.41	3	21.88	2
2,001 and more	17.86	1	22.34	1

P=0.0199; P=0.0206

influence of circulation distance on attitude toward economic income ranks fourth, on attitude toward effort sixth, and on attitude toward risks seventh. It has no significant influence on individual social demand. The farther the circulation distance, the stronger the economic demand, the attitude toward effort, and the attitude toward risks. However, it cannot influence the intensity of noneconomic demand (see table 10.21).

Sex. Sex takes seventh place among various factors in terms of relationship to comprehensive attitude. Its relation to attitude toward economic income takes second place; to individual and social demand, third place; and to risks and effort, fifth place. The individual social demand is shown in the negative. This shows that women have stronger individual social demand than men; but men have stronger demand on the other three attitudes than women (see table 10.22).

Age. Table 10.15 shows that age has the strongest influence on individual social demand; however, it exerts no significant influence on the other factors. As a matter of fact, age does have an influence on various attitudes. As its relationship with various attitudes takes on a curve, it could not be presented a with Pearson correlative coefficient, which is used to measure linear correlation.

We divided ages into seven groups to see what is the average point of attitudes in each age group, with the result shown in figure 10.3. In this chart, the seven figures from 1 to 7 represent seven different age groups: under 15, 16–20, 21–25, 26–30, 31–35, 36–45, and above 46. *P* represents visible significance.

This chart shows that people between 16 and 30 (in the second, third, and fourth groups) have strong desire for economic income, with people between 20 and 25 (in the second group) having the strongest desire in this regard; people at 15 and younger and people at 46 and older (first and seventh groups) have comparatively weaker economic demand, with people 46 and older having the weakest desire in this regard. With regard to individual social demand, people below 25 (first, second, and third groups) have strong desire in this regard, with people below 15 having the strongest individual social demand; people between

Table 10.22

Sex	Average Value of Attitude toward Economic Income Points	Order	Average Value of Attitude toward Individual Social Demand Points	Order
Men	17.83	1	24.44	2
Women	16.51	2	25.18	1
P=0.0000				

31 and 45 having weaker desires, and people between 36 and 45 having the weakest desire. Obviously, people 31 and older have weaker economic and noneconomic demands when compared with people from other age groups, and people below 15 have weak economic demand but strong individual social demand.

Like their attitudes toward economic income, people between 16 and 30, especially those between 20 and 25, have a staunch attitude toward risks; and people above 31 (fifth, sixth, and seventh groups), especially people above 46, have a weaker attitude in this regard. As far as attitude toward effort is concerned, as is the case with people's attitude toward individual social demand, people below 25, especially people below 15, tend to be more willing to make an

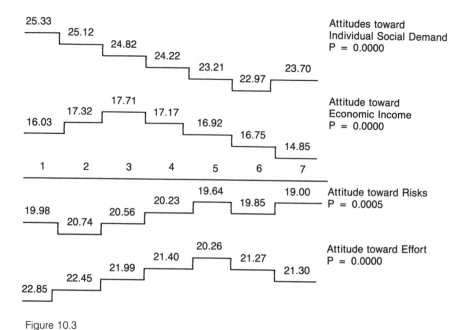

Figure 10.3

Impact of Age on Attitudes

Table 10.23
Impact of Sex

Residential Place	Average Value of Attitude toward Economic Income Points	Order
Countryside	17.38	3
Small city	17.22	4
Medium city	17.52	2
Large city	17.85	1

$P = 0.006$

effort; people between 31 and 35 (fifth group) tend to be less willing to do so. In other words, people 31 and older have a weaker attitude toward risk and effort than people in the other age groups, while people below 15 have a medium level of adventurous spirit but a stronger attitude toward effort.

Place of Residence. There exists no significant interrelationship between residential place and various attitudes, such as the comprehensive attitude, the attitude toward individual social demand, the attitudes toward risks and toward effort. Arranged in the order of countryside and small, medium, and large cities, the large city will see greater economic demand (see table 10.23).

Obviously, people in cities cherish a greater economic demand than in the countryside. (Small cities refer mainly to county seats. Their points are closer to the countryside than to the large and medium-sized cities).

Occupation. Different occupations have different intensity of attitudes, whose order is shown in table 10.24. For the purpose of simplicity, we have omitted the average points of our evaluation of various attitudes. The order, from high to low, shows the intensity of various attitudes going from strong to weak.

2.7. Summary Question on System Change

One question included in the questionnaire is: "If there is a place where wages are high and people have more chances to give full play to their ability and enhance their social status than in other places but work is extremely unstable and very demanding, competition is cutthroat, and prices fluctuate from time to time, do you wish to work and live there?" This question was designed to find the general attitude of people who fill in the questionnaire. The result is: 64.5 percent wish to; 22.9 percent don't care; 12.6 percent don't wish to. Those who say "wish to" are in the majority. What is the relationship between the distribution of answers and appraisal points of various attitudes? Table 10.25 shows the results of the correlative analysis of appraisal points of the question and various attitudes.

The correlative coefficients in the table are negative and high. This shows that

Table 10.24

Impact of Respondent's Occupation

Attitude Occupation Order		Comprehensive Attitude	Attitude toward Economic Income	Attitude toward Individual Social Demand	Attitude toward Risks	Attitude toward Effort
High	1	UAGS	UAGS	YJW	UAGS	UAGS
	2	YJW	P	MAPST	PITSF	YJW
	3	MAPST	IL	NGEP	YJW	MAPST
Middle	4	P	W	P	ECATP	P
	5	PITSF	CASTP	PITSF	MAPST	PITSF
	6	ECAPT	YJW	UAGS	AAIC	ECAPT
	7	NGEP	PITSF	AAIC	NGEP	AAIC
	8	AAIC	MAPST	CASTP	P	IL
Low	9	CASTP	ECAPT	ECAPT	CASTP	NGEP
	10	W	NGEP	W	W	CASTP
	11	IL	AAIC	IL	IL	W

Table 10.25

The Summary Question: Correlation of Response with Various Attitudes

Attitude	Pearson Correlative Coefficient	P
Attitude toward economic income	−0.2050	0.0000
Attitude toward individual social demand	−0.0834	0.0000
Attitude toward risks	−0.3692	0.0000
Attitude toward effort	−0.3671	0.0000
Comprehensive attitude	−0.4368	0.0000

with the intensification of their attitudes, people tend to be more willing to go to work and live in this hypothetical place. The correlation is highest with overall or comprehensive attitude. When we look at the form subcomponent attitudes, we see that the correlation is weakest for the first two, and stronger for the second two. In other words,, those who wish to live in this hypothetical place derive their attitudes, not from acquisitiveness, but from their acceptance of the need for risk and effort.

Obviously, factors that influence these four attitudes will inevitably influence people's response to this key question. Because of limited space, we cite here only a few examples. Tables 10.26, 10.27, and 10.28 respectively show the influence

Table 10.26
Summary Question: Impact of Use of Media

Choice % Utilization of Mass Media	Willing	Don't Care	Not Willing
Often	68.8	19.9	11.6
Sometimes	56.1	29.9	14.0
Occasionally	54.4	29.7	15.9
Never	55.6	25.9	18.5

$P=0.0000$

Table 10.27
Summary Question: Impact of Frequency of Travel

Choice % Circulation Frequency	Willing	Don't Care	Not Willing
Often	70.2	19.9	9.9
Sometimes	65.7	22.6	11.7
Never	55.8	26.5	17.7

$P=0.0000$

Table 10.28
Summary Question: Impact of Educational Level

Choice % Educational Level	Willing	Don't Care	Not Willing
Primary school	40.0	30.0	30.0
Middle school	57.0	26.8	16.2
High school or technical secondary school	63.9	22.9	13.2
College and university	73.6	19.3	7.1

$P=0.0000$

of utilization of mass media, circulation frequency, and educational level, with figures showing those who have made the choice.

Of the people who often use the mass media for news, 68.8 percent marked "willing" and 11.6 percent "not willing." Of the people who never use the mass media for news, 55.6 percent marked "willing" and 18.5 percent "not willing."

Of the people frequently on the move, 70.2 percent marked "willing" and 9.9

percent marked "not willing." Of the people who never go out traveling, 55.8 percent marked "willing" and 17.7 percent marked "not willing." The higher the circulation frequency, the more willing people will tend to be.

Of the people who marked "willing," 40 percent have received primary school education and 73.6 percent have received college or university education. Of people who marked "not willing," 30 percent have received primary school education and 7.1 percent have received college or university education. From table 10.28 we see clearly that people with a comparatively high education tend to be "willing."

3. Relationship Between Attitudes Toward Life and Selection of Occupation

What kind of relationship exists between selection of occupation, elaborated in the first part of this report, and attitude toward life, analyzed in the second part? Are there any differences with regard to the selection of occupation between people who hold different attitudes? Because of limited space, we'll make an analysis of the comprehensive attitude, totally ignoring the difference between various attitudes.

In the light of the principle of taking 25 percent of the comprehensive attitude points from both ends and 50 percent from the middle, we divided the comprehensive attitude points into high-, medium-, and low-point groups respectively for 91–111 points, 79–90 points, and 51–78 points. Now let us take a look at how people in the three groups select their own occupations.

First, let us look at the desire of people in selecting occupations. Table 10.29 shows the order of the three groups' choice of occupations.

A horizontal perusal of table 10.29 shows that different groups have different comprehensive class for each occupation. A high comprehensive class means strong desire for the selection of the occupation. Obviously, the high attitude points meant that people cherish a more positive attitude toward life; are more willing to be university and graduate students, enterprise cadres and technical personnel, individual laborers, and nongovernmental enterprise workers; and are reluctant to be cadres in administrative institutions, workers, and commercial and service trade people. For example, for the choice of individual laborers, the comprehensive class is 0.42 for the low-point group, 0.53 for the middle-point group, and 0.77 for the high-point group. For the choice of workers, it is 1.03 for the low-point group, 0.90 for the middle-point group, and 0.64 for the high-point group. For the choice of middle and primary school teachers, it is quite high for the middle-point and low-point groups. For the choice of professional people, peasants and young job-waiters, the comprehensive class is outstanding with P reaching more than 0.05, indicating that there exists a distinct difference among the groups in selecting the three occupations.

A vertical look at table 10.29 shows that the low-point and medium-point

Table 10.29
The Impact of Attitudes on Occupational Preference

Choice of Occupation	Low-Point Group		Medium-Point Group		High-Point Group		Total		
	Comprehensive Class	Order	Comprehensive Class	Order	Comprehensive Class	Order	Comprehensive Class	Order	P
UAGS	3.02	1	3.31	1	3.43	1	3.27	1	0.0000
PITSF	2.87	2	2.74	2	2.70	2	2.76	2	0.083
AAIC	2.86	3	2.55	3	2.49	3	2.61	3	0.000
ECATP	2.26	4	2.36	4	2.49	4	2.36	4	0.010
MAPST	1.42	5	1.49	5	1.32	5	1.43	5	0.044
W	1.03	6	0.90	6	0.64	7	0.87	6	0.000
CASTP	0.77	7	0.70	7	0.60	8	0.69	7	0.017
IL	0.42	8	0.53	8	0.77	6	0.56	8	0.000
NGEP	0.19	9	0.25	9	0.37	9	0.27	9	0.000
P	0.12	10	0.13	10	0.15	10	0.13	10	0.522
YJW	0.02	11	0.03	11	0.04	11	0.03	11	0.391

186

Table 10.30

Interaction of Attitude Intensity with Job Desiderata

Standard	Low-Point Group Comprehensive Class	Order	Medium-Point Group Comprehensive Class	Order	High-Point Group Comprehensive Class	Order	Total Comprehensive Class	Order	P
That can give play to one's ability	4.10	1	4.71	1	5.10	1	4.66	1	0.000
That can provide with further education	3.92	2	4.55	2	4.63	2	4.42	2	0.000
Social position is high	3.84	3	3.74	3	3.86	3	3.80	3	0.115
Work is stable	3.79	4	3.24	4	2.72	5	3.25	4	0.000
It is well paid	2.96	5	2.80	5	3.12	4	2.92	5	0.000
It is light	2.31	6	1.89	6	1.54	6	1.91	6	0.000

groups' priority for various occupations is about the same as the average result of the public, while in the high-point group the individual laborer is placed sixth, before the worker. The fact that the individual laborer, which is placed right after the worker and commercial and service trades in the other groups, is put before the worker and service trades in the low-point and medium-point groups is a significant difference.

Let us look at the standard of the occupational selection. Table 10.30 shows the difference between standards of various groups in selection of occupations.

A horizontal look at table 10.30 shows that people who hold a more positive attitude toward life tend to be more concerned about whether they can give full play to their ability and whether they will be able to further their education, and less concerned about the stability and relaxation of the work. For example, for the "ability," the comprehensive class is 4.10 points for the low-point group, 4.71 for the medium-point group, and 5.10 points for the high-point group. For the "stability," the comprehensive class is 3.79 points for the low-point group, 3.24 points for the medium-point group, and 2.72 points for the high-point group. The high-point group attaches more importance to the economic income, followed in order by the low-point group and medium-point group. For the "social position," there exists no distinct discrepancy between various groups.

A vertical look at table 10.30 shows that there exists no distinct difference with regard to the order of priority between the low-point and middle-point groups, on the one hand, and the public, on the other. In the high-point group "pay" is placed before "stability," leaving "stability" and "lightness" at the bottom of the list.

The Financial "Two-Track System": Strengthen Credit and Open Up the Nonbank Market

Jiang Sidong and Xu Xiaopo

During reform, extrabudgetary investment funds came under the control of individual enterprises. This caused investments to become smaller in scale and to slight heavy industry. In addition, the change awoke in China's enterprises an insatiable thirst for expansion. This new pressure has caused the constraints on bank credits to soften.

The vicious circle of the softening of credit constraints and consequent credit expansion has obstructed the work of readjusting and rationalizing China's microeconomic mechanism. It has forced the central government to contract credit. While this policy might hold down these unhealthy tendencies, it will not fundamentally change the behavior of the enterprises or quench their thirst for investment. A comprehensive contraction enforced by administrative means will first and foremost hold down productive investment. It may also exacerbate the problems of scale and light industry bias, leading to a repayment crisis among enterprises.

Developments in 1984 and the first half of 1985 have shown that a speedy reform of the financial system, nurturing a new mechanism and facilitating the flow and pooling of extrabudgetary funds, is the key to escaping our present dilemma. Conditions are not yet ripe for turning the specialized banks into enterprises and establishing in a short period of time a modern monetary system geared to the three traditional regulatory levers. The tactic we propose for the reform of the financial system is to adopt a "two-track" financial system. As far as credit activities of the national bank are concerned, we should perfect the existing planned control of credit and pursue a relatively tight monetary policy. At the same time, aside from funds provided by banks, we should develop the nonbank fund market, so that social funds may flow and pool over a wide area, improving investment efficiency and helping enterprises to reorganize and com-

Table 11.1

Change in the Composition of Fixed Asset Investment in Cities Surveyed

	1983	1984	1985 Jan.–June
Share of capital construction investment in gross investment	61%	64%	74%
Share of extrabudgetary investment in capital construction investment	55%	60%	72%

bine. Gradually, modern regulatory methods may be introduced into this binary financial system.

1. Softening of Credit Constraints in the Process of Institutional Reform

1.1. Fundamental Change in Funding Pattern

As reform proceeds, the funding pattern in China's economy is undergoing two remarkable changes. (1) Extrabudgetary funds have rapidly expanded and now occupy a decisive position. Taking the country as a whole, by 1984, gross fiscal extrabudgetary funds were equivalent to about 80 percent of budgetary funds. As far as the sources of funds for capital construction investment were concerned, urban state-sector capital construction investment in the first half of 1985 in the cities studied in the present survey accounted for 74 percent of the gross state-sector fixed assets investment, with extrabudgetary capital construction investment accounting for 72 percent of the total (see table 11.1. (2) Bank credit has become the main source of funds for enterprises. Since 1983, the proportion of "state circulating funds" in each enterprise's floating capital has dropped steadily; though still insignificant, the share of "enterprise circulating funds" has registered a marked increase, whereas bank credit already accounts for more than 40 percent (see table 11.2). Bank credit has increasingly become an important source for enterprise fixed asset investment. The gross fixed asset investment accomplished through internal funds in 1984 in the whole country increased by 47.3 percent over 1983; and from January to August 1985 the figure increased by 129.8 percent over the same period in 1984. This is 2.6 times as large as the increase in investments from funds raised by the enterprises themselves, which itself grew by 49.6 percent. Our survey of the sources of funds for fixed asset investment in 429 enterprises shows that the share of bank credits had increased to 31.8 percent by 1984, surpassing enterprise-owned funds and funds allocated from the state and higher authorities (see table 11.3).

These two changes indicate that the old pattern of gathering and distributing

Table 11.2

Change in Structure of Sources of Circulating Funds of State-Owned Industrial Enterprises in Seven Cities

	End of 1983	End of June 1984	End of 1984	End of June 1985
Circulating funds of the state	33.2%	31.2%	27.7%	25.6%
Circulating funds of enterprises	0.09		0.13	0.27
Bank credits	40.2	39.6	42.8	40.7
Other circulating sources funds	22.1	21.2	27.0	28.4
Payments due and payments for goods received in advance	12.4	12.2	14.0	18.4

Table 11.3

Sources of Fixed Asset Investment in 429 Enterprises in 1984

Sources	Proportion
Funds allocated by the state and higher authorities	18.3%
Bank credits	31.8%
Funds raised by the enterprises	45.5%
Of which, funds owned by the enterprises	29.1%

funds vertically solely through the state's financial network has undergone fundamental changes. The impact of banks on the activities of the national economy has increased, and foundations have been laid for further developing the new mechanism of horizontal pooling among enterprises. This is one of the major achievements of reform in the past few years.

1.2. Enterprises Do Not Have Adequate Funds for Productive Investment

Despite the rapid increase in extrabudgetary funds and in spite of the fact that the enterprises and their higher authorities own some 75 percent of gross fiscal extrabudgetary funds, each enterprise still owns very few funds. In the 429 enterprises studied, 57 percent are large or medium-sized enterprises, much greater than for the whole country. And yet, the average inflow of extrabudgetary funds for each enterprise in 1984 amounted only to about RMB 3.4 million, and the average for small-scale enterprises was less than RMB 600,000.

In 1984, the expansion of consumer demand led the expansion of aggregate

Table 11.4

Change in Structure of Enterprise Extrabudgetary Fund Expenditure

Share in enterprise extra-budgetary funds	1983	1984
Capital construction	9.2%	9.4%
Charged expenditure	45.5%	39.9%
Subtotal	54.7%	49.3%
Welfare and bonus payments	23.6%	27.0%

demand. At the enterprise level, this tendency could be seen in the ever greater share of enterprise-owned funds being used for worker and staff consumption. Consequently, the proportion used for fixed asset investment fell (see table 11.4).

In 1984, about half of the extrabudgetary funds of enterprises went to fixed asset investment. The average amount of enterprise-owned funds spent on fixed asset investment was RMB 1.7 million yuan for all the enterprises under survey, and RMB 300,000 for the small-scale enterprises. The amount of extrabudgetary funds the enterprises spent on fixed asset investment in 1985 accounted for about 10 percent of the original value of fixed assets. Furthermore, as a result of consumption taking the lead in all fields, a substantial part has been taken off the already scanty self-owned investments such as housing construction. The amount of enterprise-owned funds spent on productive investment will fall below the figures given here.

3. Softening of the Credit Constraint

At present, enterprises may still repay part of their loans before taxation (that is, a great part of these loans are actually repaid by financial authorities on behalf of the enterprises), they can still bargain with the government on tax rates and preferential treatments in tax reduction or exemption, and they can also evade taxes in various ways by taking advantage of lax tax management and enterprise financial management. However, with such reforms as changing from profit remission to tax collection, and changing from allocating funds to giving out loans, gone are the days when enterprises could rely on interest-free financial allocations for production and investment. Budgetary funds are finally strengthening their constraining effect on enterprises.

What merits our attention is that while constraints on budgetary funds are strengthening, constraints on bank credit are softening. This trend is clearly reflected in increasingly generous terms of credit and increasing amounts of overdue loans. A typical case of generous credit terms was the phenomenon of the banks' courting enterprises with loan offers. Lax credit terms will inevitably be followed by a decline in loan efficiency, leading to a further softening of pressure for loan repayment. Overdue loans owed to Construction Banks in seven cities by the end of 1984 showed an increase of 6.6 percent over 1983. By the end of June 1985, there was a dramatic increase of 44.7 percent over the same period in 1984. As a very large portion of loans issued by Construction Banks are medium or long-term loans, the rapid increase in overdue loans at the end of June 1985 reflected loans issued in 1984. Direct causes for the increase in overdue loans were the prolonged construction time span of construction projects and the inability of enterprises to repay, among other things. Overdue loans attributable to inability to repay accounted for 24.3 percent of all overdue loans owed to the Construction Bank at the end of June 1985. There are indications that with the Industrial and Commercial Bank the share of overdue loans in circulating capital loans is also increasing. Because some banks, at the request of local governments, allow enterprises to obtain new loans to service old ones so as to avoid an interest penalty, it is very difficult to calculate by exactly how much the overdue circulating capital loans have increased.

What caused the softening of the bank credit constraints? The basic reason for the softening of constraints is that at present the behavior mechanism of the economic micro-organs is not rational. At present, as the property relations between enterprises and the state are not yet clearly defined and mismanagement on the part of enterprises does not lead to bankruptcy, the enterprise budget constraint is still quite weak. Under the traditional system, the leaders of enterprises seek high production value, the expansion of the enterprise, and the prestige and honor that come with it. This gives the enterprises an impulse to expand. After a number of reforms were introduced in the field of distribution, enterprises began to seek to retain more profits, so as to promote the welfare of their staff and workers. This greatly strengthened the impulse of the profit motive, and a soft budget constraint made the enterprise's desire to expand ever stronger. The enterprises will inevitably have to go to the bank to satisfy their demands for external funds when budgetary funds become tight and the enterprise-owned production funds prove to be inadequate. Permission for pretax debt repayment and low loan interest rates have turned loans into low-cost "quasi-gifts" to the enterprises.

At the same time, another danger arises. Banks have not yet developed a way to resist the strong desire to invest. Before the banks at the local level are put under a system of management that turns them into enterprises held responsible for their own profits or losses, the constraint of their own budget is extremely weak. The banks do not have to worry about bearing the economic consequences of bad debts. On the contrary, they feel that the bigger the loans, the more interest they will reap. The specialized banks, which still earn from the "big pot" of the Central Bank, have not played the expected regulatory role in the face of enterprise expansion and the forceful administrative intervention of local governments. The softening of budget constraints of both the enterprises and the banks at the local level has left the enterprises free to compete for loans and the banks free to issue loans, neither fearing any possible adverse consequences. Such circumstances inevitably generate increasing overdue loans, resulting from inability to repay, which in turn stems from poor judgment on the part of enterprises in investment, and on the part of banks in issuing loans.

1.4. The Vicious Circle: Loosening Bank Credit and Expansion of Credit

The regulations decreed in 1984 by the Central Bank were actually issued after the event. The specialized banks' competition to issue loans forced the Central Bank to put more money in circulation so as to provide the sources for loans. The softening of bank credit constraints on the enterprises eventually led to the softening of credit control by the Central Bank over the specialized banks, which is reflected as credit expansion at the macro level. The total of loans issued by eighteen Industrial and Commercial Banks, Agricultural Banks, and the Bank of China by the end of 1984 increased by 24.2 percent compared with 1983, among which circulating fund loans increased by 20.6 percent and fixed asset loans by 52.8 percent. The total loans tendered by Construction Banks increased by 111.9 percent compared with 1983. The trend of credit expansion in the cities under survey agreed with the general trend of the country as a whole.

The expansion of credit in turn precipitated the softening of the constraint on bank credit, thereby creating a vicious circle. Credit expansion sustains the ever-increasing consumer and investment demands, leading to an all-round market boom. The booming market encourages enterprises to invest, and inflation, relatively speaking, lowers the cost to enterprises of utilizing bank loans (not only is the interest rate low in comparison with the inflation rate, but when there is increasing demand, enterprises find it easier to shift the burden of interest payments to consumers by raising the prices of their products). On the other hand, the booming market gives the banks at the local level overly high expectations with regard to the profits they may reap from the loans issued and therefore encourages them to compete with each other in granting loans. This naturally leads to the exacerbation of the softening of credit constraints. The combined impact of these two aspects may very well force a softening of the credit control of the Central Bank over the specialized banks. The economic law behind such a process of transmission of impacts is that when consumption surges ahead of production and financial and enterprise-owned funds are insufficient to sustain the corresponding level of productive investment, an objectively appropriate ratio between consumption and accumulation in the national economy, such that the level and structure of supply can match the rapidly changing level and structure of demand, can only be established passively through the expansion of bank credit.

1.5. Impact of the Vicious Circle

The vicious circle of softening constraint and credit expansion has to a great extent cancelled out the progress that had been achieved in stiffening the constraints over enterprises, and in beginning to regulate and control the national economy at the macro level. When enterprises are expecting to reap fairly high profits amid the upsurge in gross demand, they can raise their profit rate without troubling to improve their management, simply by borrowing as much as possible, expanding, and increasing their sales. According to calculations made from data collected from 429 enterprises, gross profits for 1984 increased by 1.4 percent over 1983. During the same period of time sales profits dropped from 18.8 to 15.6 percent, and the product profit rate dipped from 19.7 to 14.1 percent. In 1984, many of the enterprise economic efficiency targets were not met, and the quality of many products deteriorated drastically. Management and operation in some of the enterprises degenerated in quality. If these trends are not reversed in time, they will inevitably affect the technological progress of the enterprises, weaken the competitiveness of China's industrial products on the international market, and impede our country's industrial modernization.

2. Impact of Credit Contraction in the First Half of 1985

Credit contracted in the first half of 1985. As a result of the vicious circle of bank credit expansion, the use of administrative means became the only way to enforce credit contraction. The gross credit balance in eighteen cities at the end of the first six months in 1984 had dropped by 1.76 percent when compared with the end of 1983. At the end of the first six months of 1985 the drop was only 0.17 percent when compared with the end of 1984. It appears, therefore, that credit in 1985 did not show any sign of being squeezed. However, since the growth of both the industrial output value and fixed asset investment in the first half of 1985 was much faster than in the first half of 1984, the sharp contraction of credit in 1985 is undeniable when we consider the money demand generated by economic activity. Furthermore, the fierce momentum of credit expansion had clearly been restrained by the second half of 1984 (see fig. 11.1). The credit squeeze has had an impact on the nation's economic life in many ways. It is still too early for us to give a comprehensive evaluation on the pros and cons of the 1985 credit contraction. Here we would only like to point out four aspects that merit attention.

First, one short-term result of credit contraction is signs of improvement in enterprise management. Owing to the credit squeeze, terms for credit became harsher and greater pressure has been exerted by banks for debt repayment. Consequently, enterprises turn more and more to expensive, nonbank funds which carry with them stiffer constraints (this will be discussed in detail later). These changes have contributed to the stiffening of the budgetary constraints on

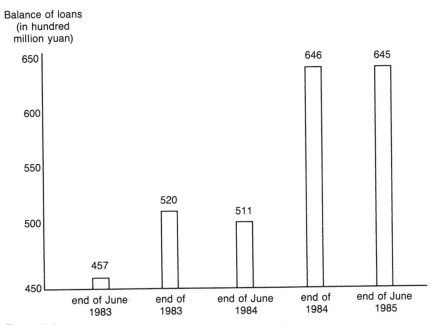

Figure 11.1

Changes in Balance of Loans in Eighteen Cities

the enterprises and may have a positive impact on the behavior of the enterprises. In the first half of 1985, there were indications of an upturn in some enterprises' economic indicators. In seven cities, the circulating funds set aside for every RMB 100 in sales income for state-owned industrial enterprises was RMB 91.8 at the end of June 1984; by the end of June 1985, it had dropped to RMB 88.5. The decline of the profits of enterprises in 1984 gradually reversed. The sales profit rate of state-owned industrial enterprises in seven cities rose from 10.5 percent in the first half of 1984 to 12.0 percent in the first half of 1985. All this goes to show that when the terms for acquiring credit funds become harsh, enterprises will have to rely more on improving management and lowering costs in order to increase profits.

Second, although the tight policy has been implemented, money for fixed assets is not yet tight. The impact of credit squeezing on circulating fund loans and fixed asset loans varies greatly (see table 11.5). From the end of 1984 to the end of June 1985, the balance of circulating fund loans issued by Industrial and Commercial Banks, Agricultural Banks, and Bank of China in eighteen cities declined. However, fixed asset loans (to state-run enterprises), equipment loans for collective-run industries, and loans for township enterprises (about half being equipment loans) all showed a fairly big increase. In the meantime, loans issued by Construction Banks also increased by a big margin. In 1984, loans tendered by

Table 11.5

Comparison Between Changes in Balance of Fixed Asset Loans and Circulating Fund Loans After Contraction

	End of June 1984 compared with end of 1983	End of June 1985 compared with end of 1984
Gross loans	−1.76%	−0.17%
Loans of circulating funds	−3.2%	−2.8%
Loans of fixed assets	+6.4%	+15.1%
Loans for the equipment of collectively-run industries	+6.1%	+13.5%
Loans for township enterprises	+9.9%	+12.9%

Construction Banks also increased by 111.9 percent over 1983, whereas from the first half of 1984 to the first half of 1985 there was an increase of 162.6 percent.

The fact that in the first six months of the year, the terms of fixed assets loans were harsher while the gross amount of loans was maintained indicates that there are many difficulties in trying to control the great upsurge in investment solely by administrative credit contraction measures, if consumption demand is not effectively restrained and efforts are not made to change the micro mechanism. This is because the strong desire to invest is aroused by the impulse of expansion at the micro level and is greatly stimulated by the upsurge in consumption demands.

Of course, a comprehensive credit squeeze of an administrative nature does have an impact on investment demand. What is most worrisome is that because consumption and nonproductive investment have shown great rigidity, credit squeezing tends to cut first and foremost into productive investment. In the first half of 1985 there were already indications of a decline in the share of productive investment in fixed asset investment. If such a trend is allowed to continue, it may lead to a serious imbalance between consumption and productive investment and further widen the gap between gross supply and gross demand.

A third aspect of contraction of credit is the growing tendency for fixed asset investment to become smaller in scale and more light-industrial. Owing to the wide dispersion of extrabudgetary funds and the rapid expansion of consumption demand in the past few years, at the same time that gross fixed asset investment expanded, the average scale of investment tended to become smaller, and investment structure became lighter (see the chapter on ''Investment'' in part III of this report). In a time of retrenchment, there is a danger that this trend may become stronger. When the amount of credit funds available to enterprises declines in relative terms, the ability of the enterprises to carry out large-scale and long-term investment is undermined. In a time of retrenchment, the risks involved in long and mid-term investment appear even more difficult to predict. All this compels the enterprises, when making fixed asset investment, to go in for profitable products that bring quick returns on investment. The investment tends to go to products in great demand, with large profit margins, and assuring quick repayment of investment funds. Compelled by stringent credit, local governments generally support such priority projects by administrative means, by granting credit loans. At present, inequality still exists in the external conditions for enterprises of different industries and different scales. Quick-profit-oriented, short-term investments on goods in great demand often tend to have fairly good immediate results. However, from the long-term development perspective and from the perspective of the national economy as a whole, such investments might be very harmful to economies of scale and even more detrimental to our efforts to lay a solid foundation for reinvigorating our economy in the Seventh Five-Year Plan.

Fourth and finally, there exists the danger of a payment crisis among enterprises. In the first half of 1985, while the industrial growth rate of most of the cities exceeded 20 percent, the balance of circulating fund loans not only declined in relative terms (decline in proportion in gross value of loans), but the absolute gross figure also declined (see table 11.5). How does one explain this paradoxical phenomenon? Part of the reason is that to cope with the stringency of circulating funds resulting from the credit squeeze, the enterprises had to rely more on commercial credit for promoting sales and purchases (see table 11.2). By the end of 1984, overdue payments owed and advance payments received by state-run industrial enterprises in seven cities accounted for 14 percent of the circulating funds. By the end of June of 1985 the figure had risen rapidly, to 18.4 percent. The problem here is that in the rapidly growing commercial credit, under the credit contraction a large proportion was the overdue payments owed by enterprises, in violation of the terms of contracts. Moreover, this kind of credit relation often involved many enterprises, one owing to the other. Should a considerable number of creditor enterprises fail to realize repayment of outstanding loans, thereby harming their normal reproduction operation, the economic life of the whole country will be seriously jeopardized. This is the so-called payment crisis. If the central government is compelled to issue large unplanned loans in a short time so as to bail out the enterprises in the event of a payment crisis, it would give rise to a new credit upsurge.

3. The Nonbank Sector: Importance and Recent Growth

We must urgently carry out reform in the financial system. In the process of institutional reform, the rapid expansion in gross extrabudgetary funds has an ever-growing impact on fixed asset investment. The vicious circle of credit expansion poses a great threat to balanced and steady development. The central government is compelled to resort to a policy of credit contraction. But while credit contraction can restrain the undesirable trends to a certain extent, it cannot be sustained because it fails to bring about a fundamental improvement in the behavior of enterprise or to quench their thirst for investment. On the contrary, it is very probable that a mandatory credit contraction carried out through administrative means will first and foremost depress productive investment and further aggravate the imbalance between gross supply and gross demand. It may also add to the tendency of investment to become smaller in scale and lighter in structure and lead to a payment crisis between enterprises. Clearly, then, timely reform in the financial system has become the key to sustaining the present urban reform.

Despite the urgent need for reform, we believe that comprehensive reform of the banking system is not possible in the immediate future. To turn the specialized banks into self-supporting enterprises and to establish a modern monetary regulatory system are admirable ideals for the Seventh Five-Year Plan. However, as of late 1985, conditions are still not ripe for carrying out such a comprehensive reform. The basic problem is the soft budget constraint of industrial and commercial enterprises. Before enterprises are put in a system in which they are held completely responsible for their own profits and losses, the state will have to undertake all obligations resulting from the mismanagement and failure of enterprises, and therefore the banks, as provider of funds needed by state-run enterprises, have no choice but to bail these enterprises out on behalf of the central government. The extent to which specialized banks are run like enterprises must be commensurate with the stiffening of constraints of industrial and commercial enterprises. If the constraints are soft, the banks' function of supervising the financial activities of enterprises must be maintained. The disintegration of such a function will seriously weaken the ability to control the enterprises. However, as long as this supervisory system is maintained, the enterprises' freedom to choose from which bank to borrow will be strictly restricted. Allowing the banks at the local level to be run like enterprises before other necessary changes are instituted will only give rise to speculation, bribery, corruption, and abuse of power because of a virtual monopoly on the supply of funds. Establishing a modern monetary regulation system before banks at the local level have become real enterprises and work under rigid budget constraints may incur a great risk of losing macro control. Based on the above judgments, it is suggested that during the Seventh Five-Year Plan period, it will only be possible for us to carry out a phased and partial reform of the existing banking system. Reform of a comprehensive nature would be undesirable.

This fact highlights the importance of the recent upsurge in nonbank financial activities, which will be described in the rest of this section. While financial reform has met with great difficulties, we are inspired by some of the new forms and mechanisms of capital flow that have appeared in the past few years: fund pooling and fund flow outside the state-run banks. These nonbank financial activities expanded rapidly in the credit contraction situation of 1985. We will describe two aspects of the nonbank sector: fund pooling and fund flow, and the emergence of new nonbank financial institutions.

Nonbank fund pooling and fund flow activities can be put in two categories: short-term fund flow activities between enterprises, and medium- and long-term fund pooling activities of enterprises and local governments. Of all the short-term fund flow activities between enterprises, the most remarkable is what has been referred to above as commercial credit between enterprises. As of mid-1985, about one-fifth of the circulating funds of enterprises were sustained by commercial credit. Overdue payments owned and advance payments received by state-run industrial enterprises in seven cities accounted for 45.1 percent of the circulating fund loans extended by banks. That is, the amount of circulating funds of the enterprises sustained by commercial credit is about half of that sustained by bank credits. The extraordinary growth of commercial credit between enterprises in a time of retrenchment involves the latent danger of a payment crisis. However, generally speaking, the rapid growth of commercial credit in the past few years reflects the fact that the demand for short-term funds by the enterprises has greatly increased with the strengthening of the horizontal economic links between enterprises. It also shows that commercial credits have taken on the function of the "paracurrency" and have acted as an important force supporting the daily production of the enterprises. If we make the best use of the situation and put on the right track this short-term fund flow (which at present is not yet guaranteed a continued and legal existence), it is highly probable that commercial credit will become one of the growth points of the new mechanisms for fund flow movement.

In the first half of 1985, the medium- and long-term fund pooling activities of the local governments and those of the enterprises in particular registered vigorous growth. Judging from the partial data, we can safely say there has been "rapid growth." In 1984, the city of Chendu made an investigation of 226 enterprises that collected funds and found that by the end of October funds collected amounted to RMB 91.83 million, an average of RMB 406,000 for each enterprise. The 26 enterprises studied in 1985 collected RMB 22.86 million in the first half of the year, average RMB 879,000 each. The long-term fund flow between enterprises mainly takes the form of compensatory trade. The scale of this flow is usually large (the average amount of funds collected from enterprises and units for 10 enterprises was RMB 2.023 million in 1985). Most of these funds were invested in the energy and raw materials sectors, and helping to supplement the investments on key construction projects.

Another important form that urban fund collection activities take is the collection of funds from society by the local government-backed profit-making companies. The fund is guaranteed by the local government. This form of fund collection is usually on the scale of more than RMB 10 million, some reaching as much as RMB 100 million. Funds collected in this way are usually used for developing tertiary industry such as constructing business blocks and marketable apartments or organizing local financial institutions. Furthermore, the funding of some large-scale fixed asset investment and key technological renovation projects has adopted the form of a joint venture between the governments at various levels, the specialized banks, and the enterprises using their financial funds, credit funds, and nonbank funds.

In the first half of 1985, compared with urban enterprises, township enterprises faced an even more stringent funding situation, and therefore the expansion of fund collecting activities was even greater. In the first quarter of 1985, 137 township enterprises in Xindu county, Chendu municipality (53.7 percent of the enterprises receiving loans), collected a total of RMB 11.07 million (that is to say, an equivalent of 70 percent of the balance of loans extended by the banks in the same period). Of the funds collected, one-third were collected from enterprises and government institutions, and two-thirds were collected directly from individual peasants. By "collecting funds" from enterprises and government institutions we mainly mean investment in related township enterprises by urban industrial enterprises. The most frequent form of collecting funds from peasants is to ask them to join the factory while bringing their own capital to be put into the factory. At a time when credit funds are in short supply, township enterprises sometimes adopt mandatory measures to collect funds from their workers. This clearly reflects the enterprise behavior of these township enterprises (which is characterized by the most rigid budgetary constraints in the country) and the close link between the interests of the enterprises and the interests of the workers.

Along with the development of various new fund flows, various nonbank financial institutions have emerged. Among these, the following call for our attention.

1. Local financial institutions. These institutions are mainly established on the provincial and municipal level and have the following characteristics. First, they have the powerful support of the local govenments, and their fund pooling activities are of an administrative nature. They may directly allocate a bloc of the local government's mobile funds and bank credit funds for their utilization or pool funds from the society on the strength of the credit-worthiness and prestige of the local governments. Second, they can collect large amounts of funds within a short period of time, and therefore can help to redistribute funds and support regional development. Third, interest rates are usually low as a result of the administrative nature of the funds. Fourth, fund allocation is greatly influenced by the local governments, and therefore a considerable part of the funds are invested in those fixed asset investment projects that are supported by the local government.

2. Interenterprise financial institutions of a mutual assistance nature. Few of these are formed on a purely voluntary basis; most have some administrative backing. The Funds Control Center formed under the auspices of the Textile Bureau of the municipality of Shanghai is based on the voluntary participation of enterprises in that industry. It regulates the enterprise-owned funds by accepting deposits and granting loans. In the province of Jiangsu, one out of every ten

economic service companies at the township levels include "financial services" in their scope of business. These companies have become parabanks that facilitate the pooling and flow of funds between the villages and township enterprises by accepting deposits and granting loans or by buying shares and joining in the investment.

3. Collectively owned financial organizations in urban areas. The "urban credit cooperatives" emerging in some cities have as their customers small collectively owned or private enterprises in the cities. To the banks, so far as these mini-enterprises are concerned, service costs are high and loans often entail high risks. For these reasons, it is often difficult for these enterprises to obtain necessary financial services. City credit cooperatives fill this gap in the financial activities in the urban areas to a certain extent. However, at present most of these collectively owned financial organizations in the urban areas are organized under the auspices of the Urban and Commercial Banks, whose main reason for supporting these institutions is to promote the welfare of their staff. As a result of this motivation, many problems still exist in the activities of these institutions. It should be noted that there exists in Chengdu a collectively owned financial organization called the "Chengdu Hui Tong Financial Company," which has the backing neither of the government nor of any specialized banks. Because this company is purely collective in nature, its budgetary constraints are extremely rigid and its activities are relatively healthy. In the four months since its establishment, it has attracted RMB 3.25 million yuan in deposits and paid out RMB 2.1 million yuan in loans. The balance is being kept as contingency reserve funds so as to maintain the company's commercial credit-worthiness. Since the establishment of the company, every single loan has been successful; there has not been a single bad loan.

4. Private banks. In regions where cooperative economy and the private sector have been growing most rapidly (such as the Wenzhou region in Zhejiang province), massive circulating funds and other idle funds have accumulated. As a result, private banks and other private financial organizations and parafinancial organizations have come into being. They have in fact become an important supplement to banks and rural credit cooperatives. The balance of deposits of the largest private bank in the Wenzhou region is about RMB 1 million. Privately owned financial organizations mostly handle short-term loans to be used as circulating funds but on occasion also grant fixed asset loans. Because privately owned financial organizations run high operational risks and are vitally responsible for their own profits and losses, the interest rates they set tend to be high.

This rapid expansion of nonbank financial activities is not happenstance. The unprecedented development of commodity economic relations and the great increase in the horizontal ties between enterprises call for a more flexible flow of funds over a wider area. The old monolithic system of state-run banks can no longer keep up with these demands arising out of the new reality. The various nonbank financial activities are to a great extent born out of the changing economic relations and have developed in the space provided by the reform. This very fact proves its necessity and constitutes its raison d'etre, and it presages the active role it will play in the new system.

4. Developing the Nonbank Fund Markets:
Main Directions for Short- and Mid-Term Financial
Reform

In view of the above analysis, we believe that during the Seventh Five-Year Plan the focus in reforming the financial system would be to open up further the nonbank fund market and activate the horizontal flow of funds. Some possible measures follow.

1. Encourage the many forms of direct fund pooling among enterprises. To pool social funds and raise the scale and efficiency of investment, the government should encourage enterprises to invest in other regions and in other industries in the form of compensatory trade, encourage large enterprises to invest in related small and medium enterprises, and promote the dispersion of funds of urban enterprises to township enterprises and the gathering of funds from society by issuing shares and bonds. A number of enterprises should also be encouraged to participate in large-scale "mixed" investment, which may even have the participation of the local governments. Fund collecting methods such as persuading people to join the factory while bringing in their own money and putting it in the factory and issuing bonus stock should be encouraged. These methods greatly stimulate fund collection and have emerged spontaneously under special Chinese conditions such as an abundant supply of labor and high demand for housing and durable consumer goods. At present some enterprises are collecting funds by issuing shares to their own staff. This method should not be blindly encouraged as it may not be conducive to controlling the increase in consumption funds and has very little impact on the investment of enterprises. (In 1985, Chengdu conducted an investigation of sixteen enterprises that collected funds from their own staff and found that the average amount of funds collected for each enterprise was no more than RMB 34,000.)

2. The horizontal flow of funds calls for the establishment of a great number of financial institutions of many types. Restriction on the establishment of financial institutions should be gradually eased. We should encourage the growth of various types of financial institutions, and financial organizations of a mutual-assistance nature, formed voluntarily between enterprises, should be given priority if obtaining help from the government. The sources of funds for such financial institutions, which somewhat resemble internal banks set up by groups of enterprises, would be the idle funds of the enterprises, or else shares and bonds may be floated. The utilization of these funds takes the following forms: (1) flow of short-term funds, including granting emergency loans to member enterprises and advancing funds on discount on the commercial bills in the hands of members;

(2) granting fixed asset loans to or directly investing in member enterprises. Support and assistance provided by the local governments or bureaus concerned will facilitate the establishment of such financial institutions at the initial stage. As soon as these financial institutions can stand on their feet, administrative intervention by the local governments and bureaus concerned should be reduced to the minimum.

Efforts to establish credit cooperatives of a mutual assistance nature among the small collectively owned enterprises and privately owned industrial and commercial enterprises in the cities should be supported. The funds of these cooperatives are collected from the member enterprises in the form of shares, and its main function is to regulate the fund flow between these enterprises. The urban collectively owned financial organizations that have the support of the banks should break off from the banks as soon as possible and be left to run their own business independently and be made responsible for their own profits and losses, so as to avoid some bad practices that have already emerged. If we ban the private banks that already exist in some areas that have well-developed privately owned industrial and commercial enterprises, then private banks will only be forced underground. This will in turn push up the price of individual funds. We might as well impose restrictions on them while allowing them to exist and persuade and guide them into forming joint-stock financial enterprises of a mutual-aid nature.

When circumstances permit, some local financial institutions should be established. The sources of funds will be local mobile financial resources, trust deposits of enterprises, and funds collected from the society through issuing shares and bonds. The funds of these local financial institutions will be utilized mainly for long-term loans and direct investment, whereas short-term regulation funds become of minor importance. The funds will be used to support major technological renovation projects, the tertiary sectors in cities, and profitable infrastructure construction. It is difficult for the local financial organizations to rid themselves entirely of intervention coming from local governments for a certain period of time after they are formed. This is because only with the support of the local government can they accumulate relatively big funds in a short period of time. However, limited intervention from the local government is not that terrifying. This is because nonbank financial institutions are after all commercial organizations with much more rigid budget constraints vis-à-vis those of the banks. Therefore they will have to give more thought to making profits; as a result, their urge to resist the unreasonable intervention of the government becomes stronger as their funds and financial strength increase.

We should permit economic service companies (or the township industrial companies) of the township government to include accepting deposits and granting loans in their scope of business. However, the relation between these companies and township enterprises should be an economic one. Dividends must be handed out for funds collected according to rules and regulations, interest on deposits must be paid on time and the proprietary rights of the investor over the funds must be guaranteed.

3. Gradually open up the monetary market and promote the flow of short-term funds. The priority at present is to put the commercial credits between enterprises as soon as possible. First of all, enterprises should be allowed to transfer bills among themselves, and nonbank financial institutions should be allowed to advance money on discount on the bills of enterprises. Financial institutions with relatively rigid budget constraints will be able to grant different discount rates according to the supply and demand of funds and the risks involved in the bills of different enterprises. In this way, the demand for short-term funds of efficient enterprises with good economic results will be met, and at the same time restraints will be put on the blind expansion of commercial credits by enterprises of low credit-worthiness. An all-around payment crisis can therefore be prevented through the market for short term funds with relatively small risk of credit expansion.

4. A long-term fund market should be formed step by step. Issuing of shares and bonds by enterprises and direct fund-collecting activities engaged in by nonbank financial institutions all point to the development of a long-term financial market. At present the practice of publicly issuing shares and bonds by enterprises is developing very slowly. This is mainly because it is difficult for the investors to make judgments on the financial situation and management abilities of enterprises or on changes in the market, thereby making direct investment in the enterprises extremely risky. However, nonbank financial institutions enjoy relatively high credibility as a result of the support they receive from the government and consequently are more attractive than individual enterprises to investors. Therefore we can adopt more of the indirect fund flow method in which funds could be collected from society through the issuance of financial bonds by financial institutions which then invest the funds in enterprises. In this way idle funds in the society could be collected at relatively low cost. While the primary market for long-term fixed assets grows, some financial institutions should be allowed to repurchase or resell bills and stocks, so as to facilitate the flow of financial assets and lower the cost of fund collecting for enterprises. Because the scale of the primary exchange of financial assets will remain small in the immediate future, developing a secondary market need not be given a priority consideration.

5. With the opening of fund markets, government regulation of financing must be correspondingly strengthened. We must consider relaxing appropriately the present provisional regulations on the issuance of shares and bonds by enterprises, as they impose too many restrictions on the interest rates of bonds and stocks and are therefore difficult to enforce in practice. To facilitate macro control and protect the rights and interests of depositors, power should be delegated to authorities for the examination and approval at different levels of the setting up of financial institutions. The scope of business for each type of institution should be regulated. A minimum among of self-owned funds should be

stipulated for each type of financial institution, in accordance with its nature and scope of business. A deposit contingency reserve fund system should be established, and the asset-liability ratio for financial institutions should be set forth and enforced. We may even impose a mandatory deposit insurance system on small-scale financial institutions. Financial institutions must establish strict bookkeeping systems and pay their taxes according to rules and regulations. Financial regulatory institutions must be strengthened. Financial organizations must be subject to the supervision and inspection of government regulatory, auditing and tax-collection departments. Financial organizations and persons violating financial rules and regulations must be punished according to law. The bankruptcy procedures of financial institutions must be set down in law, and the softening of budgetary constraints on financial institutions should be prevented.

Further opening up the fund market can bring about advantages in many fields. It will break the monopoly of the state banks and open up many channels for the flow and pooling of capital. The emergence of company shares and bonds, financial bonds, workers and staff entering enterprises and bringing with them their own funds, prize awards through selling of stocks and bonds, and other forms of fund collecting will change the former monolithic pattern of financing. The depositor can choose from a large variety of investment options according to their mobility, profitability, and other circumstances. Generally speaking, deposit interest rates of financial institutions and funds collected from society are higher than bank deposit interest rates. Therefore they can help to increase the voluntary deposits of individuals and enterprises for longer terms, thereby promoting the collection of idle funds from society. The multiple forms of financial institutions provide a wide range of services and fill up the vacuum left by the bank monopoly. The many forms of funds and nonbank financial institutions will greatly strengthen the ties between enterprises and will give an impetus to the restructuring of of China's enterprise groups centered on financial organizations.

5. Conclusion: Improve Credit Control and Promote the Financial "Double Track" System

Some people have profound doubts about opening up the fund market. They are apprehensive that opening up the fund market will bring about a new credit expansion. This worry seems justifiable. If bank credits are not made more stringent at the same time that the restrictions on the horizontal flows of funds are lifted, nonbank funds will come from the expansion of bank credit, and this will be bound to cause inflation in the total supply of money. Furthermore, should bank credit be supplied freely and without control, enterprises will continue to rely on government credit funds and will be unwilling to attract more expensive non-bank funds. Responding to the question, "Which method would you prefer to use in solving funding difficulties?" in the present survey, "Borrowing from banks" was the most favored choice by factory directors while "Soliciting funds from society'' was least favored. Naturally, enterprises choose their external fund sources according to the rigidity of the fund constraints. So long as there is a reliable source of credit funds with soft constraints, enterprises will not turn to high-cost nonbank funds with their rigid constraints.

With the fund market being opened up step by step, bank credits must be made correspondingly more stringent so as to guarantee government control over the amount of currency in circulation and at the same time make room for the nonbank fund markets to operate. We should not worry that fund markets will eat into bank deposits. On the contrary, we should encourage the growth of the fund market by gradually reducing the credit activities of the banks. In what way can we make the bank credits more stringent? If during the Seventh Five-Year Plan it is not advisable to carry out a comprehensive reform of the state bank system or adopt modern means for monetary control in all fields, then we can only strive to improve the existing planned credit control in which a comparatively stringent monetary policy is practiced through planned management. In this way, a binary system of national financial activity will take form, where credit activities of state banks and credit activities of nonbank fund markets exist side by side. In this binary system the credit activities of state banks are managed through planning whereas nonbank financial activities are regulated by market forces.

There are several advantages in having such a two-track financial system. First, the difference between the interest rates and conditions of loans in the two fund sectors can be utilized to implement the industrial policy of the state. In the process of high-speed economic growth and with the industrial structure experiencing radical readjustments, state support by means of low-interest credit funds of possible low-profit infrastructure projects or newly developed sectors with a massive scale of initial investment and a long cost-retrieval period will sustain the growth of heavy industry. The national government can base the banks' credit conditions for different enterprises on economic scale, and thus support big enterprises and big investments and control the tendency of enterprises to get smaller. On the other hand, enterprises that do not meet this test would be allowed to get high-cost external funds from the fund market. In this way those enterprises that are efficient will have the opportunity to change their production lines and merge, and thereby become large enough to qualify for bank loans. At the same time, small and backward enterprises with low efficiency would be restricted through high interest rates. Second, this system has the desirable effect of raising the overall interest rate. Furthermore, raising the interest rate by the ''two track'' interest rate system (low for bank funds and high for market funds) is more feasible than directly raising all interest rates at once. If we raise all the interest rates regardless of the specific conditions of different cases, then the tendency for the enterprises to reap quick profits would be intensified.

Third, although the access of any one enterprise to credit will vary after adopting the ''two track'' system, the total amount of low cost credit funds will be limited as a result of the ceiling set for the general scale of credit. For any enterprise, shortages will have to be made up by borrowing high-cost non-bank funds in the market, with rigid constraints on loan repayment. For large enterprises, such funds may not make up a very big portion of overall funding at the initial stage. However they will have an extremely important impact, at the margin, in hardening the enterprise's budgetary constraint by imposing a high marginal interest rate. This will inevitably restrain their urge to invest and reduce the number of unprofitable investments.

Fourth, the financial two-track system is a relatively feasible and less risky reform approach. While it is impossible to shift bank operation to an enterprise basis in the near future, and while adopting the three traditional instruments of monetary regulation carries with it great risks, the flow of nonbank funds came into being naturally in the course of economic activities of the past few years. Nonbank funds are indigenous and will not bring about ill effects because of incompatibility. The failure of these activities will not lead to an overall crisis, because they are restricted to certain regions and areas of business and the amount of funds available is extremely limited.

The basic approach of financial reform for the Seventh Five-Year Plan based on the adoption of the financial "two track" system does not exclude a partial or phased reform of the banking system, or reforms in other financial fields, such as clearing up the relationship between budgetary finance and banks, changing the interest rate structure, gradually breaking up the specialized banks, further integrating the powers, responsibilities, and interests of the banks at the local level, and so forth. All these reforms could be carried out step by step when the time is appropriate. Undoubtedly the adoption of the financial "two track" system will eventually create favorable conditions for an overall reform in the financial system. Ending the financial monopoly of the four major banks by opening up the funds market will help improve the behavior of enterprises and lay a sound foundation for turning banks into enterprises. At a time when state credit and the nonbank fund markets exist side by side in this binary financial system, we can experiment with exercising indirect regulation and control of the funds market while at the same time adhering to a planned control over the bank credit activities.

Since the present survey has not looked into all aspects of financial activities and our analysis of available data is sometimes superficial, the present report has only provided a rough and general view on the basic approach may be adopted in the financial reform. We welcome criticisms.

East Gate Books

Harold R. Isaacs
RE-ENCOUNTERS IN CHINA

James D. Seymour
CHINA RIGHTS ANNALS 1

Thomas E. Stolper
CHINA, TAIWAN, AND THE OFFSHORE ISLANDS

William L. Parish, ed.
CHINESE RURAL DEVELOPMENT
The Great Transformation

Anita Chan, Stanley Rosen, and Jonathan Unger, eds.
ON SOCIALIST DEMOCRACY AND THE CHINESE LEGAL SYSTEM
The Li Yizhe Debates

Michael S. Duke, ed.
CONTEMPORARY CHINESE LITERATURE
An Anthology of Post-Mao Fiction and Poetry

Michiko N. Wilson
THE MARGINAL WORLD OF ŌE KENZABURO
A Study in Themes and Techniques

Thomas B. Gold
STATE AND SOCIETY IN THE TAIWAN MIRACLE

Carol Lee Hamrin and Timothy Cheek, eds.
CHINA'S ESTABLISHMENT INTELLECTUALS

John P. Burns and Stanley Rosen, eds.
POLICY CONFLICTS IN POST-MAO CHINA
A Documentary Survey, with Analysis

Victor D. Lippit
THE ECONOMIC DEVELOPMENT OF CHINA

James D. Seymour
CHINA'S SATELLITE PARTIES

June M. Grasso
TRUMAN'S TWO-CHINA POLICY

Bruce L. Reynolds, ed.
REFORM IN CHINA
Challenges & Choices